BY A FLASH AND A SCARE

John E. Archer

By a Flash and a Scare

*Arson, Animal Maiming, and Poaching
in East Anglia 1815-1870*

BREVIARY STUFF PUBLICATIONS
2020

Breviary Stuff Publications,
BCM Breviary Stuff, London WC1N 3XX
breviarystuff.org.uk
Copyright © Breviary Stuff Publications 2020
The centipede device copyright © Breviary Stuff Publications
2nd Breviary Stuff edition
First published in 1990 by Oxford University Press

A CIP record for this book is available from
The British Library

ISBN: 978-1-9161586-2-7

for Helen, James and Tom

Contents

Abbreviations

Ag. Hist. Rev.	*Agricultural History Review*
BNP	*Bury and Norwich Post*
C	Cambridgeshire
CC	*Cambridge Chronicle*
E	Essex
EA	*East Anglian*
Econ. Hist. Rev.	*Economic History Review*
IESRO	Ipswich and East Suffolk Record Office
IJ	*Ipswich Journal*
JPS	*Journal of Peasant Studies*
JRAS	*Journal of the Royal Agricultural Society*
JRSS	*Journal of the Royal Statistical Society*
MC	*Morning Chronicle*
N	Norfolk
NM	*Norwich Mercury*
NN	*Norwich News*
NNLHL	Norfolk and Norwich Local History Library
NNMPG	*Norfolk and Norwich Monitor and Police Gazette*
NNRO	Norfolk and Norwich Record Office
NS	*Northern Star*
NUFO	Norwich Union Fire Office
PLC	Poor Law Commissioners
PP	Parliamentary Papers
PRO	Public Record Office
S	Suffolk
SC	*Suffolk Chronicle*
VCH	*Victoria County History*

About the author

John E. Archer was an honorary research fellow at Edge Hill University who published widely on 19th century protest and crime. His books include *Social Unrest and Popular Protest in England, 1780–1840* and *The Monster Evil: Policing and Violence in Victorian Liverpool.*

Preface

The study of nineteenth-century rural crime and protest has grown in recent years yet our knowledge and understanding of three of the more persistent covert crimes, arson, animal maiming, and poaching, have been limited and, to some extent, over-shadowed by the more dramatic episodes of collective unrest like Captain Swing, Tolpuddle, and Arch's trade union. *By a Flash and a Scare*, it is hoped, will partially rectify this imbalance but also fill one of the many lacunae.

The gestation of this book has been lengthy but in the process I have benefited greatly from the help, guidance, and ideas of many friends and colleagues. Without doubt my biggest debt of gratitude must be extended to David Jones of the University of Swansea who pointed me in the direction of rick-burning labourers many years ago. His knowledge, teaching, and writing have aided and influenced me enormously. For reasons which I, a Lancastrian, still do not understand, covert protest proved immensely attractive and fascinating to me and I was happy to pursue further research at the University of East Anglia under the patient and cheerful supervision of Gerald Crompton and Jim Holderness to whom I offer my thanks. Since then many colleagues have generously provided me with information and freely exchanged ideas and arguments. Although I cannot mention all by name I would like to thank in particular Alan Armstrong, Andy Charlesworth, Julian Harber, Roger Ryan, Roger Wells, and especially Alun Howkins, whose own research dovetails into mine, chronologically and geographically speaking. He has shown that history is a far from dull or unmelodious discipline.

I would like also to extend my thanks to all the librarians and archivists on whose premises I became a daily fixture and fitting, especially those at Norwich, Ipswich, and Bury St Edmunds who provided me with the actual newspapers and not, as I fear is becoming all too common, dreaded microfilms. The staff at the Public Record Office and the British Library were also generous with their help. A special word of thanks must be given to the Norwich Union Insurance Company who kindly allowed me to consult their directors' minute books. In more recent years my studies were greatly assisted by the award of a research grant from the British Academy and I am grateful for their generosity.

Finally, my thanks to those who helped turn a manuscript into something more respectable: Judith Cotter and Helen Wickham for their intelligent and accurate typing, Rod Pye and Ann Chapman of Edge Hill College for their photographic and cartographic services respectively, and Tony Morris of the OUP for his patience and understanding. I am, of course, responsible for all errors and shortcomings that remain.

Last but certainly not least a special thank-you to my family, to James and Tom who arrived during the preparation of this book and whose forceful presence has been, and will always be, a most pleasant distraction. Moreover they have enabled me to place my work in general in its proper perspective. And Helen, my wife, who has not only read through the manuscript identifying errors, but has both given me enormous support and provided me with a necessary and healthy escape to her garden centre at weekends. This has balanced what would otherwise have been a rather sedentary life. To them I dedicate this book.

J.E.A.

Tarleton, Lancashire
July 1989

2

I
An Introduction to Rural Protest

> My brother is uncomfortable about the state of things in Suffolk.
> They are as bad as Ireland … never a night without seeing fires
> near or at a distance.[1]

The writer of this letter, John Constable, is revered for his
unsurpassable vision of the English countryside. The tranquillity,
harmony, and timelessness of his paintings have come down the years
as some idealized golden age, transfixing the modern consciousness.
We do well to dwell on those paintings of East Anglia in the 1820s but
only if another vision, no less valid, is borne in mind; a vision of a
profoundly unequal society in which the majority of its inhabitants,
wavering between toil and charity, fought a long and often hopeless
struggle against their exploiters, the farmers and landowners.

It has become a truism for historians to attack the Constable-type
image of rural England with its thatched cottages, carthorses, and
golden wheatfields, but to little avail if the contemporary adman's
frequent and persistent message is any guide. But in challenging this
'green and pleasant land' syndrome many recent histories of the farm
workers have created, to some extent, myths of their own which
actively reinforce the artistic ones. The weight of historical scholarship
has rested firmly on those dramatic collective incidents which
occasionally shook what many suppose to be an otherwise
undisturbed society. The 'Bread or Blood' Riots of 1816, Captain
Swing in 1830, the Tolpuddle Martyrs, Bossenden Wood, and Joseph
Arch's trade union have all received their ample share of critical
attention, but these incidents, many of them short-lived, are frequently
viewed in isolation, both chronologically and in terms of perspective,
from a wider and arguably more accurate depiction of a workforce
under constant pressure from ever-changing social and economic
forces.[2] Protest which broke out between these milestones of
collective disturbance has not been subject to much scrutiny, although
David Jones's work on arson in the 1840s must be considered an

---

1   R. B. Beckett, *John Constable's Correspondence*, iv (Ipswich Record Office, 1962), 203, letter to
    Fisher, 13 Apr. 1822.
2   The following represent a small selection of the available literature: A. J. Peacock, *Bread or
    Blood: A Study of the Agrarian Riots in East Anglia in 1816* (London, 1965); E. J. Hobsbawm
    and G. Rudé, *Captain Swing* (Harmondsworth, 1973); J. Marlow, *The Tolpuddle Martyrs*
    (London, 1971); P. G. Rogers, *The Battle of Bossenden Wood: The Strange Story of Sir William
    Courtenay* (London, 1961); P. Horn, *Joseph Arch 1826-1919, the Farm Workers' Leader*
    (Kineton, 1971).

exception.[3] Riot, demonstrations, and machine breaking were not the typical responses of an angry rural workforce; although East Anglia may claim more than any other area of the country to have founded such a tradition, even there as elsewhere the weapons of protest were more varied, covert, and individual in form. Thus arson, animal maiming, animal stealing, anonymous and threatening letters, poaching, and highway robbery were the constant reminders and realities for the landed classes to remain on their guard. If reference is made to these crimes then our image of the English countryside changes — the labourers did not protest infrequently and dramatically, they protested 'all the time'.

THE CATEGORIZATION OF RURAL CRIME

With the recent growth of historical criminology historians have attempted to impose order on the various criminal offences usually classified by Victorians under the following headings: offences against the person, offences against property with violence, offences against property without violence, malicious offences against property, and forgery offences against currency. Modern scholars have found this classification unhelpful and have resorted to categorizing illegal behaviour under a plethora of headings: social crime, economic crime, rural crime, urban crime, survival crime, protest crime, crime as protest, acquisitive crime, 'normal' crime, and so forth. This search for definitions and exactitude, instead of clarifying a complex area of human behaviour, has led in some cases to confusion, and in others to misunderstanding. When a historian writes of 'social crime' do the readers fully appreciate and understand just what he or she is referring to? That a categorization of crime is necessary is readily agreed by all, but the terminology so employed has not been. In this study related to arson, animal maiming, and poaching it is plainly obvious from a review of the literature that some attempt at defining what category or categories they come under is essential. Are they all forms of social crime or protest crime? Are they a combination of the two? Recent research acknowledges that the distinction between the categories can be blurred on occasions; Jones, Emsley, and the authors of *Albion's Fatal Tree* all refer to the problems of differentiation.[4] George Rudé, in

---

3 D. J. V. Jones, 'Thomas Campbell Foster and the Rural Labourer: Incendiarism in East Anglia in the 1840s, *Social History*, 1 (1976), 5-43; id,, *Crime, Protest, Community and Police in Nineteenth-Century Britain* (London, 1982), ch. 2, pp. 31-61.

4 Jones, *Crime, Protest*, pp. 14-15; C. Emsley, *Policing and its Context 1750-1850* (London, 1983), pp. 116-17; D. Hay, D. Linebaugh, J. G. Rule, E. P. Thompson, and C. Winslow,

numerous instances, writes of a shadowy realm between social and protest crimes and eventually settles on a new subheading, 'marginal protest', for the very activities investigated here. Rule, who more than anyone has attempted to impose order on this subject, has been forced to conclude: 'it is not possible to say with exactitude how much crime of the arson kind can be regarded as social crime'.[5]

A new trend too is becoming discernible — recent research by Roger Wells on sheep stealing and Rudé on crime in general is now displaying far less confidence in defining any crime as belonging to any particular category. Wells in his excellent study concluded that sheep stealing eludes any precise categorization.[6] The root of this collective lack of historical confidence is that the more research that is undertaken the more complex the subject becomes. Only in recent years have systematic studies been undertaken of wood stealing, sheep stealing, poaching, and smuggling. The more 'ordinary' or 'normal' acquisitive crimes like theft and burglary still await investigation. Collective protest crimes — riot, strikes, and demonstrations — have been known for years and have proved most amenable to classification. Why this should be so is fairly obvious. In collective protest the motivation of the participants is clearly discernible since the authorities are confronted and forced to take notice of overtly expressed grievances. Motivation is far harder to discover in the case of a disfigured sheep in a field or a smouldering barn, especially as the arrest and conviction rates for these individual acts were so low. Put simply, contemporaries had very little to go on and historians have even less. Motivation, however, is the key to our understanding and will lead, no doubt, to more precise categorization in the future when further research has been completed. One additional and specifically historical problem serves to complicate matters further. Crime is not some absolute and fixed concept, unchanging and unvarying in definition over time; what was legal behaviour one year might well be classed illegal the next. The rule of law was extended over the countryside in the eighteenth and nineteenth centuries and in the process property owners redefined not only their own rights but also

---

Albion's Fatal Tree: Crime and Society in Eighteenth-Century England (London, 1975), pp. 13-14.

5   J. G. Rule, 'Social Crime in the Rural South in the Eighteenth and Early Nineteenth Centuries', *Southern History*, I (1979), 135-53; G. Rudé, *Protest and Punishment: The Story of the Social and Political Protesters Transported to Australia 1788-1868* (Oxford, 1978), p. 4; id., *Criminal and Victim: Crime and Society in Early Nineteenth Century England* (Oxford, 1985), p. 86.

6   R. A. E. Wells, 'Sheep-Rustling in Yorkshire in the Age of the Industrial and Agricultural Revolutions', *Northern History*, 20 (1984), 145.

legal and illegal behaviour. Wood gathering/stealing and gleaning are two clear examples of this process of 'custom to crime transition'.[7] Crime in general was not fixed or static and the same is true of protest and social crime, though one might be forgiven for concluding from the available studies that social crime always remained social crime. The study of arson shows this not to be the case. The types of people convicted, their motivation, and the communities' response to fires changed quite dramatically between 1815 and 1870, which leads one to wonder whether categorization serves any useful purpose. With these qualifications and problems in mind it now only remains for this work to classify arson, animal maiming, and poaching.

Two categories, social and protest crime, would appear to offer the most rewarding avenues of approach. At this stage it is best to keep them as distinct headings; some historians have tended to regard protest as social crime but in doing so they have failed to identify the nuances and subtleties on which others have remarked. Rudé, for example, correlates social crime with 'survival' crime and argues that protest crime was collective in character. Rule very properly draws a distinction between protest crime and crime as protest, to which latter group arson and maiming might well belong.[8] But where historians have blurred the distinction between social and protest crimes they have overlooked one vitally important issue and that is, how did the community view the action of the criminal? Certain activities — poaching, smuggling, and wrecking to name but three commonly referred to by historians — though illegal in the sense that the law proscribed them, were not viewed as criminal in any way by the labouring community. They were, in other words, popularly sanctioned activities. Although an element of protest may have been present in the mind of the poacher or whoever, it was not his primary motive. Very few criminal activities would fall under this social crime category for, as Rule observed in the case of sheep stealing, people may excuse the sheep stealer not because they positively approve of the act but rather because they sympathize with his poverty.[9] If Rule's qualification is accepted, as it should be, then Rudé's definition of social crime as being synonymous with 'survival' may well be misleading. However, Rudé's survival category does draw one's attention to the marginal areas of social crime where the distinction

---

7   See G. R. Rubin and D. Sugarman, edd., *Law, Economy and Society* (Abingdon, 1984), pp. 1-123.
8   Rudé, *Criminal and Victim*, p. 78; Rule, 'Social Crime', pp. 152-53.
9   J. G. Rule, ed., *Outside the Law: Studies in Crime and Order 1650-1850* (Exeter, 1982), p. 118.

between normal or acquisitive crime and social crime is not easy to determine. Two examples from East Anglia make this point. In the first case, police traced a stolen sheep to a Lidgate (S) labourer's wedding feast which they cut short by arresting the groom and his father. It is reasonable to assume that the meal was, or would have been, sanctioned by the wedding guests. The second is recounted by George Edwards, Member of Parliament and union leader, who recalled how his father, a God-fearing man, was gaoled 'for the crime of attempting to feed his children' when the police found five turnips in his bag.[10] This is certainly a survival-type crime but Edwards senior would have recognized the illegality of his action.

If most historians are agreed that social crime reflected a fundamental clash of values over the law there is less consensus when it comes to the question of protest. Is there a distinction to be made between social and protest crime? Certain activities — food rioting, machine breaking, and trade unionism — present few problems because they contain an element of protest supported by popular legitimacy. Arson, animal maiming, and the sending of anonymous letters are less clear. Again the element of protest would appear to be present but does that reflect the opinions of the community? There is one crucial difference between these acts and the social crimes already mentioned. The former, unlike the latter, were viewed by everybody as illegal activities. On this point there was no debate nor was there any clash between customary behaviour and statutory law. Starting a fire was, in itself, wrong. However it is the context of the fire which is important — who lit what, against whom, and why? These factors very often determined the labouring community's attitude to an incendiary fire. As will be seen, arson was viewed as a legitimate weapon of protest where the arsonist was expressing a collective grievance on such matters as low wages or unemployment. In these circumstances arson was legitimized by popular opinion and should be referred to as social protest crime.

Turning now to the rural crimes investigated in this study, poaching would appear to present the least difficulties, even though many individuals made it their profession. Men like Fred Gowing, Suffolk's uncrowned king, were quite adamant on this point — they were not thieves. This was a commonly held view up to 1870, which suggests Rudé's opinion that poaching was losing its popular sanction by the mid-nineteenth century is erroneous.[11] Country people remained

---

10 *NN*, 11 Nov. 1848; G. Edwards, *From Crow-Scaring to Westminster* (London, 1922), p. 22.
11 Rudé, *Criminal and Victim*, p. 85.

steadfastly opposed to the game laws and were keen to exercise their 'rights' on this issue.

Animal maiming, likewise, would appear to present few problems. A. J. Peacock and others have assumed maiming was the epitome of rural protest crime.[12] Oddly enough, of the three activities investigated, maiming presents the biggest problem and eludes categorization to a large extent. Historians are faced with a number of practical problems. First, it was not a very common crime, even in East Anglia, where it was most frequently executed. Second, very few maimers were caught, let alone convicted, which means the motivational factors escape our attention in most cases. Finally, there is almost no indication of how the rest of the labouring community felt about such acts. Maiming was an intensely private and individual crime, bearing many of the hallmarks of a personal grudge or vendetta. The scene of the maiming was never a focus of community attention, unlike arson where large crowds would congregate at the blaze. It may well be that the identity of maimers was well known to villagers but historians have no way of knowing that, nor is there any indication that their identities were widely known to others. We only have the negative evidence in so far as rewards were not collected nor were maimers prosecuted generally. But this cannot conclusively make maiming social protest. Moreover it will be suggested that in some cases of horse poisoning the element of protest was furthest from the mind of the perpetrator. Just occasionally a protest motive comes through in the form of a threatening letter or a defiant speech from the dock but this is in only a minority of cases. The historian is thus left to surmise or ponder on the nature of this strange crime.

Arson presents slightly fewer imponderables; more incendiaries were convicted and the context of the arson attacks are usually more clearly defined than in the maiming cases. As a weapon of social protest incendiarism can be located fairly exactly in the first half of the nineteenth century, more especially the second quarter. During this period arson not only became the hallmark of rural protest in terms of volume and frequency but also was fully supported by the labouring communities. Their behaviour and responses at the scenes of conflagration are instructive and indicative of the poor social relations between labourers and farmers. Moreover, contemporaries were convinced that the identities of the incendiaries were widely known but that communities shielded them from prosecution, despite

---

12 J. P. D. Dunbabin, *Rural Discontent in Nineteenth-Century Britain* (London, 1974), ch. by A. J. Peacock, 'Village Radicalism in East Anglia, 1800-1850', p. 45.

the enormous rewards offered. Whether arson remained an expression of collective social protest after 1852 is more difficult to ascertain. All the indications would suggest that it became less important. No longer did fires become the focuses of communal celebration or anger, nor did arsonists come so frequently from the ranks of the farm labourers as before. The higher conviction rates of the post-1850 period, in fact, allow for a more exact identification of the people involved. Children and tramps figure more prominently after 1850 and this would indicate that arson, as a weapon of social protest, was becoming more marginal. This is hardly surprising as incendiarism was frequently an expression against low wages and very high unemployment, two factors which were of serious concern to everyone in the years of depression and surplus population. However, after 1852, the advent of 'high farming' and rural migration eased the strain to a limited extent which in turn lessened the occurrence of social protest. If generalized conclusions are to be made regarding arson as a crime of social protest two points can be raised. First, Rudé's maxim that each case has to be judged on its own merits is a fair one. Second, historians have generally underestimated the high protest element, especially between 1830 and 1852. Peacock's conclusion that one-third of arson cases can be explained by 'personal pique', whatever that might be, is, on the basis of the evidence, fairly wide of the mark.[13] Arson was, generally speaking, an act of social protest perpetrated by an individual expressing a wider collective sense of grievance.

How should one regard these social protesters and criminals? The authors of *Albion's Fatal Tree* warned against a Manichaeist approach in which there were '"good" criminals, who are premature revolutionaries or reformers, forerunners of popular movements' and the bad who committed crime without qualification.[14] The temptation to romanticize the exploits of the former is strong among social historians, a perfectly understandable reaction given the qualitative differences between social and acquisitive crime. Some of them were clearly heroes in their own communities; the funeral of the capitally convicted Knockolds testifies to this fact.[15] Likewise it is difficult not to give an inward cheer when reading of Leech Borley who, having just received fifteen years transportation, jumped from the dock, ran out of the court, and across Bury marketplace to freedom.[16] However,

13 Peacock, 'Village Radicalism', p. 30.
14 Hay et al., *Albion's Fatal Tree*, pp. 10-14; E. P. Thompson, *Whigs and Hunters: The Origin: of the Black Act* (London, 2013), p. 149.
15 See Ch. 7 for a fuller account of Knockolds.
16 Borley was noted for his cross-country running, an ability which he made full use of when

the temptation to hail such men as vanguards of the working class should be resisted. One should just stop awhile and imagine meeting some of these characters in quiet country lanes in the dead of winter. Knockolds, for instance, is credited with throwing vitriol into the faces of small manufacturers. David Clowe, arrested in 1844, was a social outcast in his own parish where he was forced to live in a straw hut four-foot high and six-foot long. He had a reputation for terrifying all and sundry.[17] Whilst Knockolds was class-conscious and Clowe a member of Marx's *lumpen proletariat*, both as individuals were undoubtedly vindictive and aggressive in the extreme, and were not perhaps the sort of people to engage in conversation, let alone to whom one would wish to extend the apologia of sociology. Some of these men were, in short, brutal and wild men who operated under their own laws, not those of the state or their own communities.

CRIME IN THE COUNTRYSIDE

Any study of social protest crime must take cognizance of crime as a whole in order to place the former into some kind of quantitative and qualitative perspective. Were arson, riots, and so forth merely interesting but relatively unimportant episodes when set in the totality of rather more humdrum everyday sorts of crime? Should one even separate out artificially various criminal practices and label them social, protest, and acquisitive? And does the movement of total crime either tell us anything about rural society or bear any relationship to social protest. Answers to these and other questions are remarkably difficult to arrive at since the study of rural crime is still in its infancy. Until now historians have been drawn towards the fast expanding towns and cities where juvenile delinquency and the 'criminal classes', among other subjects, have proved attractive. Scholars have unwittingly latched on to the issues which interested nineteenth-century observers and this has given historical criminology a lopsided look. No doubt, too, this approach would implicitly conclude that the countryside was a relatively law-abiding place in comparison with the cities. Even rural historians have contributed to this notion; Horn argued that rural crime 'never assumed the threatening proportions that it did in towns'. Does such an assumption stand up even to impressionistic, let alone detailed, scrutiny? Rudé, in his comparative study of Gloucestershire and Sussex in the first half of the nineteenth century, concluded crime

---

poaching and firing stacks.

17 *MC*, 25 July 1844.

was as much a feature of the village as of the towns.[18] Looking at Suffolk, a rural county if ever there was one, in a little more detail, forces one to be even more emphatic than Rudé. In the first forty years of the nineteenth century crime rates rose far faster here than in England and Wales as a whole. John Glyde, a remarkable observer of Suffolk society, spotted another feature concerning East Anglia, the age of offenders.

According to Glyde the cohort of those under 30 for Suffolk (Table 1.1) was proportionally more criminal than the more urbanized and industrialized counties of Cheshire, Lancashire, Leicestershire, Staffordshire, Warwickshire, and the West Riding of Yorkshire, and was on a par with Middlesex. Yet Suffolk was one of the least criminal counties in the country for those aged over 30. Such figures raise all sorts of interesting questions related to work and employment opportunities for young men in the region, issues to which readers will be referred in the following chapters.

TABLE 1.1 *Ratio of criminals to population, by age, 1844-1846*

	Essex	Norfolk	Suffolk	England
under 20	1 : 873	1 : 833	1 : 851	1 : 971
20-25	1 : 231	1 : 222	1 : 218	1 : 262
25-30	1 : 356	1 : 316	1 : 292	1 : 363
30 and over	1 : 740	1 : 743	1 : 1030	1 : 753

Source: J. Glyde, *Suffolk in the Nineteenth Century* (London, 1856), 131.

Taking his investigation a step further Glyde looked at the relative criminality of town and country within Suffolk between 1849 and 1853 and found wide variations; from one criminal to 454 of the population in the Cosford Union to 1:1344 in the Mutford; but even these figures hid enormous variations within the poor law unions themselves.[19] Some of the small market towns, Mildenhall, Framlingham, Stowmarket, and Bury St Edmunds for instance, were not noted for their criminality whereas Bungay, Hadleigh, Halesworth, and Sudbury were. Similar variations existed among the rural villages of which Withersfield, a sorely troubled parish, stands out as being the most criminal parish in the county. During the five-year period it furnished one criminal to 214 of its population and yet neighbouring

18 P. Horn, *The Rural World, 1780-1850* (London, 1980), 165; Rudé, *Criminal and Victim*, p. 11.
19 J. Glyde, *Suffolk in the Nineteenth Century* (London, 1856), pp. 136-44; id., 'Localities of Crime in Suffolk', *Journal of the Statistical Society*, 19 (1856), 102-6.

Wickhambrook provided only one to 1500. Some villages were thus far more criminal than any of the market towns. One must resist common-sense assumptions that towns, with their denser populations and abundant wealth of plunderable objects, were necessarily the most criminal areas of any one county.

In attempting to trace urban and rural criminal patterns the question 'where?' has to be placed alongside the question 'what?'. Were certain offences more frequently urban crimes? A review of the cases before the Suffolk Assizes shows clearly that serious crime, ranging from murder to property offences, was undoubtedly a rural phenomenon. Of the 229 offenders only thirty-eight were town residents, or 16.5 per cent. The urban population at this time amounted to 29 per cent of Suffolk's population. Glyde concluded, 'the simplicity and innocence of peasant life exists only in imagination'.[20] An observation further reinforced by the fact that three-quarters of all crime in the county was committed by labourers.

One complicating factor in any study of rural crime must be borne in mind: criminals were relatively mobile and travelled considerable distances to commit their offences. There must have, of necessity, been considerable coming and going from town to countryside and vice versa, movement of which historians know little. Contemporaries were evidently aware of this criminal migration. Magistrates in the village of Hethersett (N), lying between Norwich and Wymondham, complained bitterly of the proximity of these two towns.[21] In fact all the villages within five miles of Norwich were subject to vast amounts of sheep and fowl stealing. At Christmas time farmers repeatedly lost their ducks and Norfolk magistrates reported farmers had given up the idea of keeping poultry for 'they only kept them for thieves'.[22] Another annual event, the sailing of the 'North Sea Pirates' from Norwich down the rivers and broads of East Norfolk, purportedly on fishing expeditions but in reality to 'poach and plunder', escaped prosecution though their intentions were well known. Likewise at Lakenham, a small hamlet on the outskirts of Norwich, farmer Underwood complained that his fields were nightly robbed of turnips: 'fellows and boys were sitting about the lanes all day long, playing cards' waiting for him to leave off work and his fields unprotected.[23] Crime migrated in the opposite direction, the end of harvest

---

20 Glyde, *Suffolk*, p. 146.
21 PRO, HO 73/6, pt. 1, Returns from guardians to the Constabulary Commission.
22 *NM*, 24 Jan. 1829; see also *NC*, 8 Sept. 1838, 19 Jan. 1839.
23 *NC*, 4. Feb. 1843; *NNMPG*, 1 Oct. 1843.

witnessed large numbers of farm labourers moving to the market towns in search of largess money and drink. Inevitably their over-exuberance led to drunkenness, violence, and boosted the trade of 'loose girls of the city'.[24] What had been tradition and custom became a law and order problem as the century progressed, and the custom itself was very much on the wane by 1870.

Much evidence exists which suggests some towns, and in particular the city of Norwich, were refuges for criminals who operated in the countryside. Were these people the 'criminal class' of the region or is the notion as inapplicable here as in other areas of the country? Superficially, looking for a criminal class in the countryside is a pretty unlikely and unproductive exercise, although Chadwick in drawing up his questionnaire for the Select Committee on the Establishment of a Rural Constabulary thought otherwise. His loaded question, number thirteen, begged an affirmative answer from the respondents. Nor was he disappointed with their replies. Not surprisingly poachers figured in many of the returns.[25] Undoubtedly East Anglia was home to a number of professional full-time poachers who in turn built up networks of receivers, dealers, and carriers. But, as we shall see, the professionals who made their living solely through poaching were only a very small minority of those who poached. Moreover, most of them were very particular in what they stole, namely game and nothing else. Pragmatism rather than any social principle directed their attitudes since poaching was invariably a summary offence if caught, whereas fowl or animal stealing carried with it the threat of transportation, at least until the mid-century. Part-timers, invariably unemployed labourers, were more likely to partake of the entire gamut of the farmyard and the game covers. The small handful of professional poachers thus hardly constituted a criminal class.

More promising are the sheep stealers, the 'notorious' gangs who operated on an extensive scale. At Broome Heath (S), for example, a gang of four were arrested; they had been responsible for killing 120 sheep in six months.[26] In another case, nine members of the Rose family, a father and eight sons, described as the 'terror of Cockfield', although arrested were never convicted because people were too afraid to testify against them. Guilty or not, the list of offences cited against them offers historians a fascinating glimpse of rural crime in ten parishes over a short period. Of the thirty-six separate offences there

---

24 *BNP*, 6 Sept. 1864.
25 PRO, HO 73/2, 5-9.
26 *BNP*, 19 July 1820.

was the theft of four sheep, one goose, one lot of ducks, eight fowl houses, five pigs, three barn robberies, five amounts of dairy produce, three house break-ins, £45 in three separate incidents, one attempted robbery, and two personal attacks. No self-respecting professional criminal would have been impressed by such a list of 'small-time' petty thieving. The common thread running through all these incidents is food, food in sufficient quantity to feed a large and presumably unemployed family. John Rose senior, rather than masterminding a gang of crooks, was clearly stealing to keep his family alive and not to make a living.[27] A more professional gang of ten from Rockland St Peter (N) were caught with twelve sheep on one of their receiver's properties and these receivers were men 'in a respectable sphere of life being farmers'.[28] Butchers are repeatedly cited as receivers and it is more than likely that they actually stole the sheep themselves since newspapers frequently commented on the expert skinning of the carcasses in the fields. The presence of 'bent' butchers, farmers, innkeepers, and shepherds suggests opportunism rather than recidivism. This is amply borne out by the example of Futter who drove seventy sheep to Norwich market where he sold them for £112. Needless to say he aroused suspicion and was arrested.[29]

The region did have its share of wild men, individuals and gangs who terrorized their neighbourhoods. Some were social outcasts, like David Clowe, as we have seen, or Isaac Tatum who was shunned by his fellow labourers.[30] Some of them were enabled by their aggression and effrontery to act with impunity. William Howell, a barn robber, was notorious, since he invariably sported a policeman's hat, a prize from an earlier battle with the law. He was eventually arrested in 1844 and hanged for the murder of a constable. His gang also contained an arsonist and animal maimer. Another policeman was murdered under similar circumstances by two barn robbers at Halesworth (S).[31]

Crime in many parts of rural Britain was laid at the door of vagrants and itinerant workers. Jones's study of Wales partly bears out the truth of contemporary accusations.[32] East Anglia was no different in so far as tramps and hawkers frequently came under suspicion

---

27 *BNP*, 3 Dec. 1834.
28 *NC*, 24 Aug. 1839.
29 *NC*, 31 July 1858. Futter was caught a second time, see *NN*, 19 Mar. 1864.
30 For Tatum see *BNP*, 11 Aug. 1868.
31 For Howell see *NM*, 10 Aug. 1844 and 21 Dec. 1844. The arsonist, animal maimer, and threatening letter writer Botwright was a member of this gang, see pp. 201-2.
32 D. J. V. Jones, '"A Dead Loss to the Community": The Criminal Vagrant in Mid-Century Wales', *Welsh Historical Review*, 8 (1977), 312-43.

during upsurges of rioting or incendiarism — it certainly did not help the hawker's case if he sold phosphorous matches.[33] But when it came to everyday crime tramps and vagrants are notable by their absence. More prominent are the itinerant workers, the Irish harvesters in West Norfolk, the railway navvies, and embankment labourers who came from all over Britain. The Irish were more victims than victimizers, on one occasion a group of them came close to death after indigenous labourers had rounded them up, tried them before a mock court, and sentenced them to death by drowning in one of the many drainage ditches of the Fenland. Their crime had been to take work away from local men.[34] The embankers in the same region were altogether a more forceful bunch, being described as 'lawless' and prone to riot and theft whenever their wages or work was reduced.[35] The railway navvies too brought in their wake minor crime waves.[36] But when all is said and done the number of professional criminals was remarkably small and hardly constitutes the nomenclature *criminal class*. On the other hand, evidence abounds in newspapers and court records to suggest that rural people in general turned to crime in times of economic distress. If there was a criminal class in East Anglia it was the entire labouring community.

The Reverend Henslow, on moving to Suffolk, was much struck by the general depravity of the local people: 'I very soon observed that certain crimes were more openly and unblushingly practiced, and far more commonly tolerated'. One old woman told him, 'Why, sir, we never think anything about taking a few turnips from the field or sticks from the hedges; it is God makes them grow, not the farmers.'[37] All historians are agreed that most rural crime was economic, 'a defence against hunger'. Beattie's observation of the eighteenth century that property crime was mainly a matter of hunger and necessity finds echoes in the Hammonds' belief that thieving was 'called in to rehabilitate the labourer's economic position'.[38] Dire economic circumstances drove labourers to petty larceny. Rudé's recent research on Sussex and Gloucestershire would appear to back this up, for the

---

33 See PRO, HO 52/9, for evidence of itinerant match-sellers from Kent.

34 *NC*, 26 Aug. 1815.

35 *NN*, 22 Mar. 1851; PRO, HO 40/17, letter from Glasse, 6 Apr. 1822. The embankers, he wrote, 'appear disposed to bid defiance to all laws, both human and Divine'.

36 *BNP*, 28 Jan. 1846; PRO, HO 43/65, letter from Col. Oakes, 24 Aug. 1843.

37 J. S. Henslow, *Suggestions towards an Enquiry into the Present Condition of the Labouring Population of Suffolk* (Hadleigh, 1844), 17-18.

38 J. M. Beattie, *Crime and the Courts in England 1660-1800* (Oxford, 1986), p. 54; J. L. and B. Hammond, *The Village Labourer 1760-1832*, 3rd edn. (London, 1920), p. 162.

value of the stolen items, food, money, and clothing, was very low.[39]

The endemic nature of poverty-induced crime in East Anglia is plain to see. In Hadleigh (S), for example, a policeman was hired to halt wide-scale petty larceny. In the space of six months he had taken seventy-five inhabitants before the magistrates.[40] During the mid-century agrarian depression potato and fowl stealing coincided with high unemployment in the Risbridge Hundred of Suffolk.[41] One labourer when asked by the *Morning Chronicle* correspondent how he managed on four shillings a week, replied:

> We can't do it on our wages, you may be sure. The truth is master, we are often driven to do many things those times that we wouldn't do if we could help it. It is very hard for us to starve, and we sometimes pull some turnips, or perhaps potatoes, out of some of the fields, unbeknown to the farmers.[42]

There was a saying in Norfolk: 'a labourer cannot be honest and keep a pig'. Surely a recognition both of the dire poverty of the labourer and his propensity to steal. Court cases of barn robbing by employees of long standing who 'bore good characters' were not unusual.[43] The threshing season was the time when farmers were most on their guard, especially if his men were wielding the flail. Loose grain would find its way into pockets and bags. One tends to forget that the advent of mechanized threshing was not simply hated by labourers because it displaced their labour but also because it lessened their opportunities to steal. One popular Suffolk folk-song of the time makes this amply clear: 'the old sow will mourn the throshin machine.'[44]

Other forms of theft — sheep, horse, and wood stealing, and highway robbery — were in the majority of cases poverty-induced crimes. In the case of sheep stealing, professionalism was apparent where sheep disappeared frequently and in large numbers — the hallmark of poverty-induced sheep stealing was the taking of choice cuts of meat from a single dead animal. The carcass, head, and entrails were usually left behind.[45] There were two reasons for this; first,

---

39 Rudé, *Criminal and Victim, passim.*
40 PRO, HO 73/8, pt. 1.
41 *BNP*, 2 Apr. 1851.
42 Taken from *BNP*, 19 Dec. 1849.
43 For examples of employees of 15 years' standing see *NM*, 22 Mar. 1845; *NN*, 7 July 1849.
44 J. Glyde, ed., 'The Autobiography of a Suffolk Farm Labourer', *Suffolk Mercury* (1894), 19.
45 See J. G. Rule, 'The Manifold Causes of Rural Crime: Sheep-Stealing in England c.1740-1840', in Rule, ed., *Outside the Law*, pp. 102-29; Wells, 'Sheep-Rustling', pp. 127-45; Peacock, 'Village Radicalism', pp. 40-4.

people stole only what they could consume immediately and, second, they wanted to escape detection. The fleece and the volume of fat were the two greatest aids to police and prosecutors. The element of protest in this form of theft is probably not as great as Peacock has suggested though. In the following case, protest, hunger, and not a little humour combined to leave the farmer in no doubt as to the thieves' motivation.

> I hant stole only one ship to night
> Resen wi becase to was so very light
> You rich and I am pore
> Wen that done i com for more.[46]

Despair drove some to commit this offence. William Woodhouse, aged 21, told the court 'that he had a mind to be transported, and he would not stop no longer in this country... They would not give me either work or money.'[47] Shepherds, perhaps more than any other occupational group, were particularly tempted into this line of business, and some may have tried to mislead their masters at lambing time by removing lambs before the employer had time to count up heads. Others appear to have gone for the final grand gesture by driving entire flocks to market and making off with the proceeds of the sale. As a crime, as Wells and Rule have observed, sheep stealing eludes precise categorization although in most cases the motive was probably poverty. It is pertinent to note that with the upturn of agriculture and hence work and wages, in the mid-1850s, sheep stealing declined rapidly, being referred to as a 'nearly obsolete offence'.[48]

It has been suggested that poverty is too simplistic and insufficient an explanation for the rural felonies which occurred. One historian has suggested that labourers could have committed crimes 'not so much as a direct result of their poverty but rather as an expression of resentment against that condition'.[49] This may well explain a whole host of property crimes, not yet alluded to, which were not necessarily protest crimes but contained within them elements of protest. Such activities appear to have become a covert alternative to overt protest. One specific but elusive crime was endemic to East Anglia before 1840, thereafter it died out almost immediately, and that was the destruction of trees, gardens, and orchards. These practices probably

---

46 *NM*, 3 Feb. 1827.
47 *NC*, 4 Apr. 1840.
48 *NC*, 2 Dec. 1854.
49 Rule, *Outside the Law*, p. 105.

have a long tradition dating back to the eighteenth century when they came within the terms of the notorious Black Act. Their high point was, however, in the years immediately after the Napoleonic Wars. One wonders if they were a substitute for arson. Although no systematic study has been undertaken such property attacks display a number of definite characteristics. There appears to have been two forms of attack. First, damage to gardens, including fruit bushes, orchards, vineries, orangeries, and greenhouses: Dering of Crow Hall (N) lost orange and lemon trees, shrubs, and greenhouses in three separate attacks.[50] In another example 500 fruit trees at Stanton (S) were cut down.[51] Most of these incidents occurred in the summer months when the fruit was ripening, a matter that was probably not coincidental. The second type of attack was to trees which did not provide edible fruit. Again the damage could be extensive, ranging from an avenue of cedars to plantations of saplings; in one case 1,800 were destroyed in a single night.[52] Trying to discover motives for these malicious acts is rather difficult. Little economic gain accrued since very little wood or fruit was taken and to put such attacks down to mindless vandalism does not really explain anything. A number of clues appear to lie in the owners of such property and these were usually gentlemen of considerable social standing. Magistrates and parsons were in fact the main victims and this would suggest they were being attacked for what they were. The parsons' fruit trees are an intriguing puzzle which may be related to their ownership of the small tithes, whereas the magistrates were probably sufferers as a result of their role in recent court cases.[53]

Resentment and protest were present in other attacks on property in the years before 1850. Numerous ploughs were cut and destroyed, harnesses torn or ripped to shreds, gigs and carts disabled, animals turned loose into standing corn, gates unhinged , and then broken or laid across the narrow country lanes at night, presumably to unseat unsuspecting farmers and poor law guardians, which made travelling at night in the 1820s and 1830s a fairly unnerving experience.[54] The Newmarket mail coach crashed into a plough and a harrow laid across its path. Another favourite trick employed by highway men was to

---

50 *NC*, 3 June and 25 Nov. 1826; *BNP*, 20 June 1827.
51 *BNP*, 30 Sept. 1829.
52 *NC*, 7 Jan. 1826, 15 Sept. 1821; *BNP*, 8 Feb. 1832.
53 See E. J. Evans, *The Contentious Tithe* (London, 1976), for a full discussion.
54 For ploughs see *BNP*, 23 Feb. 1825, 4 Jan. 1843, 11 Jan. 1843, 15 Mar. 1843; gates: *NM*, 15 Dec. 1827, *BNP*, 25 May 1836; *NC*, 3 Oct. 1840; harnesses: *EA*, 28 Feb. 1832; *BNP*, 10 May 1843; carts: *NM*, 27 Feb. 1830 and 30 Jan. 1836.

place a rope at head height across the road, thus unsaddling the rider who would be too dazed to resist.[55] Physical attacks became more brutal during the years of the New Poor Law's inception when relieving officers were beaten 'to within an inch of their lives' and when the Poor Law Commissioner Kay had himself sworn in as a special constable in order to arrest anyone who physically or verbally abused him.[56] Even travelling during the day was not without its hazards. Contemporaries recalled the resentment and pent up aggression as they rode by knots of unemployed labourers 'listlessly parading the dirty or dusty paths and roads', or 'lolling upon the ditch sides' shouting obscenities at respectable passers-by.[57] Desperate poverty drew away the veil of deferential behaviour.

If riding through the countryside, day or night, presented considerable dangers to the weak of heart then stopping at home in the winter months would appear to have been the sensible option. The clerk to the Brandon magistrates no doubt wished it was, but he became a prisoner in his own home and even then crowds of thirty to forty continued to break his windows and post threatening letters under his door.[58] It is often argued that farm labourers were respecters of the person, gamekeepers apart, and the arson attacks and the riots would suggest as much. However, during particularly parlous times, farmers, relieving officers, and the like became victims of seemingly gratuitous personal attacks. Farmers were called up at night and on looking out of their windows were shot at. Grimmer of Pakefield (S) received wounds in his neck and shoulder whereas Allday of Hingham (N) was more fortunate in that the gun misfired but his mysterious visitors did not leave until every window had been shot in.[59]

Most of these attacks on property and persons went unsolved, crimes of protest were by their very nature covert and undetectable. This being so we should be wary of Rudé's estimate that protest crime

---

55 For mail coach crashes see *NO*, 5 July 1817, *BNP*, 14 Aug. 1844; highway robbery: *NC*, 4 Mar. 1826.

56 PRO, MH 32/48, Kay to PLC, 26 Dec. 1835. Examples of assaults on poor law officials: *BNP*, 2 Apr. 1834, 30 Apr. 1834; *NC*, 18 June and 30 July 1836.

57 J. H. Kent, *Remarkes on the Injuriousness of the Consolidation of Small Farms and the Benefit of Small Occupations and Allotments: With Some Observations on the Past and Present State of the Agricultural Labourers* (Bury St Edmunds, 1844), 2; Henslow, *Suggestions*, p. 24; *BNP*, 12 Jan. 1858; PP 1839, XIX, *1st Report of the Commissioners Appointed to Inquire as to the Best Means of Establishing an Efficient Constabulary Force*, p. 136.

58 PRO, HO 52/10, letter from Smythe, 23 Mar. 1830.

59 For Grimmer see *NM*, 30 Mar. 1844; Allday, *BNP*, 9 Mar. 1836. For similar cases see *NC*, 18 Apr. 1818 and 25 June 1836.

ranged from between 4 and 10 per cent of criminal indictments in the region.[60] Admittedly he is dealing with cases that came before the senior courts but the fact is most crimes of protest never got that far. Offers of rewards, the presence of police, and the activities of farmers' property associations all proved powerless in the face of these terroristic attacks. The dark figure of unrecorded crime was probably higher for protest-type crime than for any other forms of serious offence. This can be seen by comparing reports of crime in the local press and the returns of the constabulary questionnaire. In the latter magistrates and farmers reported instances which never found their way into the columns of the local newspapers. One should also remember the primary reason for establishing rural constabularies in West Suffolk and Cambridgeshire; in both instances the high level of arson moved the magistracy to act.[61]

The accuracy of criminal statistics before 1856 and the dangers inherent in interpreting them are too well known to warrant repetition here but enough evidence survives to allow general conclusions on the movement and weight of crime in the region. Macnab believed the years 1821-51 experienced the heaviest wave of crime during the century — to what extent did East Anglia reflect the national picture?[62] Evidence from a variety of sources all points to an increase of both protest and non-protest crime after the ending of the Napoleonic Wars. One way of gauging contemporary opinion is by noting the formation of associations for the prevention of crime and the protection of property. Such associations first made their appearance towards the end of the eighteenth century in the region but between 1817 and 1828 there was a sudden burst of activity by many of the hundreds.[63] Newspapers announced the formation of nine of them in the region between these dates, and in addition the Hartismere Hundred (S) raised £500 in 1827 to establish its own rural police, a policy which continued into the 1830s when other hundreds experimented with the idea.[64] Rather basic gaol and crime statistics would seem to confirm contemporary fears. Norfolk gaol commitments showed a sudden rise after 1814 which continued until 1820, thereafter a decline until 1824, although 1822 registered a spectacular peak occasioned by the riots of that year. From 1824 to

---

60 Rudé, *Protest and Punishment*, p. 20.
61 *BNP*, 30 Oct. 1844; PP 1852-3, XXV, *Second Report of the S. C. on the Police*, p. 46.
62 K. K. Macnab, 'Aspects of the History of Crime in England and Wales between 1805 and 1860', Ph.D. thesis (Univ. of Sussex, 1965), 333.
63 *NC*, 13 June 1818, 10 June 1826; *NM*, 24 Mar. 1821.
64 *BNP*, 17 Oct. 1827.

1830 they continued to rise by 30 per cent, a trend which should have alerted the authorities to the deteriorating social and economic conditions in the region.[65] In like manner the incendiary upsurge of 1843-4 was preceded by a steady upward trend of Norwich gaol commitments from 1840. This pattern was repeated again from 1847 to 1852 when arson attacks announced the onset of the mid-century depression.[66]

The increase in the number of offenders committed to Suffolk gaols between 1814 and 1820 was less spectacular than in neighbouring Norfolk. It doubled whereas the latter had increased threefold.[67] A peak was registered in 1822 when Bury gaol, built to house eighty prisoners, reported 200 crammed within its walls.[68] By 1830 Bury gaol committals had risen to 646, rising still further to 892 by 1834. The trend reversed until 1842-3 when a sudden increase indicated growing tension. This was repeated between 1847 and 1850.[69] County committals for serious crime in Suffolk parallel the Bury gaol figures and the two incendiary years, 1844 and 1851, registered the largest peaks, 630 and 629 respectively.[70] Thereafter crime appears to have declined rapidly during the years of agrarian prosperity.

Between 1834 and 1851 regional property crimes without violence — animal stealing and larcenies — followed a slightly different trend to malicious offences against property — arson and maiming.[71] The former peaked in 1838 and then rose to a high plateau between 1842 and 1844 before dropping away sharply in 1845. Small peaks were also noted in 1847, 1849, and finally 1851. Malicious offences, on the other hand, peaked in 1836 and then dropped to a low plateau until the spectacular peak of 1844, after which they declined to a trough in 1847 before moving steadily upward to an 1851 peak. From both sets of figures it is possible to conclude that property crimes were more responsive to grain prices whereas malicious offences responded to employment trends.

Looking at the Suffolk figures for 1834-51 in a little more detail, arson declined from 1834 to 1841 when no committals were recorded.

65 R. N. Bacon, *Report on the Agriculture of Norfolk* (Norwich, 1844), pp. 154-5.
66 *NC*, 19 Nov. 1842, 12 July 1856; *NN*, 14 Jan. 1855.
67 *BNP*, 2 May 1821.
68 *BNP*, 27 Feb. 1822.
69 *BNP*, 19 June 1844; *NM*, 12 Apr. 1851; IESRO, HA II/BI/II/8, letter from governor of Bury gaol to Earl of Stradbroke, 21 June 1844.
70 Glyde, *Suffolk*, p. 117.
71 See PP 1835-52, *Annual Criminal Returns and Statistics*; W. Johnson, *England as It is* (London, 1851), p. 100.

Game law offences and animal stealing also displayed an overall downward trend but small peaks were recorded in both cases in 1836 and 1839-40 respectively. Before the arson peak of 1844, animal stealing peaked in 1842, followed by game law offences in 1843, but all three recorded dramatic drops in 1845. Whilst arson continued to fall to an 1848 trough, animal stealing recovered slightly in 1847 before receding to its 1848 trough. Poaching figures again climbed in 1846 and remained on a plateau until 1849. During the mid-century depression animal stealing was the first to peak in 1849, followed by arson in 1850 and game in 1851. However, the overall trend for animal and game thefts during these years was downwards. Comparing the three-year average 1834-6 to 1849-51, the diminution for game commitment was 55 per cent, for animal stealing 45 per cent, but arson, on the other hand, had increased two and a half times which suggests it was the hallmark of rural crime in the mid- to late 1840s.

The experience of Norfolk and Suffolk is partly repeated in the national figures between 1834-1849 when arson increased by nearly two and a half times, whereas animal stealing was down 11 per cent and game offences down by a mere 1 per cent. This suggests arson was something of a national problem from 1843 to the mid-century. This is further borne out by the evidence. Only Cumberland of all the English counties failed to prosecute anyone for incendiarism between 1843 and 1851, even though cases of arson were known to have occurred in the county.[72] Elsewhere in England, apart from the East Anglian counties of Cambridgeshire, Essex, Norfolk, and Suffolk where arson was endemic, some surprising counties ranked high on the list of incendiarism, namely and in order of precedence, Devon, Yorkshire, Somerset, and Hampshire. This might indicate rather different forces were at work where arson was concerned than in the Swing Riots of 1830. Of the forty English counties, the Swing counties were ranked in terms of decreasing importance for incendiary committals, Kent 12th, Wiltshire 17th, Berkshire 22nd, and Sussex 29th. Further research will be required to explain this rather surprising trend although Lowerson's and Wells's research might well suggest that in the case of Sussex rather different methods and traditions of protest were adhered to.[73] Another feature when looking

---

72 These observations are based on a reading of selected local newspapers and the PP annual criminal returns.

73 J. Lowerson, 'The Aftermath of Swing: Anti-Poor Law Movements and Rural Trade Unions in the South East of England', in A. Charlesworth, ed., *Rural Social Change and Conflicts since 1500* (Hull, 1983), pp. 55-82; R. A. E. Wells, 'Rural Rebels in Southern England in the 1830s', in C. Emsley and J. Walvin, edd., *Artisans, Peasants and Proletarians,*

at arson on a national scale is that the mid-century years of 1849-51 registered sixteen county peaks whereas only six counties peaked in 1844, of which five were in arable regions. Only Devon broke with this trend. Therefore arson is clearly a sensitive indicator of the seriousness of the mid-century agrarian depression.

The observations made in this chapter would appear to have important implications for the vigorous and stimulating Wells-Charlesworth debate.[74] Wells originally argued that during the gradual process of the proletarianization of agricultural labour in the eighteenth century covert protest, particularly arson, emerged and became the labourers' main weapon during the first half of the nineteenth century. In a follow-up article he changed his stance by arguing that arson had become common by the 1790s. Charlesworth, on the other hand, responded by claiming that arson remained peripheral to the mainstream of the protest movement in East Anglia, which until 1830, was characterized by collective unrest. Many problems confront historians in a debate of this kind, not least their lack of detailed knowledge concerning covert crime in general and incendiarism in particular. Moreover, arson was only deployed on a widespread scale at times of socio-economic tension and thus wild fluctuations in incendiary activity occurred. However, the overall trend for arson from the time of Waterloo to 1851 was undeniably upwards, with the 1840s becoming the boom period, especially 1843-4 when over 600 fires were recorded across the nation. Thus Wells's initial claim that arson was the enduring and characteristic feature of rural protest in the first half of the century is borne out by the facts as we know them. But historians should be wary of lumping arson with other covert crimes like animal stealing or poaching, for we have already seen that arson continued to increase whilst the other offences either contracted or, at the very most, remained static.[75] This would suggest that different economic forces provoked different criminal trends.

Arson, it will be argued, reflected the problems of under-

1760-1860 (Beckenham, 1985), pp. 124-65.

74 R. A. E. Wells, 'The Development of the English Rural Proletariat and Social Protest, 1700-1850', *JPS* 6 (1979), 115-39, and 'Social Conflict and Protest in the English Countryside in the Early Nineteenth Century: A Rejoinder', *JPS* 8 (1981), 514-30; A. Charlesworth, 'The Development of the English Rural Proletariat and Social Protest: a Comment', *JPS* 8 (1980), 101-11.

75 For further critical comment and observations of this debate see J. E. Archer, 'The Wells-Charlesworth Debate: A Personal Comment on Arson in Norfolk and Suffolk', *JPS* 9 (1982), 277-84; J. Rule, *The Labouring Classes in Early Industrial England, 1750-1850* (London, 1986), pp. 353-6.

employment, unemployment, and growing population pressure in the countryside, rather than high food prices. Charlesworth's insistence that collective protest was the hallmark of social unrest until 1830, whilst apparently holding good for East Anglia, may not be reflected elsewhere in the country. It would be misleading to believe, as he implies, that covert crimes, like arson, were substituted in any straightforward manner for collective protest after the defeat of Swing. It has already been noted how some Swing counties never became incendiary-prone whereas non-Swing counties like Cambridgeshire, Devon, Gloucestershire, Lincolnshire, Somerset, and Yorkshire did. Nor should we underestimate the labourers' choice of tactics in furthering disputes or making known their grievances. In East Anglia collective protest did not die away in the face of official repression in 1830. Between 1831 and 1834 there were at least thirty-seven recorded strikes and demonstrations and a further twenty-five riots and collective disturbances in 1835-6 when the New Poor Law was introduced. Furthermore, overt and collective protest in the region became prominent once again after 1851, well before the advent of agricultural trade unionism. This differentiation between overt collective and covert individual protest may well prove to be an artificial construct of historians seeking to impose some kind of evolutionary development on the methods and forms of agrarian unrest, as put forward by Charles Tilly in his evolutionary model from 'reactive' to 'modern' protest.[76] Anyone reading of the incendiary attacks in East Anglia between 1830 and 1850 is left in no doubt as to the overt and collective displays of anger, hatred, or undiluted joy at the scenes of conflagrations. If one separates the act of starting the fire — covert and individualistic — from the subsequent reaction which the fire engendered — overt and collective — then the dichotomy does not appear to be that great. Fires, in other words, provided outlets for displays of collective strength and unity about which the authorities could do little. All in all, the development and deployment of agrarian unrest is a rather complex matter. The happy coincidence of the invention of the strike-anywhere match, the 'Lucifer', in 1829-30, and the defeat of Swing may well be misleading us more than we realize, for technology it would seem had come to the aid of the protester at just the right historical moment.[77]

---

76 C. Tilly, *Collective Violence in European Perspective* (Washington, 1969), pp. 5-34.
77 *Everyman's Encyclopedia*, viii (London, 1978), p. 121.

2
The Farm Labourer: Work and Wages

Any study of rural protest must take as its starting-point the enormous numbers of men, women, and children who worked on the land. Strange though it may seem, and many historians have been conscious of the fact, we know so very little about them. The Census tells us approximately how many there were decennially and the registers in church and chapel mark their progress through life, but these stark facts apart, we know little of their attitudes, thoughts, behaviour, and relations both with each other and with those in power and authority over them. Too many assumptions usually pertaining to deference and passivity cloud what was often a complex and highly localized set of rural social and economic circumstances.

These men and women said little to anyone of social consequence that has been passed down to the present day, and if we are to believe nineteenth-century observers, they thought less and read nothing. They were dullards, 'always grave, moody, and silent', who 'seldom look you fairly in the face'. Plodding, 'with a slouching gait', behind teams of horses they were barely visible functionary figures in the landscape.[1] A. Armstrong and K. D. M. Snell have recently attempted to bring a touch of humanity to them by identifying their desires, priorities, and hopes in life.[2] This study, too, but from a very different perspective and set of assumptions, intends to do the same. Their crimes of darkness were, more than anything else, cries for attention writ large and by examining what they did when they did we might discover a little of their lives, frustrations, and above all exploitation. The study of rural protest, it will be shown, uncovers not a sophisticated and politically conscious class but a body of men ground down and demoralized by the economic circumstances in which they found themselves. Arson, above all, highlights the mundane daily struggle for the dignity of labour.

In 1851 there were 97,000 male agricultural labourers in Norfolk and Suffolk, or one in four of the male population. The figure for women and children is impossible to calculate since the Census failed to record the casual employment of these two groups. This agrarian workforce has resisted most attempts by historians to reduce it to an average and their contemporaries have served only to confuse matters

---

1 Anon., 'Incendiarism, its Causes and Cure', *Fraser's Magazine*, 30 (Aug. 1844), 245.
2 K. D. M. Snell, *Annals of the Labouring Poor: Social Change and Agrarian England 1660-1900* (Cambridge, 1985). A. Armstrong, *Farmworkers: A Social and Economic History 1770-1980* (London, 1988).

still more for posterity by referring to them as peasants, servants, or labourers. The first term was used frequently by those with a poetic and utopian outlook, 'servants' was a nostalgic reference to the eighteenth century with all its associated overtones of an organic and stable face-to-face community, whereas 'labourer' was the reality by the nineteenth century — landless, proletarianized, and pauperized.

By 1815 labourers were differentiated in terms of wages and work experience by their age, marital status, gender, reputation, skill, and employer. Therefore exact and definitive conclusions regarding wage movements and employment patterns are virtually impossible and this should be borne in mind over the remainder of this chapter. Who, it must be asked, came under the generic occupational description of farm labourer? A multiplicity of agrarian tasks were covered by this pervasive catch-all term: crow-scarers, backus' boys, farm servants, teamsmen, stockmen, yardmen, gang women, and casual farm workers. There were others, the professional and independent piece-workers — men like Arch who were skilled in specialist tasks, and the men who travelled with their farm machinery. All these workers had specific roles and places in the farmyard hierarchy, and even within this complex structure the labourers erected further hierarchies of their own. At harvest there was the 'Lord' and 'Lady' who set the pace of work and bargained with the farmer for the price of 'getting the corn in', and at ploughing the head team-man would lead others, in decreasing seniority, in a line of ploughs across the fields. Farm labour like most other occupations was status conscious.

All farm labourers, however, had one experience in common: they were exploited, and the banal image of the bucolic farmyard camouflages the endemic tensions and structural conflict.[3] But all labouring groups within this hierarchy were not equally vulnerable to these tensions nor were their reactions necessarily the same. Therefore, some understanding of the hierarchical structure and the economic vulnerability of the various sub-groups within it is necessary if we are to appreciate fully the context in which crimes of protest occurred.

Farm labourers began their careers at a very early age. It was not unusual for 6-year-olds to be found in the fields on a casual basis, although the 1843 *Report on Women and Children in Agriculture* regarded the age of 9 or 10 to be more common. This simple fact was, according to nineteenth-century observers, the source of the problems

---

3   A. Howkins, *Poor Labouring Men: Rural Radicalism in Norfolk 1870-1923* (London, 1985), *passim*.

of degradation and immorality found in the older farm hands. Unschooled and predominantly illiterate, children were delivered into the 'fatal guidance of vice'.[4]

Their first farm jobs were of a simple and tedious nature: stone-picking, crow-scaring, stock-keeping, weeding, and dibbling, which left permanent psychological scars. One labourer recalled: 'Suffolk labourers are often twitted as a dull lot, and no wonder. Such monotonous work as bird scaring is ruinous to a boy's mental faculties. To be obliged to look all day at the same clods and the same trees necessarily generates a stolid demeanour.'[5]

From the ages of 12 to 16 farm boys were more permanently established within the labour hierarchy when they took on servant status, known as backus' boys in East Anglia. At this stage the more intelligent were taught the rudimentaries of the specialized skills of horse or stock-keeping, but for the majority their experience was one of general labour, chopping wood, cleaning utensils, and preparing food for the farmyard animals. Whatever their abilities all of them came under the strict discipline of their masters. Some were beaten and flogged as and when their employers felt the mood and occasionally with tragic consequences. One boy died shortly after a flogging from his master, King Viall of Middleton Hall (S), who, although exonerated of blame at the inquest, felt the heat of the incendiary's wrath soon after.[6]

Children's work experience was not far removed from that of adults; they were employees from an early age, earning a cash wage, and were even more vulnerable to exploitation from their masters on account of their age and the work in which they were involved. Work conditions were harsh since crow-scaring took no account of the weather. Thus children were doubly vulnerable to prosecution. First, as employees they could, like adult workers, experience oppression and act upon their grievances through protest. Second, children were often responsible for the large number of accidental fires when, as crow-scarers, they attempted to warm themselves against the piercing winter winds. This in itself was a prosecutable offence but in the years of widespread incendiary activity a 'moral panic' would set in among landholders who tended to view all fires as malicious acts. In other

---

4   PP 1843, XII, *Reports of Assistant Commissioners on the Employment of Women and Children in Agriculture*, pp. 237-9 245-50; Glyde, *Suffolk*, p. 372.

5   J. Glyde, 'Autobiography', p. 9.

6   *BNP*, 5 Jan. 1844; Jones, 'Thomas Campbell Foster', p. 11. See also *NM*, 25 Nov. 1885, where a Norfolk labourer recalled how his master 'used to give a trashing when he liked, fault or no fault'.

words children might have, on occasion, been unfairly prosecuted and even transported for the crime of warming themselves.[7]

Children's wages, because they were regulated by custom rather than wheat prices, varied little over the period and ranged from 2*d.* a day for the youngest to 4*s.* a week for 15-year-old outdoor labourers. However the employment of children, though welcomed by parents and employers alike, appears to have had an adverse effect on the wages and the employment opportunities of those immediately above them in the labour hierarchy, the young single adult labourers. With the passing of the New Poor Law parents were keener than ever for their children to be employed from as early an age as possible since the new act stopped allowances and lowered family incomes.[8] Thus parents with young families were given preferential treatment by employers who wanted not only lower poor rates but lower wage bills.

Women too were casually employed, usually in the least skilled yet most arduous tasks. Evidence suggests they were not universally employed in agriculture and that their numbers, gangs excluded, fluctuated and then declined in the latter half of the period. However, during the Napoleonic Wars when there were severe manpower shortages in conjunction with a declining regional textile industry women gained the necessary skills and taste for field work.

Stone-picking, weeding, dropping seed, topping and tailing turnips, and harvesting were tasks commonly assigned to them. In the midwinter months, between December and February, very few were employed on the land. This was due in part to the seasonal demands of arable farming when less labour was required, but also farmers made adult men their first consideration at this time of year. It should be added, however, that farmers were never so philanthropic as to employ men in tasks which were traditionally put out to women, such as stone-picking or weeding.

The employment of women may have declined after the 1850s but the evidence is not conclusive and in some cases contradictory. It was reported in 1867:

> Everywhere I heard the same story, that women are found to be less and less disposed to go out to work upon the land. They will refuse unsuitable work; they will stay at home on wet days. Whether from the easier circumstances in which they live, or from having become intelligent enough to take a more accurate measure

---

7 For examples of accidental fires see *BNP*, 24 Jan. 1844, 15 Mar. 1859, 17 Dec. 1861; *NN*, 27 Apr. 1861.

8 PP 1843, XII. 238, 247-9; W. Hasbach, *A History of the English Agricultural Labourer* (London, 1908), p. 225.

of loss and gain there seems to be much less attraction for them in the farmers' 8d. or 9d. a day than there used to be.[9]

On the other hand, it was reported in the same year that women were taking work away from young men. In those areas where labour shortages could and did occur women continued to work in gangs. In the second half of the century pressure from moral reformers and landowners may have induced women to give up field work, when men's wages improved, for the more 'laudable' task of caring for their families.[10]

Women's wages tended to remain static over the period, although notable differentials between areas occurred.[11] However low their wages and however casual their work, women's earnings were an important contribution to the family income. It will be shown later that, where rural industries had previously existed or were in decline, the poverty of the families in those areas was greatest. When women could not gain employment in either agriculture or industry they were able to contribute to the family earnings by taking in washing, mending clothes, digging the allotments, and gleaning.

The most vulnerable, and in many ways the most rebellious, were the young single male labourers whose social and economic condition had largely deteriorated in the last decade of the eighteenth century and the first quarter of the nineteenth. By the 1830s very few young men, for instance, 'lived-in' as annually hired farm servants.[12] This transformation had profound effects on rural society. Those contemporaries with long memories idealized this employment system as the golden age of rural social relations when master and servant often worked together in 'mutual respect and attachment, which mutual dependence and mutual aid invariably create'.[13] A variety of factors set in motion the decline of 'living-in' and all have been ably recounted by Kussmaul and Snell.[14] That similar forces were at work in East Anglia, such as increasing population which provided pools of cheap day labour, fears of making a settlement, and the social pretensions of farmers — 'since farmers lived in parlours, labourers are no more found in kitchens' — are evident from the replies to

---

9 PP 1867, XVII, *Report of the Commissioners on the Employment of Children, Young Persons and Women in Agriculture*, p. 17.
10 Ibid. p. 16.
11 See PP 1843, XII, and PP 1867, XVII, *passim*.
12 *BNP*, 26 May 1824; PP 1824, VI, *S .C. on Agricultural Labourers' Wages*, p. 60.
13 R. N. Bacon, *Report*, pp. 142-3.
14 A. Kussmaul, *Servants in Husbandry in Early Modern England* (Cambridge, 1981); Snell, *Annals*, pp. 67-102.

Rural Queries.[15] However, it would be erroneous to believe that single men were simply kicked out of farmhouses in order to improve their employers' standards and qualities of living. It would appear they were keen to leave of their own volition. The food provided for indoor servants deteriorated so much, one labourer recalled, that many left the farms in the hope of improving their material and physical well-being.[16] But the *real* reason was put succinctly by the Reverend Calvert of Whatfield: 'the labourers themselves do not like the regularity of life required in domestic servants'.[17] Life under the employer's roof was clearly very restricting.

Whatever the reasons for the change the results were profound, not only for young farm labourers but also for the expansion of rural protest in the nineteenth century. They were now freed from total paternalistic supervision by their employers, especially in their leisure time when they were able to mix and talk freely with their peers, enhancing what Newby has called 'the solidarity of the taproom'.[18] Little wonder that contemporary moralists had severe reservations against the beerhouses which sprang up in every village after 1830. This solidarity was enhanced still further by two other factors directly related to the decline in living-in. First, the Settlement Laws were strictly enforced for much of this period, which meant the young were more likely to stay in the village of their birth. This led to the formation of a 'stronger village community consciousness' which in turn contributed to the protest movement against landowners and employers.[19] Second, social relations between farmers and labourers deteriorated rapidly after 1815, there being no bond of common experience between them. Physically and socially segregated, the labourers were hired and fired at will and this in turn undermined the so-called deferential relationship. As Newby argues, farm workers remain deferential so long as their self-respect remains intact, but in the 1820s and 1830s this was not the case.[20] Superficially, labourers remained in their forelock-tugging place but the sheer volume of crime, both protest and non-protest, presents a very different picture. The language of the threatening letters illustrates the ambiguities of this period rather well. Invariably they begin with polite references to the 'master', 'sir', 'mister', or 'gentlemen' before moving on to the

---

15 PP 1834, XXXIII, *Answers to Rural Queries*, given by Bevan of Rougham to qu. 38.
16 Glyde, 'Autobiography', pp. 12-13.
17 PP 1834, XXXIII, 471.
18 H. Newby, *The Deferential Worker* (London, 1977), 47.
19 Snell, *Annals*, p. 337.
20 Newby, 'The Deferential Dialectic', *Comparative Studies in Society and History*, 17 (1975). 145.

issuing of dire threats against life and property. This loss of self-respect forced labourers on a number of occasions to compare themselves with machines or black slaves. One labourer was prosecuted for calling his master a 'nigger-driver'.[21]

At about the age of 16 farm boys assumed 'the habits of men' by leaving their employer's house and becoming more independent of their parents and of their masters. This step into the adult world was not matched by any significant improvements in their standard and quality of living. Many moved in to common lodging houses of 'the most wretched description' and their security of labour plummeted, especially after the poor law reforms of 1834. Prior to this they, like the older married men, had received allowances in aid of wages or had worked in the labour gangs on the roads. Both groups led miserable existences, although married men received higher allowances, a feature which drove many into 'early and improvident marriages'.[22] However after 1834 the plight of the single men deteriorated further since they found themselves competing directly with women and children. A youth of 16 could offer his services at 1s. 6d. a day whereas women were hired for between 6d. and 1s. Marital status, not productivity or competence, likewise determined the single men's wages and their employability. Invariably youths earned between a half and two-thirds of married men and rarely worked all the year round. Many contemporaries were critical of this differential system:

> Few of the unmarried get more than 6s., the majority but 5s. per week, but, ... there can be no doubt that they [farmers] are able to get a much larger amount of work from the young unmarried men than from the married and older ones ... it is manifestly unjust to make a difference in the wages of the two classes.[23]

One response to their desperate plight was crime, a point amply borne out by respondents to Chadwick's questionnaire on the formation of the rural constabulary.[24] Furthermore, when widespread unemployment occurred among the young they occasionally viewed their plight collectively. In November 1834 at Lidgate (S) they formed themselves into what they called 'unions', perhaps an indication of a vague awareness of Tolpuddle. One of its members, George Pulham (22) was executed for firing the property of a local farmer. He

21 *BNP*, 23 Mar. 1869.
22 *The Times*, 10 June 1844; PP 1834, XXXII, 306 and 320.
23 *MC*, 5 Dec. 1849. See also *MC*, 10 July 1844, which describes 'the bad custom' as being common in 'many parishes of Suffolk'.
24 PRO, HO 73/6, pt. 1, HO 73/8, pt. 1, *passim*.

and two others had been stoning the farmer's geese on the day of the fire. At Terrington (N) the local youth formed themselves into the 'Night Jury' and went on a spree of window-breaking, gate-removing, and other minor property attacks.[25]

The national press reporters, during their East Anglia tours of 1844, noted with alarm the large numbers of young men idly congregating on village greens. When engaged in conversation the *Morning Chronicle* correspondent found they did not hesitate to speak 'bitterly of the farmers who would not give them work'.[26] Since these young men were much freer of the constraints which held older labourers in subservience, neither the discipline of regular work nor the regulations of allotment holdings could touch them. They welcomed and initiated much of the crime in rural areas.

If crime was one response then migration from the region was another escape route open to them. Both railway building and emigration to the American continent were popular, but the army proved the biggest attraction, especially when the Crimean War began.[27] This was not the first time, nor was it to be the last, that the British Army was partially comprised of dissatisfied rural labourers. At the end of the 1850s, with the war over, the movement from field to barracks continued and brought about the first labour shortages since 1815.

The young single men were the gravest social problem during the first half of the nineteenth century, although their plight was largely ignored. The usual safety nets of charities, allotments, and even the poor law itself were rarely held out to catch them in times of distress. They were the rural surplus on which farmers depended at vital times of the year. When they began to leave the land, labour shortages occurred which were eventually overcome by more extensive use of farm machinery. It is not without significance that the level of protest diminished with their exodus; they had been the rebels of the countryside.

The great majority of the labour force were adult men who covered the entire spectrum of skills from the full-time specialists — shepherds, team-men, and stockmen — to the casual, unskilled, general labourers. All too often agrarian workers have been dealt with generically under the heading of farm labour but in a study of rural

25 *BNP*, 1 Apr. 1835; *NM*, 7 June 1851.
26 *MC*, 15 July 1844.
27 For reports on army recruitment see *NC*, 18 Nov. 1854, 20 Feb. 1858; L. M. Springall, 'The Norfolk Agricultural Labourer 1834-84', Ph.D. thesis (Univ. of London, 1935), pp. 91-2.

protest this would be both uninformative and misleading. The position of the labourer in the hierarchy was reflected in his wage, security of employment, cottage, allocation of allotment, and the receipt of charity. All were, however, wage labourers, although the relationship of the cash nexus was by no means the only one that tied labour, since size of family and age could bestow rewards of charitable benevolence on the recipient from the employer.

The farmyard elite was composed of those who worked with animals. Their skill and longer working hours were reflected in higher wages, on average 2s. a week more than day labourers, and weekly perquisites. Working seven days a week, rain or shine, these men were considered by their masters to be more steady and respectable than the rest of the workforce. Court records suggest their respectability was overstated, since many were charged for all manner of crimes related to their work, from maiming and sheep stealing to theft of feed for their charges.

Beneath them came a vast army of day labourers who, as their title suggests, were hired on a daily basis and paid at the end of the week. It is almost impossible to estimate what they earned in any one year since they rarely worked every day and their wages fluctuated throughout the year due to the price of wheat, task work, and weather conditions. In fact their earnings varied from day to day. In 1849 Suffolk labourers earned 8s. a week but this was, reported the *Morning Chronicle*, 'a perfect delusion'. Thomas Campbell Foster, the *Times* correspondent, also emphasized this point in 1844 when the nominal wage was 9s.: he rarely found anyone earning this amount. Most typical was the case of John Sturman who had had five and a half day's work over a four week period. Another labourer complained, 'There's some weeks ... we only get 4s. — sometimes less than that — and in very wet weather we gets nothing at all.'[28] Deductions for sickness, bad weather, and even national holidays not only upset the precariously balanced finances of labouring families but also brought the charge of 'grinding' and 'screwing the poor' against farmers.

Farmers defended themselves against accusations of illiberality by arguing that a lot of work was done by the piece or task, but in reality this defence was untenable before the 1850s when task work was the exception rather than the rule.[29] Even where it did exist task work was open to abuse and bred considerable dissatisfaction among labourers. Price fixing was delayed until after the job had begun or even, in some

---

28 *MC*, 8 Dec. 1849; *The Times*, 16 July 1844.
29 H. Raynbird, 'On Measure Work', *JRAS* 7 (1846), 119-40; Kent, *Remarks*, p. 74.

cases, completed. One informed contemporary argued that farmers set labourers to work on task for a day or two in order to see how much could be done and then set the price so low that labourers had to work very hard to earn standard day wages. This 'infamous plan' resulted in at least one fire in the Stanton (S) neighbourhood and was the main grievance behind another at Lackford (S) where William Thompson fell out with his employer over the rate for muck-spreading. As a result he went on a 'go-slow' and was promptly sacked. A fire broke out a day later.[30]

For much of the nineteenth century labourers were paid day wages and these were related to the price of wheat.[31] This was regional customary practice but the actual correlation between wages and prices had altered by the nineteenth century. In the eighteenth century the minimum daily wage had been equal to the value of either a stone of flour or a peck of wheat, a fact referred to in a petition sent by the Lingwood (N) labourers to the House of Commons in 1841, who demanded not charity but 'fair play'.[32] During the first half of the nineteenth century Suffolk labourers had received the value of 6 pecks of wheat a week on but three occasions, which confirms Bowley's and Wilson-Fox's conclusions that East Anglia had fallen from a high wage region to one of the lowest in the space of fifty years. Between 1820 and 1844 Suffolk labourers averaged just 4¾ pecks a week.[33] This wage-price correlation was further refined by farmers who were invariably slow to raise wages in response to price rises but were quick to lower them when prices fell.[34] In addition they set maximum and minimum wage levels, above and below which earnings never deviated, whatever the price of wheat. Thus wages often ranged between 7s. and 12s. a week although wheat prices fluctuated between 38s. and 97s. a quarter. One other customary wage-fixing practice was common to the region, that of farmers agreeing the price of labour among themselves. This was designed to prevent any one farmer from being singled out as a poor employer. Needless to say labourers found this form of employer combination hypocritical since they were prevented from combining to raise wages.[35]

---

30 Ibid. 74-75; Howkins, *Poor Labouring Men*, pp. 25-9; BNP, 28 Sept. 1858, 29 Mar. 1859.
31 For examples of wage scales see NNRO, R. N. Bacon, Papers for 1844 Agricultural Report, evidence of H. Blyth; PP 1846, VI, *S .C. on the Burdens Affecting Real Property*, pp. 545-6.
32 Kent, *Remarks*, pp. 31 and 81. The Lingwood petition is quoted in full in *NM*, 6 Feb, 1841.
33 Kent, *Remarks*, p. 73; A. L. Bowley, *JRSS*, 61 (1898), 704-6; A. Wilson Fox in W. Minchinton, ed., *Essays in Agrarian History*, ii (Newton Abbot, 1968), pp. 181-2.
34 Kent, *Remarks*, p. 72; BNP, 26 Jan. 1853.
35 Glyde, 'Autobiography', p. 18.

Although wage-fixing was determined by customary practice East Anglia had relatively high and low wage areas. In Norfolk the highest were paid in the sparsely populated western and north-western hundreds where they could be up to 4*s.* a week more than the rest of the county, whereas the south-western corner and the area around Norwich were low. In the latter case the city, with its declining weaving industry, had a very depressing effect on agricultural wages.[36] At an even more local level individual parishes were identifiable as high and low wage villages. In the former the presence of a benevolent landowner like Sir John Boileau of Ketteringham and Lord Wodehouse had a positive effect on wages.[37] Conversely the most infamous low wage village was Edgefield where wages dropped to 4*s.* a week in 1833.[38] Adjacent villages were equally bad and it is hardly surprising that this area figured in the Swing Riots.

In Suffolk the western division of the county was considered a low wage region compared to the east. The differential between them was large, ranging from between 3*s.* and 4*s.* a week. However in South-West Suffolk a combination of factors, small farms, surplus labour, and declining industry, made this one of the sorriest corners of rural England. Here wages regularly fell to 6*s.* during depression years, even though in the rest of the county 8*s.* was considered the unofficial minimum.[39] Labourers in the east benefited from alternative forms of employment: herring fishing which recruited as far west as Beccles and Bungay, agricultural machine making at Ipswich, Leiston, and Peasenhall, and coprolite digging in the Colneis Hundred.[40] Cash earnings, whether daily, weekly, or task, were not the only forms of payment, as many farmers were quick to point out. References to perks and extras abound and protagonists of this form of payment translated them into monetary equivalents. Their importance increased when wheat prices rose, thus allowing farmers to avoid making money payments by substituting beer, milk, vegetables, corn, fuel, rent reductions, and so forth in their place.[41] The list is endless and the

---

36 Whereas in Suffolk and Essex the presence of Ipswich and London, respectively, had a positive effect on farm wages in surrounding parishes.

37 NNRO, Boi 117X6, Boileau Diaries, 14 Nov, 1857. See also NNRO, Boi T. 104D, MS 21470, 4 May and 5 May 1847; *NN*, 6 Feb. 1864, 5 Nov. 1864, 16 Oct. 1869, for high wage estate villages.

38 *BNP*, 24 Apr. 1833.

39 *The Times*, 11 June 1844.

40 J. Caird, *English Agriculture in 1850-51* (London, 1852), 148-9.

41 PRO, MH 32/49, Kay to PLC, Oct. 1837 which is also quoted in A. Digby, 'The Operation of the Poor Law in the Social and Economic Life of Nineteenth-Century Norfolk', Ph.D. thesis (Univ. of East Anglia, 1971), p. 156; F. Clifford, *The Agricultural*

monetary value could be quite sizeable.

The dividing line between charity and wages was a fine one and it led to further demoralization on the labourer's part. Furthermore, though such perquisites were plentiful they were sporadic and discriminatory. Team-men often received rent-free accommodation and free delivery of fuel whereas the general labourers received neither. Likewise the handing out of foodstuffs was synonymous with the truck system. Robert Chinery of Withersfield (S), for example, not only paid low wages but paid them in provisions. In 1846 he was blacklisted by insurance companies who decided his system of payment was to blame after a number of fires on his property.[42]

The question as to whether labourers were worse off when wheat prices were high or low was of interest to contemporaries. It appears all the more important to pose such a question when one remembers that up to half a labourer's wage could be spent on the purchase of wheaten flour. In the most systematic study of its kind J. H. Kent found that labourers appeared to be worse off when prices were high, as in 1816-20, 1823-31, 1838-41, but were relatively well off in 1822, 1835, 1848-52.[43] It would appear that farmers attempted to bolster up wages during times of depression. After 1852 labourers' wages kept pace with and often improved on wheat prices indicating that there were significant improvements in their standard of living. However, Kent's study brings to light the strange and puzzling fact that the relationship between protest crimes, wages, and wheat prices was uncertain. The riotous years of 1816 and 1830 are straightforward in so far as wages fell behind wheat prices, thus indicating subsistence crises. However, during the incendiary years of 1822, 1831-5, 1843-4, and 1849-52, wages were almost equal to or even in excess of the price of 6 pecks of wheat. Protest after 1830 seems to have displayed opposite tendencies to those of food riots, in that it occurred when wheat prices were relatively low. Why should this equation be reversed? The answer lies partly in the nature of the labourers' diet. In times of high prices they turned from white bread to barley and rye bread but more importantly the popularity of the potato as the staple food increased rapidly during the period.[44] The other important factor,

---

Lock Out of 1874 (London, 1875), pp. 229-49.

42 *BNP*, 30 Dec. 1846; NUFO board mins. 4 Jan. 1847. The Norwich Union refused to renew or accept insurance from this village.

43 Kent, *Remarks*, p. 81.

44 Glyde, 'Autobiography', p. 34; *BNP*, 25 Jan. 1854 and 19 Dec. 1855, when it was reported that families survived on meal and rye bread; R. Salaman, *The History and Social Influence of the Potato* (Cambridge, 1949), 530 and 539.

to be dealt with shortly, was that more labourers were more frequently employed during periods of high prices. How did the labourer regard his economic position during periods of high and low wheat prices? If we set aside incendiarism as irrefutable evidence of what they felt, the best statement came from a man interviewed by the *Morning Chronicle* in 1849 when prices were very low and wages had, in some areas, fallen to 6s. a week. When asked whether or not he was better off under low prices, he replied:

> We can get more bread for the money, and that's some consequence to the poor men like we, but they don't lower the rent to us when they lower wages. When I was getting 9s. a week I had to pay eighteen pence a week for rent, and I must pay the same now when I am only getting 6s. a week; and then I don't know how long I may be able to get 6s. The farmers have nearly got in all their seed, and then we may go about our business. And then if I ain't got no money to buy the bread, why what's the consequence if it's cheap or dear.[45]

'Viewed in this light', the reporter added, '(and many of the labourers are shrewd enough to look at the question in this way), the condition of the labourer must be bad enough.'

The labourer had rightly noted that other outgoings of expenditure were not reduced in the same proportion as his wages, and that another factor came into play during times of depression, that of unemployment. The relationship, therefore, between low wages and rural protest was not as obvious as one might have expected, yet there clearly was a correlation between the two. Insurance companies were in no doubt as to the relationship. 'Whenever wages were very low', a Norwich Union agent told *The Times*, '... and the people were badly off, or whenever it was threatened that wages would be lowered, they always found fires to commence and increase.'[46] Another point, although obvious, is worthy of note. At this time there were no institutional or customary devices in the form of collective bargaining, nor were there any organs of conciliation and arbitration to defuse conflict. Wages were determined by market forces, custom, and the individual whim of the employer, and the labourers played, on the whole, a passive role as employees without rights or powers. They very occasionally asked for wage rises, but tended to watch their employers' responses to price changes. If farmers broke the conventions of the unofficial wage controls then the reaction from the labourers was

45 MC, 8 Dec. 1849.
46 *The Times*, 7 June 1844.

often extreme, in the form of fires and threatening letters. There was no middle ground on which masters and men could meet and discuss wage rates and this meant protest was built into the system of wage determination, especially when prices were falling or slowly rising after a depression. Incendiarism was an intimidatory weapon in wage bargaining.

The most important factor in the study of rural protest is unemployment. Reference has already been made to a feature common to arable areas, that of day-to-day redundancy because of adverse weather conditions. However, on a wider scale arable cultivation governed the seasonality of farm work since farmers required a large workforce for the harvest. During particularly bad years some of these workers would find themselves without work for eleven months of the year. Underemployment and unemployment were thus considered necessary evils. Whilst it is impossible to gauge accurately the actual scale of unemployment during the period it is possible to measure the fluctuations between boom and slump years.

Arable farming, it was generally agreed, required one labourer to every 25-35 acres depending on soil conditions. Clearly large light-land farms required less labour per hundred acres than the small heavy clayland ones. In 1851 the ratio of labourers to a hundred acres was 3.25 in Norfolk, and 4.6 in Suffolk.[47] However, these figures hide important local variations. In Norfolk for example the light-land regions of the north-west appear to have been undermanned whereas in the southern unions of Forehoe and Depwade the ratio was in excess of 4:100. The West Suffolk unions of Risbridge, Stow, and Sudbury were likewise over-manned and both regions of the two counties were centres of incendiary activity between 1840 and 1850.

Descending to the parish level there were a number of villages where permanent pools of unemployment remained before the mid-century. Edgefield with 1,500 acres of cultivated land and 112 adult male labourers had for many years 70 permanently at work in the gravel pits and 40 idle during the 1833 harvest.[48] In North Suffolk the Blything Hundred reported over one-third of its men unemployed in the same year.[49] Many of these parishes were able to take advantage of the poor law emigration and migration schemes later in the decade. Over 4,000 left the region for Canada, thus relieving trouble spots like

---

47 Estimates of labourers/100 acres are based on the 1851 Census.
48 *BNP*, 24 Apr. and 21 Aug. 1833.
49 Hobsbawm and Rudé, *Captain Swing*, pp. 50-1. At Framlingham and Fressingfield unemployment reached 78%.

Blything where unemployment dropped to nothing in 1837.[50] The architects of the New Poor Law were quick to take the credit for the complete turnabout though one should bear in mind the fact that the introduction of the New Poor Law coincided with rising wheat prices and a buoyant agrarian sector. But the effects of the new law should not be underestimated since the alteration brought considerable changes in the attitude of both the farmers and the labourers. The former, conscious of the rates and the expense of maintaining people in workhouses, found it cheaper, initially, to offer the men work. The labourers, on the other hand, had used allowances in the past to supplement their wages but soon realized that their attitude to work had to change if they wanted to stay clear of the dreaded 'bastilles'. The men 'are more obliging and well behaved', one Billingford (N) farmer reported, 'if they are turned off for misconduct [they] will get no relief as formerly'.[51] Out of the 2,231 who received orders for admission to the Cosford union house in 1835-6 only 394 accepted.[52] Clearly the grim prospect of the workhouse hung over the workforce.

Farmers had few complaints during the late 1830s and early 1840s. Wheat was selling at prices unknown since 1819 and labour remained cheap and plentiful. The surplus labour problem looked as if it had been solved and this was reflected in the declining poor law expenditure: from £224,000 in 1835 to £138,338 in 1841 in Suffolk, and in Norfolk from £273,000 in 1835 to £181,000 in 1840.[53] The boom was short-lived and by 1843-4 with falling wheat prices and wages and mounting unemployment the New Poor Law faced its severest test since its inception. With the abnormally dry weather of the spring of 1844 and the uncertain political climate promoted by the Anti-Corn Law League, farmers threw thousands out of work. They reduced the cultivated acreage and allowed weeds and hedges to grow more profusely than ever.[54] The young single men bore the brunt of the redundancies while the older hands were hired and fired at will. Attempts at thinning the population were again introduced, some were sent as blacklegs to the North-East coalfields where a strike was in progress, while others moved to the Lancashire cotton mills or to the

50 *BNP*, 18 Jan. 1837; A. Redford, *Labour Migration in England 1800-1850* (Manchester, 1976), pp. 97-117. Norfolk sent 3,354 emigrants to Canada and Suffolk 787 under the poor law scheme.
51 NNRO, Bacon, Papers for 1844, reply from Hart.
52 PRO, MH 32/48, 30 June 1836.
53 Glyde, *Suffolk*, p. 188; Bacon, *Report*, p. 100.
54 PP 1846, VI, qu. 6046.

railways.[55] During the rest of the 1840s migration accelerated in response to the potato blight, high prices, the repeal of the corn laws, and the continuing high unemployment.

When the mid-century crash in wheat prices occurred unemployment rose to unprecedented heights even though poor law expenditure fell. By 1851 much of the region was close to revolt, especially where the workhouses were full to overflowing.[56] Following the depression the material welfare and security of employment for many farm workers began to improve markedly but not enough to stem further migratory flows, especially to the South-East of England where the numbers of East-Anglian-born residents rose by over 250 per cent between 1851 and 1861.[57] 'For the first time', Lord Leicester recalled in 1859, 'the demand for labour in certain portions of this county [Norfolk] had exceeded the supply — a very different state of things from what existed some years ago.'[58] Evidence to support this view came indirectly from other sources. Labourers were now leaving or abstaining from service at critical times of the year, especially at haysel and harvest time. Others were selling their labour for £7 a harvest when previously £5 had been the top rate.[59] Thus in less than twenty years the labour market had switched round completely and although this era of 'high farming' brought real benefits to the labouring community it would be erroneous to believe that they had reached their Arcadia. Structural underemployment still remained and the reality of short-term crises was ever present, as in 1867-9 when adverse weather conditions, poor wheat yields, and root crop failure brought the people to the 'verge of famine' and the young men to a point of 'insubordination and lawlessness ... which set the farmers and everyone else at defiance'.[60]

An additional factor, not as yet alluded to, influenced the labour market. The Settlement Laws, which, before 1865, made the parish, in effect, the local labour market, led to discriminatory employment

---

55 *MC*, 2 July 1844. J. S. Henslow, however, provided an interesting eyewitness account of the labourers' reluctance to migrate to Newcastle, *Suggestions*, p. 26. *BNP*, 12 Mar, 1845; *NM*, 1 May 1847, 1,000 were employed on the Dereham-Lynn line.

56 For examples of riotous workhouses see *BNP*, 2 Jan. 1850, 2 Apr. 1851; *NN*, 12 Jan. 1850; *IJ*, 8 Feb. 1851.

57 Nearly all migration was over long distances due to the absence of industry in the region. Contrast this with Redford's findings in *Labour Migration, passim*.

58 *NN*, 15 Oct. 1859.

59 *NN*, 8 July 1865, 13 July 1867. Such was the concern regarding migration that local agricultural associations asked labourers to reflect before making a decision to leave, *NN*, 10 Nov. 1866.

60 *NN*, 2 Jan. 1869, 26 Oct. 1867.

policies by farmers who were mindful of the poor rates. They were inclined to take on married men with settlements in the parish where they worked but single and non-settled men, regardless of whether they were more efficient workers, were only employed when agriculture was buoyant. These laws also caused the uneven distribution of labour. Where one or two landowners possessed the land of the parish — termed a close parish — they were in a position to cause permanent labour shortages by demolishing cottages. They forced out the non-settled poor who sought refuge in open villages, owned by a multitude of small farmers and tradesmen who invested their capital in the construction of high rent tenements.[61] The 1846 Removals Act did nothing to alleviate the problem nor to provide an incentive to landowners to halt evictions in closed parishes. Thus in localized areas the Settlement Laws led to the creation of a labour force which had no other option but to be mobile. At Great Whelnetham (S) ninety-seven families had to walk three to four miles to work because they had been unable to gain a settlement in the parishes where they were employed. Norwich, too, contained over 500 agricultural labourers, some of whom trekked up to seven miles to work because the estate villages surrounding the city had been cleared.[62] Such open parishes gained notorious reputations for immorality and Castleacre (N), above all others, was regarded as the worst. Here, 'the scum of the neighbourhood settles' turning the village into 'the coop of all the scrappings'.[63] Whether such places as Castleacre deserved their reputations as 'dens of iniquity' is a moot point — certainly if protest crime is any guide then the accusations against them are, to some extent, unfounded. What antagonized contemporaries so much was their association of open villages with agricultural gangs which were regarded as hotbeds of obscene language, vice, and sexual immorality. For their part, the labouring poor found living in the open parishes had its compensations, not least their freedom from the overbearing influences of landowners and parsons.

There was one other agrarian-related factor which affected the labour market: the use of machinery, especially the threshing-machine.

---

61 For discussions on open and close parishes see Hobsbawm and Rudé, *Captain Swing*, pp. 37 and 151-2; Digby, *Pauper Palaces*, pp. 89-96; B. A. Holderness, 'Open and Close Parishes in England in the Eighteenth and Nineteenth Centuries', *Ag. Hist. Rev.* 20 (1972), 126-39.

62 *MC*, 2 Jan. 1850. The open parish of Lakenham, a suburb of Norwich, increased by 1,000 between 1831 and 1851.

63 C. S. Read, 'Recent Improvements in Norfolk Farming', *JRAS* 19 (1858), 292; PP 1843, XII, 223.

These had been introduced during the Napoleonic Wars when the region experienced labour shortages but their numbers had continued to expand after 1815 despite the presence of plentiful and cheap labour.[64] East Anglia was by far the most important manufacturing area of threshing-machines in the country and this partly accounts for both their early introduction and continued popularity. During the winter months when the weather was often unsuitable for outdoor work, threshing by the flail in the barns was by far the biggest single task on the farm, often lasting three months. Despite technical difficulties, farmers found it profitable to use mechanical threshers which could speedily get the corn ready for market before the usual fall in wheat prices. Mechanized threshing had obvious consequences for the labourer, he was frequently laid off in winter for months. Furthermore, where machines were used, women and children were sometimes employed to feed them since neither strength nor skill were required. The labourers' anger against machinery was vented in 1816, 1822, and 1830, which saw the destruction of threshing-machines, drills, and ploughs. The immediate results of these riots were startlingly successful for the protesters as many landowners and farmers were quick to concede to their demands. But did the machines make a quick return once order was restored? In 1832 threshers reappeared in Norfolk because wet weather made autumn ploughing impossible, whereas in Suffolk the opposite occurred.[65] Here hand threshing remained very much the practice until the early 1840s when mechanization became general once more. The other great mechanical invention, the reaper, had by the time of its showing at the Great Exhibition been fully tried and tested but its introduction to East Anglia was slow. Presumably this was due to the availability of labour and the memory of the earlier riots. Trials of Bell's and McCormick's mechanical reapers were first commented on in Suffolk in 1855 and 1857 respectively, but it was in West Norfolk that they first became general due to scarcity of labour.[66]

Non-agrarian factors could have depressing effects on labourers' wages and employment. This was evident at the time of the repeal of the corn laws when labourers were used as political bargaining fodder.[67] But it was the depressed state of the well-established East

64 Hobsbawm and Rudé, *Captain Swing*, p. 319, appendix iv.
65 *BNP*, 7 Nov. 1832, 16 Jan. 1833, 26 Nov. 1834. See also N. E. Fox, 'The Spread of the Threshing Machine in Central Southern England', *Ag. Hist. Rev.* 26 (1978), 26-8.
66 Read, 'Recent Improvements', p. 280.
67 See the Barham workhouse riot of 1851 which the local whig press claimed was initiated by protectionist farmers, *IJ*, 15 and 22 Feb. 1851; *NM*, 22 Feb. 1851; and for a Tory view,

Anglian textile industry which, on occasions, had profound repercussions on agriculture. Weaving had existed in the region for many centuries, in fact Norwich's wealth and reputation were built on this industry.[68] However, it was in a state of permanent decline by 1830. The Suffolk woollen cloth industry of the Norfolk-Suffolk border region had virtually died out. By way of compensation two new industries, silk-weaving and straw-plaiting, had been introduced in the early nineteenth century in localized areas at Hadleigh, Glemsford, Lavenham, Sudbury, Haverhill, and Norwich. Even in the relatively prosperous silk industry male weavers believed agricultural labourers to be much better off than themselves. This was especially so between the mid-1820s and 1840s when the silk industry throughout Britain was depressed.[69]

Before the concentration of the weaving industry in factories had been completed at Norwich and Yarmouth, weavers in the traditional centres experienced competition and undercutting from workers in rural areas where it was common, until the late 1820s, for agricultural labourers to have looms in their cottages. Whenever they were laid off from agriculture they became 'shuttle throwers', a derisory term for less skilled weavers. At Marsham (N) one witness to the Commission reported that single men had taken up weaving in the early 1820s as the wages were higher and the employment opportunities greater than in agriculture. By the early 1830s this was no longer true: 'Anything is better than weaving. Some boys have taken to agricultural employment.'[70] At Hevingham (N) the Commissioners reported the eagerness of weavers to leave their looms and take up farm work. And at Marsham the 'weavers felt themselves to be outcasts', having 'no masters to complain to and farmers would not employ them because of the full time agricultural labourers'. This was not 'strictly true as another witness, a local farmer, said he employed weavers as labourers on very low wages. This was certainly the case at Wymondham in 1844 when weavers were reportedly undercutting the harvest wages of

NC, 15 Feb. 1851.

68 The following represents a small selection of the literature on the East Anglian textile industries: D. C. Coleman, 'Growth and Decay during the Industrial Revolution: The Case of East Anglia', *Scandinavian Economic History Review*, 10 (1962), 115-27; J. K. Edwards, 'The Economic Development of Norwich 1750-1850 with Special Reference to the Worsted Industry', Ph.D. thesis (Univ. of Leeds, 1963); id., 'Decline of the Norwich Textiles Industry', *Yorks. Bull. of Econ. and Soc. Research*, 16 (1964); PP 1840, XXIII, *Reports from the Assistant Handloom Weavers' Commissioners*.

69 *VCH Norfolk*, ed. W. Page (London, n.d.), 253 and 274; Edwards, thesis, pp. 466-7, Coleman, 'Growth and Decay', p. 121.

70 PP 1840, XXIII, 329 and 332-3.

agricultural labourers.[71]

It is quite clear from all the evidence that the decline of weaving had depressing effects on agrarian wages and employment. In some cases men lost an alternative source of income and, in others, the presence of redundant weavers could drag down farm wages. There were also more subtle effects. As time went on, weaving progressively became women's and children's work and this tied the male labourers to their own villages because of the job opportunities for the whole family, despite the poor wages and employment opportunities in agriculture.[72] Population densities in such villages were, in nearly every case, far higher than in purely rural villages in the region, thus creating potential 'blackspots' of overpopulation and surplus labour in the agrarian sector.[73]

During the period, but most especially before the mid-1850s, farm labourers, particularly the young men, had reason enough to be 'grave, moody, and silent'.

> You rarely find in these days a hedger or ditcher in the character of complainant at a court of petty sessions. He dare not, indeed, move his tongue against the occupier who employs him. His wages may be inadequate, his cottage a mere hovel, his wife half naked, and his children starving, — he may feel all this bitterly, and brood over it day and night, but not one word does he venture to utter in a tone of open complaint to any one ... He is a discontented man, and ... he has good cause to be so.[74]

---

71 For Heveningham see ibid. pp. 332-3, Marsham, p. 332, and Wymondham, *MC*, 23 Aug, 1844.

72 PP 1840, XXIII, 332-4; Edwards, thesis, p. 467; *VCH Norfolk*, ii, 271-4.

73 The average density of people per acre in Norfolk was 0.35, for Suffolk 0.34. Weaving villages ranged between 0.32 (Hevingham and Lavenham) to 1.18 (Nayland). The average density for rural weaving parishes was 0. 51.

74 Anon., 'Incendiarism', p. 245.

3

The Labouring Community and the Relief of Poverty: 'A Class Which Has Something To Lose'

Work and wages, at the best of times, were barely adequate to sustain a labouring family or even a single unmarried man. However there were safety nets, both official and traditional, which prevented outright starvation. The poor laws, old and new, provided the major assurance against this happening whereas the village charities and later the allotments contributed marginal, and in some cases significant, benefits which staved off the visit to the guardian. In these small rural communities where rich and poor were known to one another, it is commonly assumed, though hardly investigated, that charity was all important and pervading in rescuing all but the most improvident. The vast amount of informal and largely unsung charity gave rise to the myth that rural society essentially worked, that inequalities of wealth led neither to class hatred nor class envy. Social tranquillity could be bought for a florin or quarter-acre plot of land.

There was, however, one group in the countryside for whom the meshes of the safety net were frequently rather too wide, the young single men. As we have seen they were economically the most vulnerable and therefore in most need of assistance. They were rarely deemed deserving or respectable and were thus forced to live up to their already tarnished reputations through petty crime and poaching. Village charities and allotments were invariably restricted to the married or the widowed, both hallmarks of respectability. The poor laws, theoretically, offered help to all-comers but with the passing of the Poor Law Amendment Act the reality proved somewhat different. Loopholes which provided for outdoor relief favoured families whereas strict enforcement of the workhouse test fell on the young men, which pride, self-respect, and native wit told them to reject.

The one institution which does much to dispel the illusion of an innocent and caring community was the poor law, both old and new. It was a vital instrument of blatant labour discipline used by employers against their workforce, especially at times of the farming year when labour was not required. During the period under review significant reforms were introduced, especially from 1835-6 when the New Poor Law was implemented. However, it should be stressed that this hardly signified a radical departure from past practices as so many areas of the region had anticipated many features of the new act, particularly those areas which had grouped themselves into Gilbert Unions or Incorporations in the eighteenth century.[1] Thus houses of industry and poorhouses were already familiar features well before the advent of the dreaded workhouses. Under the unreformed system the poor laws were not considered unusually harsh or stringent, and the poorhouses were regarded as 'almshouses' without discipline or classification, set aside for the young, the sick, and the old. The able-bodied invariably received outdoor relief in the form of family and wage allowances. Unlike other areas of England, East Anglian labourers appear to have had few poor law related grievances. In 1830, the year of the Swing Riots, few complaints were made against poor relief, although in Hobsbawm and Rudé's opinion, when speaking of Southern England as a whole, attempts to cut down relief were 'the straw that broke the long-suffering camel's back'.[2] In East Anglia, however, the poor law and its officers appear to have become a significant bone of contention only after Swing, especially in Norfolk where, in response to the riots, poor law administration was stiffened.[3]

In some areas of this county unemployment allowances were halved between 1831 and 1835, when adult male unemployment was in the region of 15 per cent and labour rate schemes, work creation projects, and roundsman systems were taken up with vigour. Edgefield in particular became notorious both for its appallingly large labour surplus and frequent experiments at putting this surplus to work. In one scheme wages for the able-bodied were lowered to a mere four shillings a week in the hope that farmers would employ every adult male in the village. Such attempts not only served to confuse and demoralize the labourers still further but also made them more aware of the blatant opportunism of their employers. Numerous fires broke out in this and other parishes where similar experiments were being made.[4] One anonymous letter to the Brinningham overseer threatened to fire his premises and also declared that 'a mess of lead' was prepared for him. The letter continued: 'You may call your westry meetings and your labour rate meetings for the safety of the poor to

---

1   R. Taylor, 'The Development of the Old Poor Law in Norfolk, 1795-1834', MA thesis (Univ. of East Anglia, 1970), Digby, thesis, and S. and B. Webb, *The English Poor Law History*, part I (London, 1963 repr.) all deal with the unreformed system.
2   Hobsbawm and Rudé, *Captain Swing*, p. 54.
3   Archer, thesis, pp. 104-11
4   G. B. Ballachey, *A Letter to the Editor of the Norwich Mercury Respecting a Reduction of Wages in the Parish of Edgefield* (Norwich, 1833); *BNP*, 21 Mar. 1832, 24 Apr. 1833, 18 May 1833; *NC*, 9 Feb. 1833, 3 Aug. 1833, 9 Oct. 1833; PRO, HO 52/26, letter from Leck to Sir Jacob Astley, 1 July 1835.

keep thear eyes shet ... you shall be shot like a dorg before long ...'.[5]

Other moves were made to tighten up the poor law. Digby noted the introduction of permanent and paid assistant overseers and reconstituted select vestries whose task it was to restrict allowances in the hope of stemming the rising costs of poor relief which were fast becoming a major financial burden to ratepayers.[6] In consequence magisterial power declined and was replaced by ratepayer influence. The former had been regarded as unduly generous in the granting of allowances. Thus the paternalistic approach was overridden by class interest of a more capitalist nature and this bred increasing class antagonism.

The introduction of the New Poor Law from 1835 signalled the start of an escalation in violence, riot, meetings, and arson.[7] And although it has been suggested earlier that the implementation did not provide startlingly new alterations to poor relief, evidence suggests the labouring communities regarded the changeover with unmitigated horror and anger. For them, the New Poor Law was qualitatively if not quantitatively different. When all is said and done the old poor law did provide some kind of safety net into which the poor could fall in times of distress and hardship. It was regarded as a right, which they could rely on, whereas the new laws did not offer that kind of security. The Reverend Henslow, a remarkably accurate and sensitive commentator of rural life, summed up the differences between the two systems when he wrote: 'I should say that the Old Poor Law placed the ratepayers too much at the mercy of the labourers and that the New Law places the labourers too much at the mercy of the ratepayers.'[8] Henslow would appear to have a point if we are to believe the evidence of one Suffolk village where, before the implementation of the new law, paupers intimidated the relieving officers by demanding two allowances while holding clubs over their heads in a threatening manner. Within six weeks of the changeover it was reported: 'paupers doff their hats and bow and curtsey to relieving officers'.[9] More tangible differences can be discerned by simply looking at the annual poor relief expenditure which fell dramatically — in Norfolk from £306,787 in 1834 to £181,058 in 1840, and in

---

5   *EA*, 26 Mar. 1833.

6   Digby, thesis, p. 47.

7   N. C. Edsall, *The Anti-Poor Law Movement 1834-44* (Manchester, 1971), *passim*; Archer, thesis, pp. 111-32.

8   Henslow, *Suggestions*, p. 13.

9   PRO, MH 32/48, letter to PLC, 7 Dec. 1835.

Suffolk from £266,157 in 1833 to £141,536 in 1840.[10]

What differences did the labouring community perceive in the New Poor Law apart, that is, from their loss of a right? The indoor test, the supposed cessation of outdoor relief the reformed organization within the workhouse, and the adherence to out-relief in kind rather than money were the changes which angered them most. The labourers, in short, became paupers, with the grim prospect of the new stricter workhouse regime awaiting them. They were now at the mercy of professional officers, often not local men, and a board of guardians who were not only their employers but also the major ratepayers with extreme cost-conscious views.

By 1837 much of Norfolk and Suffolk had been divided into unions, Norwich was the most notable exception to this reorganization.[11] Almost from the start Chadwick's intentions of a uniform poor relief system under one centralized authority was not adhered to in the region. The harsh workhouse test was never operated to its fullest extent but that is not to say the rural poor escaped oppressive treatment; on the contrary, in the first few months of the new law's existence the poor continued to be oppressed in much the same way as before. Kay, the poor law inspector, was exasperated to find the new unions operating a system of outdoor relief to the able-bodied, particularly work schemes like digging the land. Kay, who was determined to stamp out such practices which benefited farmers at the expense of non-land occupiers and lowered labourers' wages, wrote:

> These boards are for the most part composed of occupiers [i.e. farmers], and in process of time they would under such a system have to regulate the terms upon which labourers should be hired out to themselves, ... it seems that it would in lapse of time inevitably encourage the formation of a conspiracy among employers to reduce the wages of industrious labourers.[12]

The conspiracy of employers as guardians and ratepayers was not new nor was it to be eradicated. In fact under the New Poor Law the two counties were to be notable, as we shall see shortly, for their accommodation of the employers' wishes. However in Suffolk attempts were made, initially, to follow the letter of the law. The Cosford Union offered the workhouse to 2,231 people in its first nine months and in the Blything Union 200 paupers from Westleton were

---

10 Quoted in Digby, *Pauper Palaces*, p. 108.
11 Norwich was incorporated in 1863 and Smallburgh in 1869.
12 PRO, MH 32/48, 1 May 1836.

sent to the house but the poor rates rose so dramatically the farmers quickly found them work again.[13]

Once the implementation of the new law settled down it soon became apparent that outdoor relief reasserted itself as the predominant method of payment to the able-bodied. Local guardians were able to do this by interpreting an exemption clause in the outdoor relief prohibitory orders. The most frequent evasion resorted to was the exemption due to sickness or accident in the recipient's family. In 1844 national newspaper reporters came across this practice which they regarded as humane and liberal.[14] It is hard for historians to be as charitable since the board of guardians had two objectives uppermost in their minds, first to keep poor rates as low as possible and, second, to keep a large underemployed workforce tied to the land in order to ensure an adequate supply of labour for the busy times of the farming year. Had they not employed the sickness loophole, poor rates would have increased enormously and migration from the region would have undoubtedly accelerated.

The evasion of outdoor relief continued, as Digby pointed out, well into the late nineteenth century but it was subject to small but significant fluctuations.[15] In Norfolk, for example, the poor law became progressively stricter between 1837 and 1843 when the number of outdoor recipients of relief was declining proportionally to the total number of paupers.[16] A closer inspection of the Norfolk adult able-bodied paupers shows an increasing number of them were not receiving outdoor relief in the 1840s. In 1840, 75.5 per cent received outdoor relief but in 1846 only 66.7 per cent received the same. However, by 1 January 1849, the number had risen to 81 per cent and carried on rising to 84 per cent by 1860.[17] Therefore, the number of adult able-bodied receiving outdoor relief in the first six years of the 1840s was significantly lower than during the whole period under review. This was to have some bearing on the wave of arson in 1843-4. In addition, as will be seen, the workhouse was offered to many able-bodied in the mid-1840s but they declined the offer, preferring to 'shift' for themselves through crime and charity.

East Anglia was notorious for another aspect of poor law administration, first identified by Foster in 1844 and described in detail

---

13 PRO, MH 32/48, 16 Apr. 1836 and 30 June 1836.
14 *The Times*, 6 July 1844.
15 Digby, thesis, p. 158.
16 Bacon, *Report*, pp. 162-97.
17 By 1843 the % of adult able-bodied paupers receiving outdoor relief had dropped to 64. After 1849 it never fell below 73%.

by Digby.[18] This was the 'Ticket System', an illegal practice which the Poor Law Commission had no idea existed. Guardians claimed they needed evidence of the applicant's 'reasonable diligence' in seeking work. In fact the system not only worked against the labourer but also kept poor rates down since a labourer had to have a ticket signed by every employer in his parish stating that they had no work to offer. The whole process of applying to the board, having the ticket signed, and then receiving relief took, according to Foster, ten days during which time the applicant received no relief. The. system had, in the reporter's words, a 'nasty and deliberate twist' because some farmers, it was claimed, refused to sign the ticket on the grounds that they could offer work to the labourer at half the recognized wage rate. A labourer who refused to take the job received no relief and a persistent offender was committed to gaol under the Vagrancy Act for 'refusing wholly or in part' to maintain his family.[19]

When *The Times* exposed this harsh practice the PLC investigated the popularity and distribution of these tickets and discovered the system was neither universal nor widespread, being restricted to nine unions in the two counties. Whether this abuse was fully suppressed after the scandal of 1844 is difficult to determine since the *Bury Post* reported in 1860 that labourers 'usually' had to take a list to the poor law guardians with the names of their previous employers and others who had no work to offer.[20]

Foster's explanation for incendiarism was built around the hatred for the system. One labourer told him: 'The men will say I get nothing because master would not sign the paper — therefore master shall get nothing and fires his stacks'.[21] Walsham, who was called in to investigate the abuse, was convinced no such relation existed between the two. He was able to cite examples of unions which had experienced a large number of fires where the system was not practised.[22]

It was the workhouses, however, above all else, which came to symbolize the oppression of the New Poor Law. Their existence brought dread to many labourers, even though the majority never actually entered them. The strong antipathy against workhouses dated

---

18 Examples of the ticket can be found in PRO, MH 32/80; *The Times*, 21 June 1844. See also A. Digby, 'The Labour Market and the Continuity of Social Policy after 1834: The Case of the Eastern Counties', *Econ. Hist. Rev.* 28 (1975), 75.
19 *The Times*, 21 June 1844.
20 *BNP*, 11 Dec. 1860.
21 *The Times*, 21 June 1844.
22 PRO, MH 32/80, letter to PLC, 10 July 1844.

back to the reforms of 1835 when the workhouse test was applied more stringently than it was in the years that followed. The bad reputation and physical presence of these houses were to haunt rural communities until well into the twentieth century. So great was their hatred and fear that 'they will starve to the last pinch rather than enter the unionhouse'.[23] Reports from Newmarket in 1860 stated that the labourers: 'would contrive to struggle on from day to day with one or two stinted meals of potatoes or turnips' rather than enter the workhouse. Other reports stated that men would sell all their worldly possessions to eke out their existence in order to keep their liberty.[24] Evidence supporting the labourers' dread of the workhouse is overwhelming; for instance at the Thingoe house in 1844 the only inmates were thirty old men, yet there had been many applications for relief from young labourers who had only been offered the workhouse — none however had accepted the orders.[25] Obviously some would have found work but for many the alternatives were crime or survival on an even lower standard of living. Henslow observed: 'The repugnance of the poor to the confinement of the house, and their natural dislike to those regulations to which it is necessary they should submit when there, induces them to support hardships with a determination which it is painful to witness, and scarcely possible for persons in easy circumstances to comprehend.'[26]

Why was there such antagonism against workhouses, especially in an area of England where they had been in existence for well over fifty years? Much of the hatred was based on the new rules imposed by the Poor Law Commission, and these new rules compared very unfavourably with the rules under the old regime. Life in the unreformed houses was often represented as some idyllic existence where discipline was lax, where the food was plentiful, where movement in and out of the house was unrestricted, and where sexual relations between married and unmarried were promiscuous.[27] One labourer told a gentleman named Bree of Stowmarket that: 'I was in the house three years about 20 years ago; wonderful times, Sir — you

---

23 *The Times*, 11 June 1844.
24 Glyde, *Suffolk*, p. 183; *BNP*, 10 Jan. 1860; PP 1836, VII, *S.C. of the House of Lords on the State of Agriculture*, p. 204.
25 *The Times*, 15 June 1844.
26 Henslow, *Suggestions*, p. 11.
27 Glyde, *Suffolk*, pp. 172-3; PRO, MH 32/48, Kay to PLC, 3 Oct. 1835. Discipline in the Stowmarket workhouse was, he reported, 'almost as lax … as a brothel'. Food in the unreformed houses ranged from 194 oz. to 265 oz. per week whereas a soldier received 168 oz. and a farm labourer a mere 122 oz.

could not flog a man out of the house then.'[28] Reorganization must have come as a great shock not only to the inmates but even to the employed labourers as well. Workhouses took on the appearance of prisons and it was not long before they gained a reputation as such. The Reverend Cobbold of Wortham quoted one good and 'honest' labourer: 'Master I will never go into a workhouse. Never. I see no reason why I should be sent to prison, and shut up in the closed walls and doors of such a place, when I never wronged any man, and do not deserve to lose my liberty.'[29] The association between prisons and workhouses was a strong theme whenever the labourers' voices were raised in protest. During the trials of incendiaries or in the reports of prison inspectors the theme constantly recurred: 'The Union and the Gaol are one — both prisons; the Union a worse prison than this.' Many paupers went to great lengths to be transferred from the workhouses to the gaols. In East Suffolk in the year ending 31 March 1843, 111 paupers were gaoled for disorderly conduct in workhouses. In 1846 the *Bury Post* reported that crimes of breaking union house property had become so common that 'scarcely a week passes without the wanton destruction of glass and earthenware belonging to the guardians'.[30]

Another bone of contention was the segregation of the sexes in the workhouses, or as one labourer told the *Morning Chronicle* correspondent, 'as long as I can arne a sixpence anyhows, they sharn't part me from my wife'.[31] This and the lack of food were the two main reasons for the workhouse riots between 1835 and 1870. In the late 1840s and early 1850s many 'desperate and successful' attempts by married men on the married women's wards were made. The police were invariably called in to quell the riots and in one case a constable lost his life in the fracas which followed.[32] The inmates also made determined raids on the food stores, eating all the cooked meats and cooking all the raw. At Barham (S) house which rioted with depressing regularity between 1850 and 1853 one inmate said, 'Hunger is a sharp thorn, it is enough to make us do what we would not.'[33]

---

28 *BNP*, 3 July 1844.
29 Revd R. Cobbold, 'Parochial Features of Wortham 1828-1870, (in IESRO, HA 11/A13/10). The labourer was Thomas Goddard.
30 *BNP*, 11 Apr. 1843 and 15 Apr. 1846. It was common knowledge in Suffolk that paupers received less food than prisoners and this acted as a spur to get transferred to gaol.
31 Quoted by *BNP*, 12 Dec. 1849. Sir John Boileau received a threatening letter in 1851 which accused him of being 'one of the first to separate man and wife in the union', NNRO, Boi 69/117 X 6, 12 Nov. 1851.
32 *NM*, 24 June and 1 July 1848.
33 *BNP*, 12 Jan. 1848, 9 Feb. 1848; *NC*, 15 Feb. 1851, 21 Feb. 1852, 28 Feb. 1852, 6 Mar.

After 1853 when agriculture picked up and the rural workforce either began to leave the land or else were employed more steadily throughout the year, we see a rapid decline in both anti-poor-law protest and indoor relief. But when all is said and done the poor laws, particularly the New Poor Law, did much to sour an already desperate situation in which relations between employers and employees were at their most antagonistic between 1835 and 1851.

Whilst the pervasive presence of the poor laws did little to mitigate rural poverty which stood face to face with extravagance, charity could assume a vital function both for the labouring families and their benefactors. As recipients of food, fuel, and clothing, to name but three, the poor's weekly incomes could be supplemented, especially during the winter months, by these vital doles. The benefactors, on the other hand, bought peace, social tranquillity, and a much needed boost to their reputations in the neighbourhoods. There is no doubt, too, that they felt the act of giving would be rewarded in the hereafter. The Reverend William Andrew, in a moment of disarming honesty, wrote in his diary on 21 December 1840: 'Snow — I gave to each about five shillings in clothing. O What a privilege to be the Lord's Almoner! Remember me, O God, for good! Enlarge my heart! Let not my left hand know what my right has done!'[34] The following year his right hand was doling out vast quantities of soup to people who had trudged eight miles through deep snow to his door, and all this, including the recipe for the soup, was faithfully recorded once again in his diary, presumably for God to weigh up at the day of reckoning.[35] One cannot but be impressed by the sheer amount of charity in East Anglia; the local press is full of instances of 'roast beef and plum pudding' at every Christmas. Likewise, local one-off celebrations were frequently reported, as in the case of the coming of age of W. E. L. Bulwer, when a gigantic feast for 2,000 labouring people from five Norfolk villages was laid on. Ten years later these same people rioted against Bulwer because of his tendency to appropriate land left to village charities.[36]

That benevolent charity was intended to be an act of conspicuous consumption and a means of keeping the poor in submissive deference was apparent to contemporary critics of rural society. The Anti-Corn Law League's newspaper, the League, in an article headed,

1852; *NM*, 12 Jan. 1850; *IJ*, 21 Feb. 1852; *NN*, 21 Feb. 1852.

34 O. Chadwick, *Victorian Miniature* (London, 1960), p. 54.

35 Ibid.

36 *BNP*, 10 May 1820; Hobsbawm and Rudé, *Captain Swing*, pp. 154-5.

'Not Charity, But Justice', observed: 'Doubtless these things are sometimes kindly intended, but they are far more frequently the result of ostentation and feudal pride.'[37] This is amply borne out by the obituary of the Countess of Albemarle. Its language is refreshingly honest and clear and the lady's motives explicitly stated:

> The inhabitants of Kenninghall and the neighbouring parishes were constantly visited by the late lamented Countess of Albemarle, who very condescendingly entered with her amiable daughter, Lady Sophia, into the wretched abodes of those who were lingering under sickness and poverty, relieving them with clothing, medicines, and other necessaries, suitable to their wants. She likewise manifested as great a concern for educating the rising generation, always placing all the poor children of Quidenham, and many of Kenninghall and other places, at reading, writing, and sewing schools, thereby fitting them for servitude, and good and useful members of society.[38]

In return for such generosity the poor were expected to be grateful and hence deferential. If the right behaviour was not forthcoming then the wrath of the benefactor could indeed be great. The Earl of Albemarle, widower of the Countess, gave all his workers gifts of food but one of the recipients, Robert Collings of Kenninghall (N), who had received sixteen pounds of beef, eight quartern loaves, and six pints of strong beer, was caught poaching in one of the Earl's plantations the day after receiving this dole.[39] He was gaoled for six months with hard labour for this offence.

Benevolence was highly selective, the worthy poor were rewarded whilst the unworthy went hungry and presumably compounded their unworthiness by poaching and crop stealing. The former were invariably identified as belonging to large families, hence reducing the single men's chances of a free meal, or else worshippers in the established church, which only a minority of labouring families were in the nineteenth century, especially after 1830 when non-conformity spread rapidly.

One Suffolk man recalled instances of injustice in which he placed the blame firmly at the parson's door:

> The poor who went to chapel were spoken of in terms of contempt, and scornfully treated by many a parson and by the squire. To attend church, make a bow, or a curtsey, to their so-called betters, and be grateful for their wretched situation in life in

---

37 *League*, 6 Jan. 1844.
38 *NC*, 13 Dec. 1817.
39 *BNP*, 4 and 18 Jan. 1826.

which they were placed, were classed among the duties of poor men and women. And if any of them failed to observe their obligations they were excluded by the parson from charities and other benefits enjoyed by their church-going neighbours ... During winter, blankets, pieces of flannel, and coals were distributed in many parishes only to such labourers as attended church. Private benevolence was as strictly limited as charity bread. The distribution of these things were generally in the parson's hands, and it is a notorious fact that they were almost always manipulated in favour of church-going men and women, and against Dissenters. Though the oppressed villager might cry out, there was, unfortunately, no appeal.[40]

These recollections were not simply the jaundiced views of dissenters. Local newspapers recorded similar instances on many occasions. At Hingham (N) children received free clothing if they attended church, not once but twice, on Sundays. At nearby Shelfanger (N) the rector altered a charity bequest to 'the industrious poor' to include only those who attended his services.[41]

Charity, no doubt, carried with it the stigma of poverty, albeit worthy poverty, which did little for the villagers' self-respect. Ashby of Tysoe recalled how the vicar's wife handed out red flannel which one inhabitant proceeded to wash 'the charity out on it'. In such circumstances red cloth took on the uniform of dependent poverty as the women of four Suffolk villages were no doubt painfully aware when the Earl of Bristol gave out seventy-two bright red cloaks.[42]

The clash between charity on the one hand, and the villagers' self-respect on the other, was evident in one important area that was to cause mounting tension during the nineteenth century: the status of charitable lands left in trust.

At Brandon (S) and Horsford Heath (N) villagers were prosecuted by trustees of 'poor lands' for cutting broom and turves. In the latter village they continued to exercise their rights which were eventually upheld in the law courts.[43] One of the lengthiest disputes arose at Ixworth (S) where the poor wrote to the Charity Commissioners in 1857 accusing Sir Charles Lamb of misappropriating the rent from trust land. Lamb, in his defence, claimed the rent was being used for their benefit as he was paying towards the poor rates, a common

---

40 Glyde, 'Autobiography', p. 64. For similar comments see J. E. Ritchie, *Christopher Crayon's Recollections: The Life and Times of the Late James Ewing Ritchie, as Told by Himself* (London, 1898), pp. 10 and 37.

41 *NN*, 21 Nov. 1846, 26 Jan. 1861, 30 Jan 1864.

42 M. K. Ashby, *Joseph Ashby of Tysoe, 1859-1919* (London, 1974), p. 46; *NC*, 4 Jan. 1817.

43 *BNP*, 30 July 1861; *NN*, 28 July 1866.

method of paying trust monies at this time, but the villagers found this unacceptable and for many years felled trees on the land despite the dangers of court fines. Finally in 1866 they discovered that much of the money was actually being paid towards the reparation of the parish church and, furthermore, the Commissioners had endorsed this in 1857.[44]

Another long-running dispute arose at Little Walsingham (N) where 'dissatisfaction in some, nearly amounting to tumult' was reported. Meetings and petitions to the Commission were met with the rebuff that charities were 'a reward and not a right'. The Charity Commissioners clearly had the interests of landowners at heart. Five years after the initial protest Partridge, the local Independent minister, took up the cause once more by not only claiming that £160 was still owed to the poor but that funds from two other charities had been misappropriated as well. In a rousing sermon Partridge entreated his congregation to 'combine, and go collectively, but peacably to the church doors and demand it ... Cursed is he that opposeth the poor. The parish must combine, some individuals might perhaps suffer, but the great men could not oppose the entire parish (cheers).' His role as the village 'Hampden' was short-lived however, he learnt to his disgust that the poor had unwittingly signed away all their rights in 1861.[45]

The renewed interest in parish charity and trusts brought with it a new level of political consciousness, albeit of a very localized and narrow kind, but it did represent a significant step forward. Village meetings, organized by non-conformists, were held and their research into parish records unearthed charity deeds. Only Felthorpe (N) appeared to have an unlikely champion in their rector, the Reverend Brickdale, who acted as their spokesman when an inspector of charities arrived in their village. In gratitude the villagers signed a petition of thanks which also spoke of the discontent which had troubled them for many years but 'did not dare open our lips'.[46]

Like commons' enclosures, townlands could be and were subject to 'improvements'. In 1796 a piece of fenland had been granted to the poor of Marham (N) with a rent charge for the grazing of animals and turf cutting. Local farmers felt that this form of land usage was wasteful and pressed for its cultivation; in return they were to buy

44 BNP, 24 Dec. 1861, 13 Nov. 1866; W. White, *History, Gazetteer and Directory of Suffolk 1844* (Newton Abbot, repr. 1970), p. 701.

45 NN, 25 Jan., 1 Feb., 15 Mar. 1862, 14 Dec. 1867, 4 Jan., 25 Jan. 1868.

46 NN, 3 Mar. 1866. See also W. White, *History, Gazetteer and Directory of Norfolk 1845* (Newton Abbot, repr. 1970), p. 780, which states that money had been set aside for the repair of the poor's cottages.

coals for the parish. To some this appeared reasonable but to the majority of the parish such improvements struck at their very livelihood. Small traders were threatened with the loss of cheap grazing land, for others who made a living from turf cutting the dangers were obvious, 'whilst for the majority a change in fuel supply was expensive and inconvenient. Their ovens were designed to burn only turf, and conversion to coal was estimated at 30s. per oven. In 1869 the Marham people put their case to the Charity Commissioners and were heartened when the leading landowner Villebois was won over to their cause. Their success was limited as eleven labourers were soon in the courts for breaches of the peace against two of the farmers. In March the women were mobilized into action against contractors who had begun to mark off the dykes. With tin boilers and frying pans they set up a cacophony of 'rough music' and then charged at the trustees. The police who were present in force, quickly formed, in the best of English traditions, a square around the trustees and arrested twenty-eight women who were charged with affray and the levelling of ditches. Their efforts were, however, not in vain, for the Commissioners responded with new proposals that gave the poor twenty acres for turf cutting and between forty and fifty acres for allotment gardens.[47]

Other villages began to have limited victories also. At Gooderstone (N) the poor took their case to the courts and won. At Great Ryburgh (N) the villagers were warned not to set foot on the 'turf common' (which had been let at £10 a year) for fear of disturbing the game. So upset were they that they repossessed the common and refused to hand it over until a rent of £40 was agreed upon.[48] At Aldburgh (N) the parishioners resorted to a number of novel tactics when they discovered that £140 of the £160 a year income from the parish estate was going into the pockets of wealthier villagers. They nominated a former farm labourer turned shopkeeper named Henry Flatman for the position of parish warden. Twelve voted for the farmers' candidate (due to plural voting he received thirty-eight votes) whilst Flatman received seventy-two votes from as many voters. The farmers reacted in predictable fashion, 'if the labouring class will dare to vote in these matters contrary to the wishes of their masters, they are to have the moving ticket — that is, they are to be paid off'. A meeting was called by the poor at which they set up a subscription to raise funds for the protection of labourers who

---

47   NN, 6 Mar., 13 Mar., 3 Apr., 24 Apr., 8 May, and 30 Nov. 1869.
48   For Gooderstone, NN, 26 Mar. 1870; Great Ryburgh, NN, 9 July 1870.

refused to conform to their employers' orders.[49] This was, perhaps, the nearest Norfolk labourers ever came to forming a trade union before 1872.

From the small number of cases alluded to it is obvious that charity, instead of oiling the creaking joints of paternalistic and rural organic society, was producing, in its own right, an issue to be questioned and fought over. The emerging energy and confidence of village communities from the 1850s onwards can be seen in their methods and tactics of revolt. Further research in this and other counties may well show a direct relationship between the emergence of charity disputes and the formation of agricultural trade unionism. Even if the link cannot be proved, the whole question of charity rights dispels once and for all the notion that the rural people had subsided back into passive and accepting quietude as a result of the relative prosperity of the high farming era. One must remember that trade unionism did not emerge from nothing, it was built on years of oppression and fermenting hatred. The high-handed dispensation and administration of charities did contribute, if nothing else, to the growing awareness and consciousness of villagers' rights and their position within rural society.

Only in one area of charitable benevolence was self-respect and a measure of independence handed back to the labouring communities and that was in the granting of garden allotments. Like everything else to do with charity, the spread and growth of allotments was patchy and had much to do with landowners' paternalistic whims, consciences, and, in some cases, social strength, and dominance. Inevitably, therefore, allotments never became a general feature of the East Anglian countryside during the period. However, where they were found village communities reaped a genuine benefit from them and in nearly all cases were saved from the ignominy of the poor law.

Allotments emerged as a direct consequence of rural protest in the region. They were, in fact, the only serious attempt by philanthropic landowners at ameliorating the labourers' appalling social and economic plight. Moreover, these same landlords, shaken by both the protest and their own paternalistic neglect, hoped the allotments would provide the foundation or cornerstone for a revitalized paternally structured community in which they would reassert leadership and care in return for deference and social peace. It also provided them with an opportunity to remind their farming tenants of the benefits of traditional virtues in place of the stark cash nexus.

49 *NN*, 7 May and 8 Aug. 1870.

Almost to a man the farmers were hostile.

The allotment system was a response to the deteriorating social relations in the rural communities, as the 1843 *Select Committee on the Labouring Poor* pointed out:

> The practice of parcelling out fields in small allotments for cottage tenantry may be traced back to the end of the last century ... but it was not until 1830, when discontent had been so painfully exhibited amongst the peasantry of the southern counties, that this method of alleviating their situation was much resorted to.[50]

Although advocated in the final decade of the eighteenth century allotments do not appear to have been introduced then to East Anglia. In fact the first reference and the distinction of granting the first allotment would appear to belong to Sir Henry Bunbury, a large landowner in West Suffolk, who handed out land to his labouring tenants at the end of 1816 shortly after the 'Bread or Blood' Riots. However, until 1830 allotments were very few and far between; the local press refers only to Terrington (N) in 1818, Barningham (S) in 1822 (a year of riots), Nowton and Barnham (S) in 1829.[51] The Swing Riots and the wave of arson which followed brought an immediate response; the introduction of the New Poor Law in 1835-6 and the renewed wave of arson in 1843-4 and 1849-51 likewise initiated a similar response from startled landowners. In all, over fifty parishes introduced sizeable allotment schemes between 1830 and 1851 as a direct result of rural protest.[52]

Introduced as a precautionary measure against incendiary attacks and as a preventative rather than as a cure, allotments did not necessarily guarantee against rural protest. There were notable examples where allotments prevailed on an extensive scale in villages infamous for discontent; Barningham, Frettenham, Heydon, Hitcham, Ixworth, and Walsham-le-Willows experienced a combination of fires, riots, and strikes. The failure of Walsham (S) was conspicuous by virtue of being subjected to an extensive inquiry by William Kent, who sadly observed that the village had not only been the scene of five arson attacks in less than twelve months, but was also the parish

---

50 PP 1843, VII, *S .C. on the Labouring Poor (Allotments of Land)*, p. 203. For a fuller discussion on allotments see D. C. Barnett, 'Allotments and the Problem of Rural Poverty', in E. L. Jones and G. E. Mingay, ed., *Land, Labour and Population in the Industrial Revolution* (London, 1967), pp. 162-83; Archer, thesis, pp. 475-532.

51 C. J. F. Bunbury, ed., *Memoir and Literary Remains of Lt. Gen. Sir H. C. Bunbury Bart.* (London, 1868), 197; *The Times*, 10 July 1844; *BNP*, 27 May and 18 Nov. 1829.

52 Sixteen parishes introduced allotment schemes at the end of 1830 and a further twelve were in existence by 1833.

which possessed the highest acreage of allotments in the entire county. Those prejudiced against the system argued that this was hardly surprising since allotments 'had actually done harm by increasing the amount of pauperism in the parish', a sentiment shared by Chadwick.[53] Critics feared the system would give rise to a 'race' of peasant smallholders as was to be found in Ireland at this time.

The granting of allotments were not simple acts of philanthropy on the landlords' part since they asked for and received a rent, usually at the current rate for agricultural land, although in some cases the rents were excessive. Thomas Campbell Foster found rents to be as high as £8 an acre which he regarded as indefensible.[54] The size of individual plots likewise varied from one village to another, from two acres down to thirty perches, but the most common size was a quarter of an acre. Given the intensive cultivation and spade husbandry employed on these plots, labourers gained very substantial yields of potatoes and wheat far in excess of anything farmers could hope for on their extensively cultivated fields. Allotments could provide an addition of between 1s. and 2s. a week to a labouring family's earnings, which in nineteenth-century terms was a very substantial improvement indeed.

To many county landowners the allotment system became not only a cheap, convenient, and effective panacea for checking social indiscipline but also a vehicle through which they could reassert their power and influence over village communities which had been slipping away since the ending of the Napoleonic Wars. They, as much as the labourers, were distressed to see paternalist links being steadily eroded by the obviously strengthening capitalist relationship between employer and employee. For this reason, allotments as a form of social control may be considered a paternalistic anomaly within a capitalist economy. This reassertion of landlord influence within the village structure put the farmers very much on the defensive. They viewed any landlord directives with suspicion and, in a few cases, with open opposition. Many thought their workers would become thieves of seed corn and potatoes, while others maintained the men would 'waste' their strength and energy on their own plots and not on the employers' fields.[55] The root of their antipathy was more than likely blind prejudice. The labourer 'must not forget', explained an employer,

---

53 *BNP*, 23 Oct. 1844; S. E. Finer, *The Life and Times of Sir Edwin Chadwick* (London, 1952), pp. 86-7.
54 *The Times*, 10 July 1844.
55 PP 1843, XII, 265.

'that I am the farmer and he is the labourer'.[56] They feared above all else the loss of their monopoly as the sole occupiers of land and predicted that a race of independent peasant proprietors would emerge as a result. Thus farmers were 'up at arms' whenever landlords mooted the idea, 'and by their united efforts broke down many a scheme ... Their determination to prevent the labourer from having a bit of land actually induced some of them to sign a pledge, declaring that they would employ no labourer who held an allotment.'[57] This reaction in Barking (S) was by no means unusual but what makes it interesting is that the scheme was put forward by Lord Ashburnham in 1843-4 when the parish was seriously affected by incendiary fires and threatening letters. At Columbine Hall, tenanted by John Boby — a notoriously unpopular farmer — the incendiary took the trouble to return after the first fire to complete the work of total destruction. In an anonymous letter to Ashburnham, an 'old servant' complained:

> it generally believed that you had ordered Mr Moore your steward to allott small parcels of land at a fair rent for benifit of the Pore many applications has been made but none let more would have been but the labourers are afraid of their masters as it has been insinuated it injure them with the farmers as they would lose their work if they applied.[58]

The 'absurd jealousy', as Foster called it, of the farmers was altogether unfounded. As Irish-type peasantry of smallholders scratching a living did not materialize; furthermore, labourers applying for plots had to fulfil numerous conditions set by landlords and vicars. Invariably land was given to the deserving poor who were subjectively defined as 'honest', 'industrious', and 'respectable'. A labourer, in order to pass this moral means test, had to come from a family free of criminal tendencies and a family of long standing within the village and hence settled there. His work record was also relevant, and those who had actually worked for the landlord were given preferential treatment, as were those with a record of long service with one master. Labourers with large families who had managed to stay clear of poor relief, except in exceptional circumstances, were also likely candidates. All this applied to 'needy' widows with children to support, and old men with a history of 'honest toil'. One other aspect was taken into account —— that of regular attendance at the Established

---

56 Clifford, *Agricultural Lock Out*, p. 33.
57 Glyde, 'Autobiography', p. 40.
58 IESRO, HA 1/HB6/1b/24, 57, 59, 60, 62. See also J. Harber, 'Incendiarism in Suffolk 1840-45', MA diss. (Univ. of Warwick, 1975), p. 42.

church. Once the allotment was granted, the competitive ethic was injected into the allottee by offers of incentives — rent reductions and cash prizes — for the best maintained plots and cultivated crops. By all accounts the labourers were sufficiently motivated to work till eleven at night in winter, or put in two hours at dawn before they went to work.[59]

Vegetable growing was not only profitable but also morally and physically uplifting. Beershops and game preserves were no longer meant to be the labourers' traditional haunts. Certainly if they were caught adding a bit of meat to their home-grown diet they were immediately stripped of their land. 'The men', Bunbury maintained, 'were more afraid of losing their Allotments than going to jail: a proof of the operation of the practice as a moral check.'[60] These plots of land were credited with enormous powers; the Reverend Henslow's flock at Hitcham (S) was 'notorious for witchcraft, drunkeness, poaching, sheep stealing, and immoral habits' in 1839 when he arrived. However, by the time of his death in 1861 his recalcitrant parishioners, by means of allotments and firework displays, were the very models of virtuous rusticity.[61]

Allotments were, therefore, useful as a means of social control, discipline, and conditioning, but we should not overlook one drawback contained in the logic of the initial distribution of land to the community. The men and women who were granted land were already those perceived by landowners to be law-abiding and deserving. The more troublesome villagers, the unemployed, the unattached, and the irreligious presumably never made it on to the short-list of applicants, thus they were given no alternatives to compounding their already poor reputations by maintaining their drinking and poaching habits. Further research at a local level may well reveal that the allotment system may have driven a wedge into the labouring community over the course of time, dividing the respectable from the disreputable, leaving the latter isolated and the former more

---

59 PP 1843, XII, 265. At Shotesham labourers managed to fit in two hours on their allotments during their lunch break.

60 For an example of a poacher losing his allotment see *The Times*, 10 July 1844. Between 1824 and 1844 Bunbury evicted only one man on account of crime.

61 Anon., *Biographical Sketch of the Revd John Stevens Henslow* (London, 1861), 9-12. His firework displays were the subject of much harsh criticism in 1844, the year he introduced them. Henslow, through the medium of the local press, announced that if the people wanted fires then they ought to be given them. Modern psychologists would probably applaud his reasoning and his methods. The pyrogenic displays on the rectory lawn quietened the neighbourhood, while all around incendiary fires continued. See also J. Russell-Gebbett, *Henslow of Hitcham* (Lavenham, 1977), p. 75.

firmly attached to the social and economic mores of the landed elite. They now had, after all, 'a little stake in the county' and became, in the words of the Select Committee on the Labouring Poor, 'a class which has something to lose'.[62]

---

62 PP 1843, XII, 261; PP 1843, VII, 226.

4
Incendiarism: Annual Survey 1815-1834

INTRODUCTION

Historians had, for many years, contented themselves by describing the protest of the years from Swing to Arch in no more than one paragraph. Between these two famous landmarks lay *terra incognita* where 'burning ricks and farm buildings ... told the tale of an angered, desperate people'. Protest of this kind, it was argued, 'bore the mark of a pre-industrial age'.[1] In more recent years Hobsbawm and Rudé have concentrated on incendiarism in 1830 only, but they did at least recognize that this form of crime became the characteristic mode of protest 'only after 1830'. Since then two studies have carried forward our knowledge. A. J. Peacock, in a short essay, 'Village Radicalism in East Anglia 1800-1850', has brought much new evidence to light but his approach was mainly of a descriptive nature. David Jones, in a more detailed and analytical article, which again concentrated on East Anglia, studied the crime in far greater detail but he limited his perspective to only two years.[2] The present study is the first attempt to examine incendiarism over a long time span and in relation to other forms of covert agrarian disturbances. Before embarking on a systematic analysis of this most secretive and enduring crime of social protest it will be necessary to survey some of the events of the nineteenth century which are relevant to this study.

But, first, what criteria were employed in determining what constituted arson attacks? It has been necessary to accept the observations and findings of the law courts, insurance companies, and news reporters of the period. We must take on trust the accuracy of their evidence but it is worth pointing out that the insurance companies had well-trained and experienced fire investigators whose job it was to inquire into each claim. Farmers, too, had little to gain from reporting fires which had occurred on their property as having been incendiary in origin when in fact they had been accidental, since their insurance policies could have been placed in jeopardy. The historian has other important evidence by which to gauge the accuracy

---

1 R. Groves, *Sharpen the Sickle; The History of the Farm Workers Union* (London, 1949), p. 25; T. Barker, ed., *The Long March of Everyman* (London, 1975), p. 91.

2 Hobsbawm and Rudé, *Captain Swing*, p. xviii; Peacock, 'Village Radicalism', pp. 27-61; D. J. V. Jones, 'Thomas Campbell Foster', pp. 5-43. In addition there are two dissertations: S. W. Amos, 'Social Discontent and Agrarian Disturbances in Essex 1795-1850', MA diss. (Univ. of Durham, 1971); J. Harber, 'Incendiarism in Suffolk 1840-45', MA diss. (Univ. of Warwick, 1975).

of contemporary reports. Lightning, for instance, caused many accidental fires but it is easy to discount this natural phenomenon as the alleged cause of incendiary fires. Likewise the invention of steam threshing machines and steam locomotives brought in their wake an increased fire risk to farming property. The insurance investigators were able to establish with ease the fires caused by sparks from such machines. Accidental fires were started in most cases by natural combustion (overheating) and by the carelessness of children and servants. In the first case, overheating was seasonal and usually gave warning of itself, or else left sufficient evidence of the fact since this type of fire burnt from the centre outwards (whereas incendiary fires burnt inwards). Farmers knew when stacks were growing warm or were at risk when they had been constructed of green hay after the haysel. In the case of children and servants the truth was often eventually brought to light by the persistence of the police, parents, and employers. They were susceptible to pressure.

In some of the examples of arson it has been deemed necessary to treat them with scepticism and caution because contemporaries were unable to ascertain the cause of the fires. Some have been discounted as being probable accidents whilst others have been included because they caught light at times of the day, or rather night, or in months of the year when accidental causes seemed the least likely explanation. There were 'tell-tale' signs which characterize them as being incendiary in origin, such as fresh footprints in the vicinity, occurrence during the nights of winter weekends, simultaneous fires breaking out in different places, and lastly the type of property fired was often itself a clue. Thus the study of fire causes has not been ignored, but has in fact been examined in considerable detail.

Despite all the academic interest in the major explosions of collective protest over this period, it is incendiarism which became the prime weapon of the rural war. In fact after 1830 fire became the hallmark of social protest for much of this period as Table 4.1 indicates. The number of fires listed in that table may well be an underestimate of the actual total since incendiary attacks were not universally reported in the local press or in insurance company records. Newspapers were more likely to miss instances of fires during years of greatest social unrest, as in 1843-4 when it was argued that reports of fires only led to further outbreaks on the grounds that imitation was a motivating factor. One reporter also noted that small fires ceased to be newsworthy. Likewise, unsuccessful attempts at incendiarism often went unnoticed, until a more serious fire occurred on the same property when the papers reported the previous attempts.

TABLE 4.1 *Incendiarism in Norfolk and Suffolk, 1815-1870*

Year	No. of Fires		TOTAL	Year	No. of Fires		TOTAL
	Norfolk	Suffolk			Norfolk	Suffolk	
1815	3	8	11	1843	40	44	84
1816	5	22	27	1844	76	142	218
1817	1	7	8	1845	32	21	53
1818	6	7	13	1846	32	27	59
1819	2	7	9	1847	15	20	35
1820	7	12	19	1848	17	27	44
1821	7	11	18	1849	27	51	78
1822	19	45	64	1850	30	45	75
1823	1	10	11	1851	40	35	75
1824	3	9	12	1852	29	25	54
1825	4	3	7	1853	17	9	26
1826	2	0	2	1854	22	17	39
1827	4	1	5	1855	12	14	26
1828	3	2	5	1856	7	16	23
1829	9	7	16	1857	11	16	27
1830	28	19	47	1858	10	22	32
1831	53	11	64	1859	17	18	35
1832	52	12	64	1860	8	7	15
1833	58	14	72	1861	15	25	40
1834	33	17	50	1862	6	7	13
1835	17	8	25	1863	11	14	25
1836	13	7	20	1864	19	23	42
1837	10	7	17	1865	18	18	36
1838	3	5	8	1866	11	14	25
1839	4	1	5	1867	13	12	25
1840	6	7	13	1868	32	28	60
1841	11	4	15	1869	11	12	23
1842	15	10	25	1870	18	15	33
				TOTAL	975	997	1,972

Sources: Local newspapers, 1815-70; *The Times*, 1843-4; *Morning Chronicle*, 1844; PRO, ASSI 33/12-14; ASSI 35/276-90; HO 64/1-6; IESRO, HA 11/B1/11/2, NUFO, board minutes, 1840-51.

There were 1,972 fires in Norfolk and Suffolk between 1815 and 1870, an average of thirty-six fires a year or three a month. Whilst presenting these figures in this way may seem misleading, given the cyclical and seasonal nature of the crime, it does, however, emphasize the scale of incendiarism. In forty-six of the fifty-six years there was on average one incendiary fire a month in the region. None of the exceptions occurred after 1850, which is a surprising observation as historical opinion believes social protest to have declined to almost nothing after this date. If the figures for each county are taken separately another important fact comes to light. On the whole the figures run along a parallel course but their troughs coincide more frequently than their peaks. Furthermore, one would expect two arable counties in the same region to have had similar, if not parallel, trends of incendiary activity, but they differed or even diverged at five major points. Suffolk, in the first ten years of the period, experienced more than twice as much incendiary activity as Norfolk. Second, this trend is reversed in the first six years of the 1830s when Norfolk had a much higher incidence of arson. This would suggest that this incendiarism was the result of the defeat of the 1830 Swing Riots which were far more extensive in Norfolk than in Suffolk. Third, the explosion of fires in the 1840s in Suffolk is very notable even when compared to the considerable peak of Norfolk. In the former county the arson rate rose from almost nothing to well in excess of 100 in 1844 and then declined very sharply, whereas in Norfolk the peak was neither as large nor was the trough so deep in 1845. Incendiarism may, therefore, be regarded as a more persistent feature in Norfolk than in Suffolk. Fourth, both counties experienced an upsurge in mid-century but numbers in Suffolk peaked in 1849, and in Norfolk in 1851. And lastly, from 1855 to 1870 Suffolk had more incendiary fires every year than Norfolk, 1860, 1867, 1868, and 1870 excepted. The patterns of incendiarism from 1815 to 1870 are striking and raise several questions. It is hoped that this and the following three chapters will find answers to these questions about the enigmatic crime of incendiarism.

INCENDIARISM: A NEW EXPRESSION OF GRIEVANCE

Some historians regard incendiarism as a traditional form of social protest.[3] Fires, for instance, had been lit occasionally during eighteenth-century food riots — occasionally being the operative

---

3   See Ch. 10 for further comments on the idea that arson was 'traditional'.

word, for incendiarism on a widespread scale was a nineteenth-century phenomenon. Charles Mackie thought it sufficiently unusual to warrant a mention as late as 1807 when he was compiling the *Norfolk Annals*, and J. H. Kent regarded 1816 as the year in which the 'first race of incendiaries' became active. Bunbury likewise recalled 1816 as the year when incendiarism first appeared, as did the *Bury Post* which lamented the fact that Suffolk 'must bear the disgrace of having given birth' to 'that dreadful practice of burning farmers' property'. The scale of incendiarism during this year of machine breaking was, in comparison to later years, small.[4] Peacock, in his detailed book on the 'Bread or Blood' Riots, referred to only twenty-two fires in Norfolk and Suffolk between 1815 and 1816.[5] Small though this number was, it signified a new departure from more traditional modes of protest. In 1822, again a year of riots and collective demonstrations, incendiarism on a large scale became a primary weapon in the protester's arsenal. In that year over sixty fires have been recorded and such was the novelty of the scale of the fires that Constable was moved to write that the rector and the squire had forsaken the village because of their fear of the fires.[6]

So novel was incendiarism as a form of protest that sufferers, with the aid of solicitors, resurrected the dormant provisions of the Black Act which, had it remained in force after its demise in 1827, would have produced disastrous consequences for local ratepayers. This act allowed a victim of incendiarism to be compensated by the hundred in which he resided. In 1816 the *Suffolk Chronicle* actually published the relevant sections of the Black Act together with advice to its readers on how to make a claim, and thereafter it was used extensively in that county. In Norfolk the use of this act was described as 'unprecedented' in 1823 when farmer Wrench claimed £140 damages from the inhabitants of Holt. This was not so, because Balls claimed that maximum £200 from the hundred of Happing in March 1819.[7] Obviously the repeal of the act had a profound effect on the fire insurance companies who must have benefited enormously after 1827.[8] Further evidence also suggests arson, before 1830, was of a relatively low order. First, the annual committals for arson in England

---

4   C. Mackie, *Norfolk Annals* (Norwich, 1901), 60-1; Kent, *Remarks*, p. 41; Jones, 'Thomas Campbell Foster', p. 5; R. H. Mason, *The History of Norfolk* (London, 1884), 482 n. 1; Wells, 'Development', *passim*; *BNP*, 17 Apr. 1822.

5   This figure was based on a close reading of A. J. Peacock, *Bread or Blood* (London, 1965).

6   Beckett, *John Constable's Correspondence*, iv. 203.

7   *SC*, 18 May 1816; *NC*, 27 Mar. 1819.

8   Hobsbawm and Rudé, *Captain Swing*, pp. 56 and 340.

and Wales between 1810 and 1829 never rose above forty-seven, and that was in the exceptional year of 1822. In fact, for all other years there was less than one committal a year per county.[9] Second, the Norwich Union Fire Insurance Minute Books also record a similar pattern. They show only eighteen claims in 1822 and no more than nine a year between 1821 and 1829.[10]

From such evidence it is possible to conclude that in no year before 1830, 1822 excepted, did the number of fires attain the level and frequency of the post-1830 period. Nor should we be surprised by this observation. Let us consider for a moment one simple question, so obvious that it is often overlooked by historians of social protest who tend to ask the question 'who', rather than 'how'. How were the fires ignited? There were a number of techniques: hot coals or cinders, smouldering peat, fireballs, tinder-box and flint, pipe, and 'Lucifer' matches. Any self-respecting incendiary would choose the box of friction matches. They were light, portable, concealable, cheap, and effective — in fact superior in every respect to all other methods. The point which really has to be emphasized in the context of this study is that the 'Lucifer' matches, as sold in every village store, only came onto the market in 1830. This proved an absolute boon to would-be incendiaries.[11] Without wishing to sound facetious one could argue that new technology found an eager market ready and waiting to take full advantage. The matches' practical, almost liberating, effect can be seen in the example of Christopher Birch who started eight fires in South Norfolk in 1850 as he staggered home from the public house. In 1820 Birch would have been faced with a practical problem — it conjures up the unlikely picture of a drunken man staggering, not only under the influence of drink, but also the weight of a brazier. Similarly a tinder-box and flint was not a particularly effective method of starting a fire in heavy rain or high winds, the latter meteorological condition being much favoured by incendiaries. The essence of a successful incendiary was his speed and stealth and the 'Lucifer' match with its effective ignition allowed him to strike the match and then escape across the fields. The 'Lucifer' or 'strike anywhere' match thus opened up a whole new vista for the angry labourer.

---

9 Figures quoted in *Captain Swing*, p. 56.
10 My thanks are extended to Roger Ryan for allowing me to quote these figures based on his research of the Norwich Union Fire Insurance Minutes 1821-9.
11 *Everyman's Encyclopedia*, viii, 121; *NC*, 29 June and 3 Aug. 1850.

ANNUAL SUMMARY 1815-1819

The restoration of international peace in 1815 marked the beginning of a protracted rural war in East Anglia. The apparent arcadia of the war years — it certainly became that in retrospect, with its high wheat prices and economic prosperity for farmers and landowners alike — came to an end when agricultural depression set in almost as soon as the fields of Waterloo had been cleared of the dead. And from the same fields returned many thousands of soldiers, formerly agricultural labourers, who expected, in return for their services to king and country, work, wages, and low food prices. In this they were to be bitterly disappointed. Their enemy was now the farmer, the parson, the squire, the miller, and the poor law official; their battleground the very parishes of their birth, and their weapons were now an arsenal of torches, mallets, and pickaxes.

These early years of 1815-16 marked the first serious outbreaks of collective disturbances and incendiarism in East Anglia. The story has been expertly constructed and recounted by Peacock in *Bread or Blood*, a book whose very title echoes the battle-cry of the rioters. In addition to this study there has recently appeared a short but useful corrective by Charlesworth.[12] For these two reasons it has not been deemed necessary to retell the same story in any great detail, except to bring out some salient features which have a bearing on the later years of trial and tribulation for the labouring classes.

In 1815 a feature occurred which was to be repeated in 1829. In both years serious signs of anger were evident months before the large explosive demonstrations of protest in 1816 and 1830 respectively. Even before the ending of the Napoleonic Wars, William Mason, 'the champion of the rights of the poor', was arrested with others for destroying fences recently erected as a result of a parliamentary enclosure act at North Lopham (N).[13] Further to the south at Gosbeck (S) twenty labourers gathered and destroyed two threshing machines. Sir William Middleton, a leading landowner and by all accounts an unpopular one — 'his life in Jamaica had spoiled him, and made him a loose fish in many ways' — had to obtain an escort home for himself and the other arresting magistrates when they were confronted by an angry crowd at Ipswich.[14] As was so often the

---

12 Peacock, *Bread or Blood*; A. Charlesworth, *An Atlas of Rural Protest in Britain 1548-1900* (London, 1983), pp. 146-8.
13 *NC*, 4 Mar., 1 Apr. and 29 July 1815.
14 *SC*, 25 Feb., 4 Mar., and 8 Apr. 1815; *NC*, 4 Mar. and 8 Apr. 1815; Glyde, 'Autobiography', p. 11. Sir William's father was known as 'Bags' because he was once caught rummaging

case in later years and in other counties the law dealt leniently with them. After one month in gaol the nine convicted men returned to Gosbeck to their previous employers and remained there for many years.[15] Scenes of anger and hostility were evident in Norwich less than a month later when Coke, the leading agriculturalist of his day, faced a riot from anti-corn law supporters whilst attending a cattle show on Castle Hill. Only the presence of the military and the reading of the Riot Act prevented the disturbance from escalating.[16]

After a brief lull, during which Waterloo and the harvest were won, the all too familiar signs of trouble shattered the peace once more. The start of the threshing season was marked by the destruction of another machine at Holbrook (S), and by November fires were fast becoming a new and regular feature of rural protest. In two Norfolk villages, Croxton and Whissonett, it appears arson was now being employed in anti-enclosure disputes.[17] However, collective protest remained the norm, when in late November a hundred labourers gathered from Kenton, Ashfield, and Monk Soham (S) and destroyed three threshing machines in the area.[18]

The year 1816 began badly for the labourers; their wages were reduced and many were without employment. Unprecedented numbers were forced to seek poor relief and the low wheat prices of January to April were of little compensation or consolation to the unemployed and an even greater deterrent to the farmers to find work for the men. The local press, sensing trouble ahead, reported increases in theft, invariably petty, and poaching. The latter produced unusually bitter fights between poachers, 'drawn up in battle array', and keepers.

The fires began in March, and significantly one was on the property of the Terrington (N) overseer, which destroyed dressing machines and flax used by unemployed.[19] The first threshing machine was broken in North Essex at Mile End Heath in early April, and by the seventeenth of the month the anti-machinery riots had spread into Suffolk. This marked the start of five and a half weeks rioting in the region. It would be erroneous, however, to perceive the riots as one

---

through labourers' food bags in order to see what they ate for dinner.

15 Glyde, 'Autobiography', p. 11. See also Hobsbawm and Rudé, *Captain Swing*, p. 75, where the rioters of Lower Hardres, the first village to rise in 1830, received only a caution and three-day prison sentences. The same leniency was extended to Norfolk's first Swing rioters at Paston.

16 *NC*, 25 Mar. 1815.

17 For Holbrook, *SC*, 5 Aug. 1815, *NC*, 15 Oct. 1815, 20 Jan. 1816; Croxton, *NC*, 6 Jan. 1816; Whissonett, *NC*, 25 Nov. 1815.

18 *SC*, 20 Jan. 1816; *NC*, 2 Dec. 1815, 20 Jan. 1816.

19 *NC*, 16 Mar. 1816.

single uprising, and they were certainly not one or even a series of food riots, as Charlesworth correctly points out.[20] There were waves of unrest interspersed with a full-scale arson attack in Suffolk. The objectives of the demonstrators too were quite different and depended, to a large extent, on the locality where the protest was occurring. The first wave, from 17 to 29 April, running in a band to the east of Bury in a south-easterly direction to Hadleigh, was associated with farm machinery and low wages. The second began on 3 May in the south-west corner of the county, continued until 22 May, and was again associated with the use of machinery, though Haverhill experienced a food riot. This region was also notable for a large concentration of incendiary activity. The third wave began on the Suffolk-Norfolk border on 16 May at Brandon and moved northwards into western Norfolk and south into the Fens. These riots, concentrated into one intense week, were the bitterest and most famous of all the 1816 disturbances; the ones to which Peacock referred as the 'Bread or Blood' Riots. As this catchphrase implies, the demand for lower food prices was probably the important grievance, but wages, the poor law, and enclosure were also cited by the crowds. There were other pockets of trouble in the same month in Norfolk; around 19 May four villages west of Wymondham experienced anti-machinery demonstrations and Norwich itself had three days of rioting. Finally, to the north of Swaffham, on 26 May, food riots and low wage protests were reported.[21] Thus the disturbances were widely dispersed in the region and the grievances aired by the assembled workers were quite disparate. Even the rioters themselves could in no way be described as a homogeneous section of the rural workforce, especially in the market towns like Norwich or Bury where other occupational groups were heavily involved.[22] Although one contemporary recalled 1816 as the first year when incendiarism became a significant and worrying problem the fires actually played a fairly peripheral role to the main events. The actual number of arson attacks more than doubled the previous year's total, twenty-seven compared with eleven, but the volume was low when compared to the post-1830s. The main increase in incendiarism lay in Suffolk with twenty-two fires, heavily concentrated into the first fortnight of May when arson was virtually a daily happening and acted as a kind of back-up pressure to the rioters' demands. At Cockfield, for example, a

---

20 *NC*, 20 Apr. 1816; Amos, thesis, pp. 23-4, Charlesworth, *Atlas*, pp. 146-8.
21 See May and June edns. of the local press and Peacock, *Bread or Blood*, chs. 6-10.
22 *NC*, 18 May, 25 May 1816, 24 Aug. 1816.

threshing machine was the object of the incendiary's torch, likewise at Clare; at Haverhill it was the maltings, and at Drinkstone the local magistrate, Grigby, who was very active in restoring the peace to the county, lost a barn for his public spiritedness.[23] Incendiarism, as a weapon and tactic in its own right, had yet to be fully installed in the labourers' arsenal.

The troubles of 1816, perhaps perceived as a short-lived and singular event, were soon forgotten and to a large extent forgiven. Rioters left over for trial from the previous year were discharged at the 1817 assizes.[24] What had constituted normality for a whole generation returned; wheat prices regained their wartime levels and averaged 100s. a quarter for much of the year. The little trouble there was occurred in Suffolk where millers received threatening letters and in one case were visited by the incendiary. The boom mentality was evident in other disturbances. Enclosures of wastes and village greens continued, sparking off a typical anti-enclosure riot at Cowlinge (S). Again the judge treated the men leniently, lecturing them on their 'mistaken notion of what they conceived a right belonging to them', before releasing them.[25] In the months after the 1817 harvest incendiarism in Suffolk was high by previous standards, five in the space of three months, which led one insurance company to run a business-recruiting campaign. Their special offer, a pessimistic one, promised any property owner insured with them a reward after every incendiary attack. Given the circumstances of later years, with their enormous increases in incendiary activity, this promotion would cost the company absolutely nothing since rewards were never collected.[26]

Conditions improved for the labourers in 1818 when wheat prices began to fall steadily whilst their wages held up. Even employment, when compared to previous years, was reported as being good thanks to the clemency of the weather. Incendiarism on the other hand did not diminish. Of the thirteen fires, six occurred in Norfolk, more even than in 1816. This was a new and disturbing development noted by both the Norwich Union Insurance Office and property owners in East Dereham, where they formed an association for the prevention of crime.[27] Exning in Suffolk, too, began what was to become a long

---

23 For Cockfield, *SC*, 27 Apr. 1816; Clare, *NC*, 18 May 1816; Haverhill, *NC*, 11 May 1816; Drinkstone, *SC*, 11 May 1816.
24 *NC*, 12 Apr. 1817.
25 The fire was at Brandon Mills, *SC*, 8 Nov. 1817. Woodbridge millers received anonymous letters, *SC*, 4 Jan. 1817. For Cowlinge see *NC*, 9 Aug. 1817.
26 *NC*, 27 Sept. 1817. The County Fire Office was the company in question.
27 *NC*, 13 June 1818.

association with arson. The four fires that year spread panic through the ranks of the Exning farmers who requested and received the aid of a Bow Street officer to investigate their problem. This gentleman met with early success, the arrest and conviction of 14-year-old John Webb. His triumph was short-lived as two more fires were lit and anonymous letters posted, threatening to burn all the farmers out.[28]

THE 1820s

The steady and inexorable descent towards depression was evident by 1820: 'Ruin stares us in the face' reported the *Bury Post*. Unemployment increased as wheat prices continued their long fall; a whole generation of farmers, quite unused to and ill-prepared for depression, remained indifferent and apathetic.[29] By the end of the year the Norfolk press too had noted a similar indifference which they feared might lead to a repeat of 1816.[30] Their powers of prophecy could hardly be described as miraculous foresight since the evidence of impending trouble was there for all to see. The tell-tale signs of game law convictions rose by 45 per cent in Norfolk, and highway robbery and burglary became commonplace.[31] At Hadleigh robberies reached such epidemic proportions that another Bow Street officer was sent down from London. Dressed as a farm labourer and circulating among the locals in the pubs, he finally captured a gang of four, but only after all the leading inhabitants had received death threats and one farm had been burnt.[32] Incendiarism was probably the best barometer of the true state of affairs, it more than doubled the previous year's total.[33]

The year 1821 brought no respite, with farmers giving up their tenancies despite rent and tithe reductions. Wages were generally lowered to 9s. a week and unemployment was described as 'frightful'. In one village there were as many as seventeen able-bodied without work in June and in another forty-five people were forced in to Rollesby (N) house of industry. The apathy of the previous year was now replaced with 'fearful foreboding' of the approaching winter

---

28 *NC*, 10 Apr. 1819; *SC*, 15 Aug. 1818 and 24 July 1819; *BNP*, 26 July 1820. Exning had nine fires and numerous threatening letters between 1816 and 1821.

29 *BNP*, 5 Jan. 1820.

30 *NM*, 9 Dec. 1820.

31 *NM*, 9 Dec. 1820; HO 52/2

32 *BNP*, 8 Mar. and 12 Apr. 1820.

33 In Norfolk the seven fires were widely dispersed throughout the county whereas in Suffolk the dozen fires occurred to the east of Ipswich.

among Norfolk farmers.[34] Large rent and tithe reductions, anything up to 30 per cent, did little to ease the strain in the new year; neither did one county meeting attended by 6,000 farmers and landowners, where lower taxes and higher import duties were demanded. However, not for the first or last time, one of the basic catalysts of agrarian distress and ultimately protest came to the fore — bad weather. Heavy and continuous rain put paid to any outdoor work in January 1822, forcing the already high unemployment even higher. The labourers' response was immediate, unprecedented, and intimidatory. In the first six weeks of the year twelve fires illuminated the night skies of East Anglia. Some were enormous, the Chediston (S) fire caused £1,000 worth of damage to buildings and corn; others were preceded by dire threats promising death and destruction to the recipients. At Nettlestead (S) farmer Moore, who had only recently completed building a new barn burnt down in 1820, lost this too.[35] The fear generated by these fires, great though it was, paled into insignificance when panic ensued at the onset of the riots.[36]

They began in the South Norfolk parishes of Burston, Gissing, and Shimpling on 14 and 15 February, where labourers broke or dragged threshing machines to the parish boundaries. During the first week of disturbances trouble spread eastwards in Norfolk and southward into Suffolk. However, from 28 February onwards the Norfolk demonstrations — the word riot could hardly be ascribed to the peaceful gatherings which had taken place until then — entered a new and more desperate phase. The Winfarthing labourers turned on the ranks of constables and farmers surrounding Doggett's farm where, despite earlier promises to discontinue using his machine, a thresher was at work. One gentleman was dismounted, the machine broken, and the constables forced to retreat under a hail of stones. This area around Diss fell very much into the hands of labourers who set up day and night patrols in order to prevent arrests.[37] By now the local authorities were clearly alarmed and regular army reinforcements were ordered to be sent in. Letters to the Home Office drew comparisons to the state of Ireland and 'Captain Rock's Corps'. Surtees, the most active of the justices, reported 'there comes instances of men putting their scythes at the end of poles, which brings us nearly upon a par

---

34 *NM*, 31 Mar. and 14 Apr. 1821; *NC*, 23 June 1821; *BNP*, 7 Nov. 1821.

35 For Chediston, *NM*, 23 Feb. 1822; Nettlestead, *NM*, 26 Jan. 1822. At least eight Suffolk parishes received a spate of anonymous letters in early Feb., see *BNP*, 13 Feb. 1822.

36 For the fullest description of the 1822 riots see P. Muskett, 'The East Anglian Riots of 1822', *Ag. Hist. Rev.* 32 (1984), 1-13.

37 *NM*, 23 Feb. and 9 Mar. 1822; *NC*, 23 Feb. and 30 Mar. 1822; HO 40/17.

with the Irish rebels'. And Lieutenant Colonel Ray, clearly a worried man, wrote:

> Threatening letters are circulated among us most liberally and the fire Brand, the most formidable of weapons, is the portion of those who persist in the use of threshing machines or any way are obnoxious to the party. At present thank God — I have escaped without letter or fire Brand but after tuesday next [i.e. 5 March] I must expect my portion of notice from them, for on that day ... I have orders from Mr Lee and the Magistrates ... to parade troops on Sturston Common adjoining the town of Diss.[38]

Fortunately for Surtees, Ray, and the others, the East Anglian labourers never resorted to the extreme terror tactics of Captain Rock's band in Ireland but the worst was yet to come, for from 4 to 6 March the riots in Norfolk escalated and moved northwards to Wymondham, where machine breaking had begun late on Saturday 2 March. Here two bands of men separated, one going south-west and the other south-east. The former, headed by a musical ensemble, cleared over a dozen machines in the Attleborough neighbourhood.[39] The Wymondham group was finally dispersed on 6 March and seven of them were sent up to Norwich, itself in a 'feverish temper'.[40] The worst of the disorders in Norfolk had finally come to an end after three weeks.

In Suffolk the disturbances also continued in the first week of March when the Cratfield and Laxfield men destroyed six threshing machines.[41] At nearby Hoo more labourers assembled on the green and passed the following formal resolution: 'that all threshing machines, whether in use or not, should be destroyed immediately; that all farmers who insisted on continuing the use of them should be burnt; as well as their property, and that all corn drills and mole ploughs should be demolished without loss of time.[42] This remarkable resolution is unique. At no other time was incendiarism, and by implication murder, advocated in such a formal and public manner by

---

38 For Irish parallels see *BNP*, 13 Mar. 1833; PRO, HO 40/17, 12 Mar. 1822; IESRO, HA 247/5/85, letter from Ray, 1 Mar. 1822.

39 *NM*, 9 Mar. 1822; *NC*, 9 Mar.-30 Mar. 1822; *BNP*, 16 Mar. 1822; PRO, HO 40/17, letters from Surtees, 6-7 Mar. 1822; IESRO, HA 247/ 5/87, letter from Ray, 7 Mar. 1822. One of the band was arrested for 'voluntarily playing the clarinet'.

40 PRO, HO 40/17, 6 Mar. 1822. At this time the Lord Lt. of Norfolk, Wodehouse, received a dramatic note written in a hurried and large scrawl: 'What the consequences will be for this town and neighbourhood if soldiers are not sent cannot at present be stated.' Wodehouse passed it on to Peel, describing its contents as being 'of an alarming nature'.

41 *BNP*, 20 Mar. 1822.

42 *BNP*, 13 and 20 Mar. 1822.

a large body of people. It shows clearly how arson, though an individualistic method of protest, could become the collective desire of the labourers. To what extent this meeting influenced the following events is hard to assess, although we might infer the point — the burning of farmers' property — was taken very much to heart. Machine breaking in Suffolk ceased for over a month but the remaining twenty-six days of March witnessed fourteen fires, despite the presence of nightwatchmen on many farms. The fires were concentrated in two main spots, one close to the Norfolk border where machine breaking had been prevalent, and the other further south in central Suffolk. In one instance a threshing machine was the specific target as it had been covered with haulm before being fired.[43] In most other cases the damage was mainly to stacks of corn.

Public excitement began to mount at the end of the month when in Ipswich, which had been free of riots and fires until then, a large fire on 28 March destroyed the property of Byles, the corn miller, amidst 'great rejoicing' among the labouring community. Another large landowner received an anonymous letter threatening fire if he dared to use his threshing machine. On other farms cart harnesses were cut to shreds, but most worrying of all to the mayor were the papers found around his town on Saturday, 30 March.[44] Addressed 'To the inhabitants of Ipswich', the circular continued:

> Prepare for the grand meeting on the Corn Hill on monday next at nine o' clock and render your assistance round the town to burn the courts, Mr. Cobbolds, Mr. Edgars, Mr. Roes and Mr. Stewards premises down our party is now five Hundred and fifty seven strong any one that would wish to join us meet us on the Corn Hill in the evening.[45]

Come the night of 2 April no meeting took place, a welcome anti-climax no doubt to the authorities, but there followed three fires in quick succession and an anonymous letter that must surely warrant some kind of award for its sheer length.[46] Though complicated, the grievances listed in the letter are full and inclusive of virtually every problem from the price of beer to the Settlement Laws. In typical fashion the writer implied that he was a member of a well-organized group ready and waiting only for the word of command. The 'Secret

---

43 *NM*, 23 Mar. 1822, at Finningham.
44 *NC*, 6 Apr. 1822; *BNP*, 3 Apr. 1822.
45 PRO, HO 40/17, letter from Quilton, 31 Mar. 1822.
46 PRO, HO 40/17, letter from Gooch, 4 Mar. 1822. One of the fires took place on the property of a farmer who had just given evidence at the assizes against an incendiary.

Avenger', for it was he, concluded: 'Once more for the last time as my pen is nearly stumped up and my *Horse* is waiting to conduct me to another scene of action. We have three men amongst us that are able and are continually employed in making [fireballs?] sufficiently convenient to carry several in their pockets ready for distribution ...'

During the remainder of the year the two counties experienced sporadic outbursts of machine breaking. In the first week of April machines were destroyed at Woodton, Poringland and Kirstead (N), a previously unaffected part of the county, but the final episode in Norfolk occurred back in one of the original trouble spots, Winfarthing, where two carpenters led a crowd of twenty labourers who unceremoniously pushed a threshing machine into fourteen feet of water.[47] In Suffolk machine breaking continued in mid-April and two more were broken in July at Burgate and Bedingfield. No doubt in this instance the rioters were clearing away the machinery in anticipation of the threshing after the harvest. This was certainly the case in Foxhall, Norton, and Mendham between September and December.[48]

Both Charlesworth and Muskett correctly point out that the 1822 disturbances were far more serious and sustained than in 1816 when labourers had been joined by other occupational groups[49] During the two months of machine breaking in 1822 more than forty parishes became involved and an estimated fifty-two machines were broken. The localized nature of the disturbances meant the riots were certainly as impressive as the later Swing Riots and far more emphatic and particular in their hatred of machinery, as nearly all the demonstrations were connected with the use of machinery. Whilst the riots obviously disturbed the equanimity of major landowners and magistrates — at the height of the troubles over 250 special constables were sworn in, the yeomanry deployed, and the regular army sent for — the 123 people brought before the courts received relatively mild sentences, usually twelve months imprisonment or less, perhaps reflecting the fact that many of the convicted were described as being 'quiet, honest and respectable men'.[50] Convicted rioters who were not agricultural labourers often received slightly heavier

---

47 *NM*, 6 Apr. 1822; for Winfarthing see PRO, HO 40/17, letter from Lee, 25 Sept. 1822; *NM*, 12 and 26 Oct. 1822.

48 *NM*, 20 July 1822; IESRO, HA 247/5/103, letter from Shawe, 4 Sept. 1822; *NM*, 4 Jan. 1823. After harvest bands of men paraded through half a dozen parishes in the Loddon Hundred looking for threshing machines, *IJ*, 21 Sept. 1822.

49 Charlesworth, *Atlas*, p. 148; Muskett, 'East Anglian Riots', p. 2.

50 *NC*, 16 Mar. 1822. Many of the accused were able to obtain good character references.

sentences; Goose, a farmer, and Wink, a carpenter, received two years.[51] More disturbing than the riots and demonstrations, which at least gave the gentry and farmers the excitement of the chase, was the unprecedented upsurge of incendiarism. No amount of soldiers, yeomanry, constables, nor even the large numbers of labourers employed as nightwatchmen, could halt the fires, as the example of Cracknell's property at Stonham Aspal (S) indicates.[52] Each farm in this village had two men on nightly guard duty and Cracknell himself had five men on watch when the fire broke out on his premises. When confronted by such powerlessness the Lord Lieutenant of Suffolk met with eighty justices in April to discuss the fires and the methods of preventing them which, by then, posed 'a more dreadful threat'.[53] Surprisingly, nothing was done in the end to fight this 'most formidable of weapons', except to urge sufferers to make claims under the stipulations of the Black Act. Unlike the rioters, convicted arsonists received no mercy from the assize judges. Noah Peake and George Fortis were hanged for a fire at Diss. Peake claimed 'By a flash and a scare' it was intended to alarm farmers and induce them into making a more ample allowance for the poor.[54] These two labourers had also been involved in the machine breaking at Winfarthing, the only time during the period when machine breakers turned to arson. They were interesting in other respects since both had been in the army during the Napoleonic Wars, and Fortis had actually served at Waterloo. This led some contemporaries to believe there was a 'regular system of organization and communication' behind the riots but this conspiracy theory must be considered unlikely. This is not to say that the machine breakers did not proceed without a certain amount of discipline. Mr Wright of Kilverstone (N) informed the Home Office that the people conducted themselves with civility and without violence.[55] Very often a band of fife, drums, clarinets, and horns preceded the marchers and were used to regroup the men after a melee with the yeomanry — in such cases village custom and army practice coincided to useful purpose. Norfolk magistrates also noted that disbanded soldiers 'were among the foremost in exciting disorder'; it would seem then that service to one's country conferred certain individuals with leadership qualities which could be utilized in

---

51 *NM*, 20 July 1822; *BNP*, 3 Apr. 1822.
52 *SC*, 23 Mar. 1822.
53 PRO, HO 52/3, letter from Duke of Grafton, 8 Apr. 1822; *NM*, 27 Apr. 1822.
54 *NM*, 20 Apr. 1822. Peake also admitted writing 'warning letters'.
55 PRO, HO 40/17, 12 Mar. 1822.

fomenting trouble.[56]

On one matter we are certain — the use of threshing machines decreased significantly after 1822. Landlords wrote to their tenants asking them to give up their machines, and occupiers 'abjured the use of threshing machines on penalty of five pounds' at Wingfield, Metfield, and Marlesford (S), if only for a year. Two years later the Reverend Collett of Kelsale (S) reported machinery was 'now generally, and by all liberal men, disused'.[57] Later events during the Swing Riots suggest the 1822 disturbances put an effective brake on the use and spread of machinery in North Suffolk and South Norfolk.[58] For that reason alone the men of these two areas could count themselves victorious.

The labourers may have ended the year in jubilant mood but their employers began 1823 bitter, disappointed, and squeezed from all sides. It was they who had borne the brunt of the labourers' anger during the riots and fires and it was they who carried the major burdens of high poor rates, taxes, and low wheat prices. What they feared above all else was a continuation if their landlords, tithe-owners, and the government did not take notice of their plight. They assembled at Norwich, at a vast county meeting to give vent to their anger. Upwards of 6,000 packed St Andrews Hall to debate agricultural distress and listen to the radical farmer William Cobbett. The meeting ended in spectacular confusion when the normally deferential tenantry voted in favour of Cobbett's resolution and petition, often referred to as the 'Norfolk Petition'.[59] Cobbett himself, along with most political contemporaries, regarded this petition as an important and significant shift in middle class public opinion towards the radicals' cause. More realistically, seen in its proper and limited context the 'Norfolk Petition' resembles something approximating a modern by-election in which temporary hostility to an unpopular government is both short-lived but spectacular none the less. Whether moved by the petition and the subsequent founding of the Cobbett-inspired *The Norfolk Yeoman's Gazette*, landowners and rectors reduced rents and tithes still further, by as much as 50 per cent in some cases.[60] They could perhaps live with an angry workforce but to withstand the

---

56 PRO, HO 40/17, letter from six JPs, 2 Mar. 1822.

57 Hobsbawm and Rudé, *Captain Swing*, p. 61; Muskett, 'East Anglian Riots', p. 10; *BNP*, 10 Mar. 1824.

58 See next section of Ch. 4, 'The Swing Years 1830-1833'.

59 *NM*, 4 Jan. 1823; *Political Register*, 11 Jan. 1823; G. D. H. Cole, *The Life of William Cobbett* (London, 1927), pp. 278-9; J. Sambrook, *William Cobbett* (London, 1973), pp. 133-4.

60 See *Norwich Mercury* and *Bury and Norwich Post* between Jan. and Mar. 1823.

verbal attacks of their natural allies, their tenants, in the rural war was unthinkable and beyond them.

These reductions, together with the enormous charitable hand-outs to the poor which liberally pepper the columns of the local press, were enough to restore tranquillity to the region for the next five years. It was a case of arcadia restored as something approximating normality was apparent, for as wheat prices rose so the number of fires decreased, to become infrequent reminders of past tensions. In fact in 1826 Suffolk appears not to have had a single incendiary attack and Norfolk reported only two. It was around this time that an important shift began to take place. Between 1815 and 1824 Suffolk had had two and a half times more fires than Norfolk but from 1825 onwards the position was reversed, with Norfolk becoming the epicentre for incendiary activity for many years to come. Despite the relative quiescence in incendiary activity there were exceptions, as Cartwright of Ixworth (S) could testify with two fires.[61] Shepherd Taylor of Dilham (N), who was to gain the unenviable reputation of being one of the most arson-prone farmers of the nineteenth century, had only one fire, but this was enough to destroy his entire farmyard, causing over £5,000 worth of damage, being the costliest fire in the region before 1830.[62]

The apparent downturn in incendiarism may well have been a reflection of the improved conditions for labourers who appear to have been more fully employed than in the early 1820s. In 1825 the *Bury Post* reported: 'for some years past any one might ride across the country at this season [winter] without seeing a single labourer in the fields', but ditching and draining work was renewed with the farmers' growing confidence in stable corn prices.[63] Having said that, attacks on property, and theft in particular, fill the pages of the local newspapers. Associations for the 'mutual protection of property' sprang up during the mid-1820s in Aylsham, South Erpingham, East Lexham, Blofield and Walsham, Eye, and Hartismere, because of the 'alarming' increase in crime.[64] Deep resentment and social unrest were simmering just below the surface, waiting quite literally for a spark.

The poor harvest of 1828 cut short the threshing season the following winter, leading inevitably to high unemployment. Wages too remained low, around 9s. a week, the same rate as in the mid-1820s

---

61 *BNP*, 30 Mar. 1825.
62 *BNP*, 19 Sept. 1827. Taylor suffered six fires on this farm and had a threshing machine broken in 1830.
63 *BNP*, 12 Jan. 1825.
64 *NC*, 31 Dec. 1825, 10 June and 25 Nov. 1826; *NM*, 13 Dec. 1828; *BNP*, 17 Oct. 1827.

when wheat was fetching 10*s*. a quarter less. Thus nearly all the ingredients were present for a resumption of hostilities — it was just a question of time. The labourers were a long-suffering, one might almost say stoic, group of workers but it became evident in 1829 that even their patience was now running out. Incendiarism increased sharply, trebling 1827-8 numbers, with ten fires breaking out before harvest, suggesting that the hunger-gap period was still a time of considerable tension, or as the East Anglian saying goes, 'while the grass grows the horses starve'. The same was true of the neighbouring counties of Essex and Cambridgeshire where fires were lit with depressing regularity. Again the scale of the fires was, on occasions, enormous: John Beddall of Finchingfield (S) lost seven corn stacks, three barns filled with corn, and all his buildings. His brother, Samuel, just over the border in Essex, had suffered a similar catastrophe the previous week.[65] The Norfolk courts overflowed with cases; magistrates reported 'the increase of crime was most alarming ... the farmers had given up the idea of keeping poultry for they said they only kept them for thieves'.[66] Sheep too were being stolen in unprecedented numbers over to the west in the Fens. The crucial turning point came at harvest when labourers were to discover what the immediate future held for them in terms of winter employment. Again the weather intervened; heavy rain made the harvest not only late but poor in yield, thus prospects for threshing that winter looked bleak.[67]

The Swing Riots, which Hobsbawm and Rudé date from 28 August 1830, when the labourers of Lower Hardres in Kent destroyed the first threshing machine, started a year earlier in East Anglia. Even as the harvest was being gathered in, men were assembling and destroying the hated machines in Ashbocking, Otley, Stonham Aspal, and Wetheringsett (S).[68] The twenty-seven men and one woman convicted at the sessions in Ipswich and Woodbridge had to regard themselves fortunate when the courts passed sentences of only one month's imprisonment on them.[69] Norfolk, as yet, remained free of rural disturbances but it too was experiencing its own problems which became enveloped in the Swing events of the following year. Norwich, being a major textile centre then in the throes of depression, was caught up in a long-running and notoriously bitter weavers' dispute

---

65 *BNP*, 14 Jan. 1829.
66 *NM*, 24 Jan. 1829.
67 *BNP*, 23 Sept. 1829.
68 *BNP*, 30 Sept., 28 Oct., 4 Nov. 1829.
69 *BNP*, 28 Oct. 1829.

which spilt out into the surrounding country villages, where rural weavers undercut the more radical and militant city workers. The road leading out of Norwich to the south was dangerous for the cloth carriers, who were waylaid by hooded men and doused with vitriol. On one occasion the city weavers marched south to Saxlingham Nethergate and fought with the rural men.[70]

If warnings and advance notice were needed, all the evidence suggested 1830 was going to be a difficult and dangerous year. The propertied classes received an unequivocal message from the 'poor labourers in the Hundred of Cosford' (S), who, in an open letter to the *Suffolk Chronicle*, issued a direct and moving message of despair and threats.

> ... because of oppression the poor of the land mourn who are our oppressors Mr. Editor we trust you know we who plough the grateful soil and store its golden produce well know it is not scarcity thanks and praise be to God for an abundance though we cannot have it and yet know no reason why should not for who more deserves it are we not subjects under the same king under the same government that we are thus tyranised when called upon to defend our king and country have we not fought boldly valiantly and honourably for our king country and those oppressors who are now enjoying twenty thirty and forty thousands yearly while numbers of our class are starving weigh'd down with oppression and worn out with vexations we shall shortly fight for ourselves we count it an absolute right for us to rise for support for our wives and beloved children who are as dear to us as the children of the great are to them our side is strong and hang as it were by a thread ready ripened for a revolt and we shall ere long hoist our flag to shake off our oppression think not Mr. Editor think not this threat of your country obstinate turbulance we are drove to it but that a better day and better motives of live and let live may prevent those dire evils is the hearty desire your poor fellow creatures who feels to much the effects of these times.[71]

In 1830 the 'thread ready ripened for a revolt' broke.

THE SWING YEARS 1830-1833

The year of the Swing Riots, 1830, has perhaps received more attention from students of rural protest than any other year. The Hammonds' moving and partisan account, together with the superbly detailed national overview by Hobsbawm and Rudé should need no

---

70 *NM*, 19 Dec. 1829.
71 *SC*, 5 Dec, 1829.

introduction.[72] From the pages of these two books we learn of the turmoil which overtook the southern and south-eastern counties of England when labourers went on the march, destroying threshing machines, attacking poor law officials, kindling incendiary fires, mobbing vicars and farmers for lower tithes and higher wages. The ubiquitous and mysterious Captain Swing emerged in twenty-one counties threatening death and destruction to anyone unwilling to make improvements. The fires, too, bore witness and gave credence to the sincerity of his threats. Arson, in a wave of national fury, swept the English countryside for the first time in its history, which has led Wells to describe Swing as being a unique phenomenon.[73] And so it was when Swing is viewed in its national context, but when the riots are placed in an East Anglian context, they represented a phase of rebellion which had been waged for over a decade. They were, arguably, the third chapter of a long-running serial of rural protest.

There was a surprising continuity with the riots of 1816 and 1822, especially in Norfolk, which suggests Captain Swing should not be viewed in isolation from the earlier troubles. Most riot-prone villages in 1816 and 1822 remained unaffected, whereas previously untroubled parishes in close proximity to those experiencing trouble earlier rioted. Norwich apart, there was very little overlap between the three rioting periods. In fact, overlap between 1822 and 1830 occurred in only eight South Norfolk parishes, a region which not only became an incendiary flashpoint in later years but also the centre for trade unionism in the 1870s. In all eight cases the point at issue in 1822 had been the use of threshing machines. However, in 1830, riots in six of the parishes were concerned with low wages and tithes. Only Winfarthing and Attleborough had machinery destroyed in both 1822 and 1830 but interestingly enough only chaff engines, drills, ploughs, and carts were demolished in 1830, not threshing machines. This suggests there were none left to destroy, a conclusion in part supported by the absence of machine breaking in nine other rioting South Norfolk villages in 1830.

While machine breaking was the dominant form of protest in North Norfolk, it was the anti-tithe demonstrations which lent the Swing Riots their most distinctive flavour as they often brought labourers and farmers together in a temporary and unlikely alliance against tithe-owners. With two distinct and separate elements confronting them, the magistracy and landowners turned on each other in a remarkable display of uncertainty and collective loss of

---

72 Hammonds, *Village Labourer*; Hobsbawm and Rudé, *Captain Swing*.
73 Wells, 'Social Conflict', p. 515.

confidence. Their experience in dealing with the earlier troubles appears to have counted for little and it could be argued that their dithering and uncertain behaviour at the start of the riots did much to fuel and extend them throughout the region.

Despite evidence of mounting tension in the winter of 1829/30, and the riots of the southern counties, there was a period of comparative calm in East Anglia before the demonstrations began on 15 November. By mid-October there had been only half a dozen fires in the entire county, though some were close to future trouble spots. At Witton, for example, the Lord Lieutenant, Colonel Wodehouse, lost his entire farm and threshing machine through fire.[74] However, by the last week of October and the first fortnight of November incendiarism was certainly playing the role of 'curtain raiser' to the riots when ten fires broke out in the Swing heartland. At Briston, labourers looked on in sullen silence as three stacks belonging to a leading county magistrate, Sir Jacob Astley, burnt. The enormous sum of £1,000 was offered by him for the conviction of the perpetrator but it was never claimed.[75] At North Cove (S) eight burning stacks illuminated the night sky on 13 November and could be seen from both Norwich and Bury, a distance of some forty miles.[76] This sudden upsurge of incendiarism caused consternation among landowners, four of whom sent out an address to labourers with the promise of further large rewards for information. It began:

> Fellow Countrymen
> There have been fires at Briston and Stody, in this neighbourhood, and it is our duty to call upon you to combine with us in the most strenuous manner to discover the perpetrators. It is for the honour of our county, it is for our credit as men, that we must find out and punish these cowardly miscreants. Englishmen were never assassins! Englishmen were never incendiaries ...[77]

The jingoistic and xenophobic nature of this address was to become a typical feature during the Swing Riots.

Machine breaking began in the most unlikely of places, Paston, a small village a mile from the North Sea in North-East Norfolk, and spread inland over the following week.[78] Like the labourers of Lower

---

74 *NM*, 23 Oct. 1830.
75 *NM*, 13 Nov. 1830. By this time rumours were spreading through Norwich of fires burning in all the surrounding market towns.
76 *NM*, 20 Nov. 1830.
77 *EA*, 23 Nov. 1830.
78 *NM*, 20 Nov. 1830; Lt. Col. J. R. Harvey, *Records of the Norfolk Yeomanry Cavalry 1780-1908* (London, 1908), p. 247.

Hardres in Kent, the rioters received no more than a severe reprimand; in addition gentlemen 'of high respectability', including Colonel Wodehouse, ordered the discontinuance of threshing machines wherever their influence extended.[79] The Norwich Union Fire Office likewise announced an increase in premiums on farm properties and 'that policies insuring farming stock be void if threshing machines be used on the premises'.[80] It seems the insurance companies and the landowners were aiding the labourers in their work. Paternalistic concessions of this kind divided the Norfolk magistracy, some of whom believed the rioters had to be stopped vigorously. Lord Suffield, the leader of the hardliners who believed the Lord Lieutenant's approach was the turning point, recalled: 'All the labourers near me were content until they heard of the North Walsham resolution.'[81] This recommended owners and occupiers to discontinue their threshing machines and increase wages to 10s. a week. The evidence would appear to support Suffield for in the final week of November the rioting not only escalated and spread but protest became more varied. Tithe disputes began to figure more prominently in South Norfolk, arson made an unwelcome return, and physical violence to property owners occurred. At Irmingland, in the heart of the Swing region of North-East Norfolk, two 'gentlemanly looking' strangers were seen driving away from a burning stack 'as fast as the horse could go'. The fire was accompanied by an explosion 'and the discharge of something like a rocket which flew the distance of two hundred yards across the fields'. The *Norwich Mercury* observed: 'The fires are not the work of our own people — it is so un-Englishlike.'[82]

Outsiders immediately came under suspicion for these and other fires. A campaign began on 26 November to round up any unlikely looking characters, especially if there was circumstantial evidence that could be used against them. At Swaffham a day and night patrol was established to keep an eye on 'vagrants and outsiders'; at Walsingham the bridewell immediately became crowded with Irish and foreign vagrants.[83] Thomas Berney, a leading magistrate, informed Melbourne

---

79 *EA*, 23 Nov. 1830; *NC*, 20 Nov. 1830.

80 PRO, HO 52/9, letter from board of directors, 22 Nov. 1830.

81 R. M. Bacon, *A Memoir of the Life of Edward, Third Baron Suffield* (Norwich, 1838), 330. For the resolution see PRO, HO 52/9, 24 Nov. 1830.

82 *EA*, 30 Nov. 1830; *NM*, 4 Dec. 1830. At Reepham Lord Astley was stoned out of the village after telling the labourers, 'Ditch water was too good for them', PRO, HO 52/9, 25 Nov. 1830.

83 *NC*, 4 Dec. 1830; PRO, HO 52/9, 29 Nov. 1830.

of the arrests of four Italians, one Frenchman, and a black man. He bemoaned, 'the whole county is overrun with foreigners', some of whom had come from Kent, a fact of some significance to magistrates who recalled what had occurred there earlier in the year. One man named Browne, from Maidstone, was arrested whilst carrying sulphur, fuses, and flints. It transpired he was a cracker-maker and one of his companions was Samuel, born in South Carolina and the black man alluded to above. Other vagrants had come from another Swing county, Sussex, thus allowing conspiracy theorists to weave elaborate plots.[84]

The week beginning Monday 29 November marked the climax of the Norfolk riots when virtually every region of the county was in turmoil and 'nearly in a state of revolution'. Previously unaffected areas to the west and south of Norwich experienced strikes, machine breaking, and tithe demonstrations. The city itself was not only surrounded by riots but experiencing them also.[85] Arson had virtually died out during the height of the disturbances between 29 November and 3 December but on Saturday 4 December it returned to the Swing-affected areas. At Lingwood the fire acted as a catalyst for a machine breaking riot. Here the labourers helped fight the flames and were rewarded with drink for their efforts. Thus fortified, they crossed the lane to a farm opposite, destroyed a machine, and then marched off into the night towards Strumpenshaw in search of more.[86] Thereafter arson and machine breaking died away in the county, leaving the clergy of South Norfolk as victims of violence and intimidation until 8 December when the Swing Riots ceased.

The Suffolk disturbances were quite different in character, far less widespread, and much less intense than in Norfolk. Even the incendiary activity failed to follow a parallel pattern in so far as the fires played the role of final curtain to the riots rather than as a curtain raiser as in Norfolk. The disturbances began almost a fortnight after Norfolk in the northern half of the county at Bacton on 29 November, by which time farmers and gentry in the Bury neighbourhood had ordered the destruction of their machinery and the Suffolk Fire Office had refused to insure new policies where machines were employed.[87] However, machinery was not the main

---

84 *NM*, 4 Dec. 1830; PRO, HO 52/9, 2 Dec. 1830.
85 PRO, HO 52/9, 30 Nov. 1830, Wodehouse in a hastily scribbled note to Melbourne wrote, 'I tremble for this town [Norwich]. The mob are trying to force into Norwich and to unite in great force.' *NM*, 4 Dec. 1830.
86 *NM*, 11 Dec. 1830.
87 *BNP*, 1 Dec. and 8 Dec. 1830.

grievance of Suffolk labourers; low wages were. As in South Norfolk, the Suffolk farmers were able to redirect labourer hostility on low wages by advising their workers to negotiate lower tithes. This alliance worked well enough until the week beginning 6 December when the disturbances spread to all areas of the county. But only in the south-west did serious trouble occur where the Withersfield labourers took the lead. Here, 'the excesses of the peasantry were greater than we have heard', reported Colonel Brotherton, 'Armed with scythes, flails and other implements, fit for the work of aggression', the men threatened to take the farmers' corn by force. They broke two threshing machines, the only recorded incident of machine breaking in the county during the riots. Six of the Withersfield men were transported, making it the most harshly treated parish in the county.[88] By 11 December the riots had virtually exhausted themselves, but this date marked the start of an incendiary campaign of nine fires which lasted until the end of the month.

The Swing Riots ended in Suffolk on a rather bizarre and sensational note when on 16 December the authorities caught their Captain Swing. A sighting was made of 'a man in a gig' passing through Stradishall dropping threatening letters as he went.[89] At Stoke-by-Clare a farm steward, named Brown, eventually caught up with him. It transpired that Swing was none other than Joseph Saville, a 53-year-old straw-plait manufacturer who, while making a rather circuitous route home to Gamlingay (C) from Great Yarmouth, had been dropping letters out of his gig. At Debenham, a few days previously, he had told villagers 'that in Norfolk, things were going on well and here they must show a little more spirit — Master Swing must come amongst them'.[90] At the time of his arrest Saville clearly had many more letters to dispose of as a parcel of written papers was discovered in his gig. When taken into custody he attempted to hide the letters in a privy but they were extricated with a pair of tongs for posterity. His letters were, by any East Anglian standards, unusual to say the least and were clearly religiously inspired and anticlerical in tone. To give the reader some indication of their content a few examples from his parcel are cited below:

> Will you farmers and parishioners pay us better for our labour?
> If you will not we will put you in bodily fear.   Swing

---

88 *EA*, 28 Dec. 1830; *BNP*, 22 Dec. 1830; PRO, HO 52/10, letter from Revd Mayd, 6 Dec. 1830; HO 40/27/3, letter from Col. Brotherton, 13 Dec. 1830.

89 *EA*, 21 Dec 1830.

90 PRO, HO 52/10, letter from Revd Chevallier, 17 Dec. 1830.

O ye Church of England Parsons, who strain at a knat and swallow a Camel. Woe — Woe — Woe be to you! Ye shall one day have your reward.

England! beware that you do not bring vengeance down upon your heads by robbing the Poor.   Swing

If you don't behave better and give the poor man his due I will visit you, or my name is not, Swing

You Clergy, ye Vipers, you love Tithes, Cuminin and Mint: ye are Men-eaters and not soul-savers, but ye are Blind Blind leaders of the blind, twice dead plucked up by the roots.[91]

As one local newspaper reported at the time, he was 'actuated in his calling he says, by the word of Scripture which denounces woe to the oppressor, and in fact some of his notices are garnished with texts from the Holy Writ, "Woe unto you, Scribes and Pharisees etc."'.[92]

As will have been gathered by now, Saville was something of a religious fanatic and, at the time of his arrest, was a Primitive Methodist and member of the Bible Society. Previous to this he had been a Methodist and before that a Baptist. He was also given to chopping and changing his occupations, having been a baker, miller, and a corn merchant. His politics though were a little more stable, as he was a reader of Cobbett's *Political Register* and a keen admirer of Hunt, two radical *bêtes noires* at this time. In Gamlingay he was an extremely popular and charitable man, as a character reference from four parish officers testifies.[93] It transpired that he had established a sick society and Sunday school, and had provided dinners for widows at Christmas, given potatoes, coal, and allotments to the poor, as well as lowering rents to his tenants. This impressive track record no doubt swayed the judge at his trial, and Saville must have considered himself fortunate in receiving a one year gaol sentence together with a £50 fine.

The East Anglian Swing Riots, with the exception of the machine breaking region of North Norfolk, were notable for the alliance between farmers and labourers, amounting, according to one eyewitness, 'almost to a case of conspiracy'. This collusion was, however, short-lived if incendiarism is used as a barometer to measure the state of social relations between them. In 1831, whilst the trials of

---

91 PRO, HO 52/10, letter from Garey, 18 Dec. 1830. Other examples of his letters can be found in *EA*, 18 Jan. 1831; C. Day, *An Address to Those whom it may Concern* (Ipswich, 1831), p. 23.

92 *EA*, 28 Dec. 1830.

93 *BNP*, 5 Jan. 1831.

over 220 rioters were taking place, the Swing campaign appears to have been continued by other methods. Incendiarism returned on an unprecedented scale to Norfolk, whilst in Suffolk nine of the eleven fires occurred before mid-March, in parishes of high unemployment. Rectors and vicars, previously victims of verbal and physical intimidation, became the incendiaries' primary targets. One of the fires, though occurring on farmer Martin's premises at Rendham (S), was aimed at his landlord, the Reverend Wade of Blaxhall. Martin, a month prior to the fire, received an anonymous note advising him to remove his corn, 'for it was determined to burn the premises, as the landlord ... was a Devil'.[94] At Knapton the Reverend Cook had his harnesses slashed and his corn stolen. Very occasionally some of their brethren were moved to make Christian gestures as in the case of the Barningham (S) rector who started a tithe-free allotment in his parish.[95] Threshing machines too were still being destroyed but it would appear they were fast becoming a social liability. At a farm auction at Higham Green (S) one machine fetched only 10s.[96] In Norfolk, where fires occurred in every month of the year save June, the epicentre lay in the Swing heartland between Guist and Happisburgh. Here farmers and landowners became 'panic stricken' for they noted a change in the character of the targets; no longer were these lone stacks in isolated fields, but farm buildings were increasingly coming under attack. There were twenty-three such attacks resulting in greater destruction. At Rudham a barn, five wagons loaded with corn in the straw, a wheat stack, three dressing machines, a threshing machine, a haycutter, and a bullock shed were destroyed at a cost of £1,500 to the insurance company.[97] Large rewards were still offered but to no avail and the county magistracy met in December to debate the establishment of patrols.[98] One hundred, Launditch, recognized that the incendiary could conceivably have come from the ranks of the local labouring population when they issued a handbill which attempted to dissuade the indigenous people from such acts. Its arguments rested on five points:

> How wicked such burnings are in the sight of God.
> How foolish such burnings are in respect to their own wants.

---

94 *BNP*, 26 Jan. 1831.
95 *EA*, 29 Mar. 1831.
96 *BNP*, 28 Sept. 1831. In the 22 parishes of East and West Flegg (N) no machines were used in 1831, PRO, HO 52/14. However, where there continued to be machines trouble was reported, see *EA*, 2 Aug., 25 Oct. 1831; *BNP*, 18 Sept. 1831.
97 *EA*, 26 Apr. 1831.
98 NUFO archives, 1831 circular, no reference.

How little these burnings injure the property of the corn grower.
How thoroughly un-English these burnings are.
How dangerous to themselves these burnings are.[99]

It is doubtful whether these words of advice were heeded since the reaction of people in general during periods of incendiarism became much more volatile and, indeed, much more disruptive. The Reepham firemen were stopped on the way back from a fire at Great Witchingham (N) and were 'shockingly maltreated'. At North Barsham (N) 2,000 simply stood and watched the flames, and at Little Massingham (N) bystanders were heard 'vociferating with fiendish triumph — a rare fire [i.e. a wonderful sight], a hell above ground, a glorious sight, etc.'. Whereas at Hemsby (N) labourers 'threw into the fire anything they could find', and at Happisburgh (N) onlookers felled a farmer attempting to extinguish a fire on his property.[100]

Threatening letters, too, became common. In the far west of Norfolk, on the border with Huntingdon and Ely, Swing complained of the employment of Irishmen at harvest.[101] Further east in the Tittleshall district where 'labourers seem to regard their employers with aversion' anonymous notes became 'general' during the summer months. They complained of farmers switching to scythes and using rakes to gather up any possible gleanings, normally the traditional booty of the poor.[102] Standing sheaves of corn were damaged, cut, or thrown into ditches. After a fire in the parish leading proprietors established a horse and foot patrol to combat incendiarism.[103]

The police force at this time largely consisted of inadequate and unenergetic special constables and local village constables who had the impossibly large task of protecting property and arresting offenders. Blyth told the Home Secretary that men were needed who could 'descend to the very heart of society', and John Ensor of Rollesby Hall urged the cabinet minister to establish a police force 'regularly armed and trained and converted into a kind of National Guard'.[104]

The year 1832 witnessed no respite in the frequency of fires until March, when a temporary lull occurred until November, the fires then returning with an even greater intensity. Whole areas of the region

---

99 *EA*, 6 Dec. 1831.
100 *BNP*, 9 Nov. and 2 Nov. 1831; *EA*, 22 Dec. and 27 Dec. 1831.
101 *EA*, 2 Aug. 1831.
102 *EA*, 30 Aug. 1831.
103 *EA*, 15 Nov. 1831.
104 PRO, HO 52/14, letter from Blyth, 26 Nov. 1831. The Martham surgeon, according to Blyth, 'had heard no less than twenty labourers in the course of the night declare their joy' for a fire which had taken place locally.

remained unaffected, such as South and South-West Norfolk and much of Suffolk. The main concentrations were in Aylsham (5 fires), Gunthorpe (4 fires), and Corpusty (3 fires) in North Norfolk, and Neatishead and Hainford further south — in all there were twenty-one fires in this belt. Unemployment remained at a high level despite the first wave of emigration to America from the East Dereham region.[105] In November it was reported that farmers were generally returning to the use of threshing machines, so much so that by the beginning of that month more wheat and barley had been threshed and brought to market than was usual at that time of the year. This was mainly due to the poor weather after harvest that had prevented ploughing.[106] One farmer, John Savoury of Syderstone (N), steadfastly, some might say foolishly, refused to give up using his threshing machine which the entire village had boycotted, thus forcing him to bring in outsiders. For his troubles he suffered two fires during which no one helped; in fact they went further by sabotaging his watercarts.[107] Low wages, high unemployment, the use of threshing machines, and the fact that three fires occurred on the property of parsons suggested that all the grievances of the Swing Riots had returned once more.[108] Although the fires abated during the spring and summer months tranquillity was not yet restored. Large-scale strikes and Reform Bill celebrations spread considerable unease among the gentry; 'the spirit of dissaffection which now pervades no small part of our rural population, whose diabolical passions are urging them on to every kind of crime and insubordination', Robert Orris warned the Walsingham Sessions, was surely going to usher in 'still more terrible and devastating scenes' the following winter.[109]

His fears for 1833 proved to be well-founded. Arson increased in both counties, mainly in response to the tightening up of poor law administration at parochial levels. Parsimony exceeded all bounds of humanity at Edgefield (N) where regular unemployment among the able-bodied was in the region of seventy at any one time and with as many as forty unemployed throughout the harvest period. The parish vestry resolved to reduce wage rates to 4s. a week for able-bodied men, with an additional shilling for each wife and child. The local

---

105 BNP, 11 Mar. 1832. However, of the 29 Briston people who arrived at Yarmouth for the boat to America, 20 changed their minds and returned home, BNP, 25 Apr. 1832.

106 BNP, 7 Nov. 1832.

107 EA, 17 Jan. and 31 Jan. 1832.

108 BNP, 19 Dec. and 26 Dec. 1832; EA, 18 Dec. 1832.

109 BNP, 18 July 1832. For strikes see BNP, 18 Apr., 6 June, 18 July 1832; EA, 5 June and 30 Oct. 1832.

press was horrified:

> One shilling a week for a woman or a child! It is not two pence a day, and will not even fill their bellies with potatoes! Talk of Ireland, this is real starvation point! Transport the people to America, New South Wales; send them to Walsingham Prison, or Norwich Castle; sell them for slaves, hang them, shoot them, any thing rather than this living death.[110]

The sad irony is that many did languish in gaols though the people who fired the properties of four of the vestry committee on separate occasions escaped detection. At nearby Brinningham two fires were lit and numerous anonymous letters sent to those connected with the poor schemes, one of which was written by pauper blacksmith, Josiah Turner.

> G. Furnance
> You termed yourself to be a friend to the poor of this parish and to those that come to your doors in distress, how can you behave in this shameful way whereby you go in danger every day and all you farmers around, your houses and you must leave them for they shall be in flames but you G.F. shall be a dade man, prepear yourself to die for a mess of lade is got lit for you moore and moore beside you, you may call your westry meetings and your labour rate meetings for the safety of the poor to keep thear eyes shet these meetings ear no goes they bring on fires robrey murders and such like you shall be shot like a dorg before long; bean you surprised at this ... be not afraid to shew this to your brother man eaters, look on your supper of lade, take warning you bloody weel barrow set.[111]

The 'bloody weel barrow set' suffered in Wymondham after the vestry altered the poor regulations when three farms and twelve stacks were destroyed by fire.[112] In Suffolk the fires were mainly confined to the northern central part of the county where Wortham and Worlingworth accounted for three fires each. In Norfolk the timing of the fires departed from the normal pattern even though the first and last two months of the year accounted for the majority of them. November had eighteen alone, but there was a large gap between mid-March and mid-July when no fires were reported. This intermission ended with a spectacular outbreak of nine fires in July and August, no doubt as a result of the light harvest that year. One feature of incendiarism which was to become common in later years was

110 *BNP*, 24 Apr. 1833.
111 *EA*, 26 Feb. 1833.
112 *NC*, 23 Nov. 1833.

prominent in 1833, when fires often occurred in pairs over a short period in the same neighbourhood. In January there were four fires to the east of Norwich, two of which occurred on consecutive days at Loddon and Heckingham. In March three fires occurred within a week at Stanhoe and Bircham, at Edgefield two fires in four days, and this pattern was repeated in August and again in the last three months of the year. Taking the year as a whole the concentration of outbreaks had moved north-westwards to the Docking corner of the county, where eighteen fires had been reported. The Edgefield area continued to be a persistent trouble spot with eight fires; and further south the villages between Norwich and Wymondham accounted for a further seven. Nearly half the fires in both counties were on property other than isolated stacks, which signified the growing determination of the incendiary to cause as much damage as possible.[113]

There was a considerable diminution of fires in Norfolk in 1834 whereas in Suffolk the number increased. In Norfolk the epicentre was still located in the north-west of the county, and in Suffolk the first four fires of the year occurred in the north-east, which prompted the most important landowners in that area to call a meeting of the Blything Hundred where night patrols were established.[114] Onlookers at fires still continued to display a considerable degree of disrespect and animosity; at Kessingland (S) they threw stones at the firemen and at Lidgate (S) looting was carried out during the confusion of the fire.[115]

Two important national events occurred that year, the first was the sentencing of the Tolpuddle labourers, and the second, the passing of the New Poor Law. Both passed by virtually unnoticed in the region. It was left to Ipswich mechanics to parade and petition in favour of the martyrs.[116] Perhaps unaware of the events taking place elsewhere, labourers in North Suffolk and South Norfolk struck for higher wages and more work. At Mendlesham (S) the 'novel scene' was of the unemployed forcing the employed out on strike with the avowed intention of 'dictating' terms to farmers. The far larger strike in the Eye (S) neighbourhood lasted just three days and was begun by labourers who had heard farmers had signed a 'round robin' which outlined a wage reduction to 8s. a week. They were determined 'to oppose combination by combination' to keep up their wages, and in

---

113 The largest fire in 1833 was at Chilton (S) where everything but the house was destroyed, *BNP*, 28 Aug. 1833.
114 *BNP*, 29 Jan. 1834; *NC*, 15 Feb. 1834.
115 *NC*, 11 Jan., 29 Nov. 1834.
116 *BNP*, 9 Apr. 1834.

this they were successful.[117] With regard to the passing of the New Poor Law, only one village appeared alert to the dangers which were about to overtake them. At Hillington (N) labourers armed with sticks and bludgeons, though offering no violence, made their feelings known to local magistrates regarding the impending changes to poor relief.[118]

The twenty years from 1815 to 1834 experienced over 500 fires, an enormous number by the standards of other English counties at this time, but the prime feature of these early decades was the collective and often non-violent protest and demonstrations. The riots of 1816, 1822, and 1830, together with thirty-seven strikes between 1831 and 1834, would suggest as much. The following twenty years, from 1835 to 1855, were perhaps the worst of the nineteenth century, if not the worst in the entire history of the landless labourers. Their response was, with the exception of 1835-6, rather more vindictive, covert, and terroristic. The occurrence of arson, which became the first and last resort, almost doubled that in the earlier period.

---

117 NC, 7 June 1834; BNP, 7 May and 24 Sept. 1834; PRO, HO 52/25.
118 NC, 11 Oct. 1834.

5
Incendiarism: Annual Survey 1835-1870

1835-1841: THE INTRODUCTION OF THE NEW POOR LAW

In 1835 with the implementation of the New Poor Law Cobbett predicted 'another RURAL WAR .... more durable and mischieveous than the last'.[1] The whole gamut of the arsenal of rural protest was brought into action to halt the new law: from the quasi-legal and loyal petitions to Parliament through to open and collective displays of violent riot. However, because of the increasing effectiveness of law enforcement bodies, opposition became covert and was characterized by physical violence towards poor law personnel and incendiary attacks on their property. These displays of protest, although localized and often focused on the new workhouses, were more protracted and more persistent than the previous short-lived rebellions of 1816, 1822, and 1830. In the context of rural England as a whole the people of Norfolk and Suffolk, in keeping with their reputation as sowers of rural discontent, fought the most vigorous rearguard action experienced between 1835 and 1837.[2]

The different techniques of protest employed by opponents of the New Poor Law were, perhaps, indicative of their growing sense of desperation. Protest began peacefully and passively enough with petitions and meetings. In May 1835 a Stradbroke shoemaker and Cobbett disciple, named Mills, addressed over 500 labourers at Horham (S) despite prior warnings from the magistracy that the meeting would be considered illegal.[3] These defensive tactics however soon gave way to more aggressive action in the Docking Union of North Norfolk in June which had the unenviable task of being the first union to implement the new law. It began in the village of Great Bircham where labourers were the first recipients of the new form of relief; they were offered tickets for flour and shop goods in place of the usual cash payments. They called a general strike in the neighbourhood and wandered from farm to farm checking that no blackleg labour was being used. Physical violence only broke out when the largest farmer, Kitton, employed strike breakers on 29 June, setting off a cry from the strikers: 'We are bound in a bond of blood, and

---

1 *Political Register*, 13 June 1835.
2 N. C. Edsall, *The Anti-Poor Law Movement 1834-44* (Manchester, 1971).
3 *BNP*, 27 May and 3 June 1836; see also Edsall, *Anti-Poor Law*, p. 34. There were many other petitions 'praying' for the total repeal of the new law, see PP 1837-8, XVIII, pt. 1, *S.C. on the Administration of the Relief of the Poor*, p. 48; IESRO, HA 11/B5/25 for an undated petition from Wickham Market; *BNP*, 27 May 1835 from Palgrave.

blood will be spilt before this is finished.' And spilt it was when two blacklegs and a farmer were dragged from their horses and ill-treated. After futile and unsuccessful attempts by the authorities to arrest the ringleaders the labourers went on the rampage, stoning farmhouses, throwing down haycocks, and turning out horses and cattle into the standing corn. At Kitton's home 400-500 assembled and broke down his doors and windows and then fired his furniture in the house. Another group meted out similar treatment to three other farmers who were forced to flee across the fields with their families. By early July the army and coastguard were able to restore order, forcing labourers to drift back to work.[4] This episode caused consternation in the county; magistrates informed the Home Office of the limited strength of the law enforcement agencies and emphasized the fear and panic running through the ranks of property holders, with farmers refusing to give information against known rioters and many others refusing to be sworn in as special constables. One letter to the Home Secretary reported: 'The farmers though unanimous in favour of the Poor Law Amendment Act are intimidated by the labourers, and from a fear of damage to their property by Incendiarism and otherwise, are deterred from taking an active part in the preservation of the peace.'[5] Dragoon guards and Metropolitan police were drafted in to aid the besieged magistrates.

The next notable disturbance broke out in East Suffolk, scene of petitioning earlier in the year, where the Thorndon men demanded their 'usual pay' on relief day but were refused. Three titled landlords led a successful charge on the crowd and scattered all before them.[6] All through this district late in 1835 guardians were assaulted and gates were taken off their hinges and laid across the lanes at night. When Ipswich introduced the new law in December and altered the existing workhouse so as to conform with the new regulations: 'Windows had been blocked up, iron bars placed in front of them, the wall surrounding the building ... heightened', riots erupted on the streets and spilt out into outlying villages.[7] Violent assemblies took place at

---

4   NC, 4 July, 11 July, 18 July, 8 Aug. 1835; BNP, 8 July, 15 July 1835; PRO, HO 52/26, numerous letters, see especially letter from Parry to Lewis, 1 July 1835; Digby, thesis, p. 172; Peacock, 'Village Radicalism', pp. 37-8.
5   PRO, HO 52/26.
6   BNP, 7 Oct. 1835; NC, 10 Oct. 1835; PRO, HO 52/27, letter from magistrates 3 Oct. 1835.
7   Glyde, 'Autobiography', p. 44, Edsall, Anti-Poor Law, pp. 35-6; BNP, 23 Dec. 1835; NC, 19 Dec. 1835; NM, 26 Dec. 1835; PRO, MH 32/48, Kay's draft of his annual report, 30 June 1836; PRO, HO 52/27, letter from Grimsby, 17 Dec. 1835, and letters from Fox Mande to PLC, 19 Dec. 1835.

Snape, a notorious poaching village, and Blythburgh where 300 marched on Bulcamp workhouse armed with pickaxes and crowbars with the intention of demolishing the new building.[8] At Semer workhouse, whose inmates had gained a reputation for intimidation and violence — they had reduced it to a 'state of incipient demolition' — chamberpots and pails were thrown from the windows and paupers made their feelings known by defecating on the floors of the wards. It was here that a well-aimed rock felled a magistrate whilst he was reading the Riot Act. Again troops were brought in to quell the disturbances.[9]

After a short lull over Christmas riots broke out once more at Badingham, Laxfield, Stradbroke and Iken.[10] Organized collective disturbances came to an end by March 1836 in Norfolk, after riots at Grimstone, Kenninghall, and Cromer.[11] This gave way to more clandestine and violent action: Heckingham house of industry was badly damaged by an incendiary fire and relieving officers were attacked and left 'insensible'. After the Heckingham fire poor law inspector Kay sent out a 'very secret' circular to all unions ordering them to search all workhouse wards at night for tinderboxes.[12] Such precautions were inoperable at Sudbury where a spectacular fire burnt down the workhouse in the process of construction. Spectators gathered and obstructed the fire engines and police. The *Bury Post* reported: 'the poorer classes made no secret of their satisfaction clapping their hands, shouting, and some even going down upon their knees to thank God for having heard their prayers.'[13]

Only one major peaceful demonstration took place in 1836 and this was at Bury St Edmunds where 2,000 gathered to hear the leader of the poor law opposition, the Reverend Maberley, a Tory of the old school who had toured through five other eastern counties trying to whip up support for his cause. His leadership came too late to the region and he was effectively muzzled by his bishop who ordered him to remain in his parish.[14]

---

8 PRO, HO 52/27, letter from Bence, 29 Dec. 1835, letter from Earl of Stradbroke, 8 Jan. 1836; *BNP*, 30 Dec. 1835.

9 PRO, MH 32/48, draft annual report; HO 52/27, letter from Cooke and Calvert, 24 Dec. 1835; HO 52/26, letter from magistrates' clerk, 6 Jan, 1836; *BNP*, 6 and 20 Jan. 1836.

10 *BNP*, 30 Dec. 1835; *NM*, 2 Jan. 1836; Glyde, 'Autobiography', pp. 44-5.

11 PRO, HO 52/30, letter from Gurney, 7 Feb. 1836; HO 73/7, pt. 1, returns from Fakenham and Great Massingham; Digby, thesis, p. 172; *NC*, 12 Mar., 2 July 1836.

12 PRO, HO 64/6, circular from Kay; *NC*, 30 Apr. 1836; *BNP*, 27 Apr. 1836.

13 *BNP*, 30 Nov. 1836.

14 RO, MH 32/48, letter, 9 July 1836; HO 52/30, letter from mayor, 28 Sept. 1836; *BNP*, 28 Sept. and 5 Oct. 1836; Edsall, *Anti-Poor Law*, p. 41; F. H. Maberley, *To the Poor and their*

During 1836-7 further fires broke out on poor law property; women in the Rollesby house of industry (N) destroyed half the building when the sexes were segregated for the first time and two guardians at Bircham and Hethersett (N) lost stacks.[15] However, by 1837 guardians and magistrates were able to congratulate themselves on having weathered the storm of protest and on implementing the new law in the region. Moreover they felt more secure through their enthusiastic introduction of migration and emigration schemes to Yorkshire and Canada. Pressure from overpopulation was relieved in the north-eastern hundreds of Suffolk and the troublesome parishes of Edgefield, Creake, Briston, Saxthorpe, Wood Dalling, Reepham, and Heydon (N). Because of this the movement of arson in Suffolk, at least, swung from the east to the southern and south-western corners of the county and it was here that incendiarism became a permanent feature.

From 1838 to 1841 incendiarism almost completely ceased, 1839 having the lowest number of fires on record during the post-1830 period when only five occurred in both counties. It was apparent that years of high wheat prices, contrary to earlier years in the century, were also years of tranquillity. The agrarian sector was at this time buoyant and employment regular. This latter fact was reflected in the very low poor law expenditure figures. One other point which suggested some semblance of relative well-being in rural areas was the Suffolk labourers' mild flirtation with Chartism.[16] Such political and economic aspirations were never experienced by labourers in times of economic distress when they did not have the inclination to think beyond the limited horizons of work and wages, and even during this period of relative prosperity Chartism only took root in Norwich where the weavers were already recognized militant radicals, and in East Suffolk, where the anti-poor law movement had been most vociferous. In the former, delegates were sent out from the city to the rural villages but with little success, leading to a disappointed and angry speech from Vincent on a visit to the Norwich branch where 'He vented a vast quantity of spleen against the landowners, farmers

Friends (London, 1836); Digby, _Pauper Palaces_, pp. 211-12. Maberley was also active in the anti-Roman Catholic Emancipation movement and was later involved in defending Suffolk incendiaries in 1844. Between 1835 and 1860 he was the vicar of Great Finborough (S) and an obituary of this fascinating man appeared in the _Gentleman's Magazine_ (1860).

15 _NC_, 25 Mar., 19 Nov., 3 Dec. 1836.

16 For Chartism in East Anglia see A. F. J. Brown, _Chartism in Essex and Suffolk_ (Chelmsford, 1982); H. Fearn, 'Chartism in Suffolk', in A. Briggs, ed., _Chartist Studies_ (London, 1959), pp. 147-73; WEA Eastern District, _Chartism in East Anglia_ (Cambridge, 1952).

and particularly the agricultural labourers, whom he considered little better than brutes.'[17]

In Suffolk, however, Chartism did take root in rural areas, albeit briefly, but even here the presence of non-agricultural workers at the machine works at Ipswich, Leiston, and Peasenhall may have been important.[18] Some of the country meetings attracted between 1,000 and 4,000 listeners at Friston and Saxmundham in 1838, but this sudden growth was never sustained, nor too did it pose the same kind of threat as the more limited but more radical branch in Norwich, where pike-heads were being manufactured and stored for the intended revolution.[19]

THE 1840s

With the downturn of wheat prices in 1842 there came an increase in the number of fires. After harvest in Norfolk ten fires broke out, which in itself gave little indication of the coming explosion; but there were other danger signals. Crime in general increased: sheep stealing, animal maiming, and implement breaking in particular. Henslow, writing two years later with the benefit of hindsight, claimed that he had sensed an ominous change in 1842.[20] From October 1843 to December 1844 incendiarism throughout England reached an unprecedented scale. During the Swing period about 300 fires had occurred, but a conservative estimate for this fifteen-month period would be in the region of 600.[21] Every county from Cornwall to Cumberland experienced some form of rural protest during 1844, but it was in Essex, Cambridgeshire, Suffolk, and Norfolk that arson proved to be most constant, spectacular, and persistent. 'You have a very different state of things now to meet to what you had in 1830-31', warned the *Northern Star*, 'Misery has advanced with giant strides since then.'[22]

The fires began to sweep over the two counties after the 1843 harvest and again large rewards were offered, with the usual

---

17 *NC*, 3 Dec. 1842. For Norwich Chartists see editions of *NC* between 1838 and 1840; PRO, HO 40/46, letter from Clarke and Tipple, 25 July 1839. NNRO, LLC/3/4, letter from Wodehouse to Russell, 11 Mar. 1839.
18 Fearn, 'Chartism', p. 151; Brown, *Chartism*, pp. 39-60.
19 NNRO, LLC/3/1, letter from Loftus to Wodehouse, 5 Mar. 1839. Blacksmiths in Norwich and Little Snoring were discovered making pike-heads.
20 *BNP*, 16 Oct. 1844.
21 Estimate based on a sample of local newspapers for 1843-4.
22 *NS*, 23 Dec. 1843.

unsuccessful results.[23] Many of the fires caused considerable damage: Riches of Hingham (N) lost everything except his house; Buck of Hawstead (S) lost two barns, outbuildings, horses, stables, and the produce of 37 acres of corn. In November the farm and infamous Red Barn at Polstead (S) (scene of one of the century's most famous murders) had been fired for the third time: the last completed its destruction. Other farmers were such frequent victims that little remained of their farms. Among them were Smith of Rickinghall (S), Hicks of Hadleigh (S), Taylor of Stanton (S), Silverstone of Great Saxham (S), and Harman of Costessey (N).

The number of fires gradually increased from fourteen in October and fifteen in November, to twenty-three in December, which marked the zenith for Norfolk and most other British counties. In Suffolk the fires continued to increase, with twenty in March and twenty-one in June, thereafter they subsided until November which recorded eighteen instances. As the months progressed concern in the local press remained muted and gave little indication of the real fear experienced by many landowners. This was partially due to bewilderment on their part, for they were at a loss to explain this upsurge of protest, but they also held the common belief that the more that was written on incendiarism the more fires there would be. However, there is evidence of widespread fear and dismay in public documents which contain frequent requests to the Home Office for rewards and for policemen. An anonymous letter from a Suffolk farmer was notable for its immediacy:

> It is with pain that I address you upon the state of the county of Suffolk at the present time, what is to be the end God only knows, since last Saturday the hand of the Incendiary has been nightly at work, the Heaverns have been illuminiated by the under-mentioned fires, at Coddenham, at which the House, Barns, and stacks with — several *Horses* were destroyed. A large fire at Foxhall Heath about 3 Acres destroyed, on Monday a large fire at Thetford of Agricultural produce, Tuesday night at *Framlingham* also another Fire was plainly seen the same evening of Bury, Wednesday at Naughton in which a large quantity of cows with Barns etc. destroyed, and several fields of wheat and Beans, have been partly mown down such is a faithful picture of Suffolk at the present time ... 9 o'clock Thursday night another Fire in the direction of Stowmarket.[24]

In May, Lord Ashburnham's agent, J. K. Moore, wrote 'scarcely a

23 PRO, HO 43/64-6, requests to the Home Office for rewards, 1843-4.
24 PRO, HO 40/59, 19 June 1844.

night passes without a fire'. Three weeks later he complained 'incendiarism has rather increased than diminished in this neighbourhood ... three fires were seen from hence at nearly the same time'. By June, 'The alarm and dread', he wrote, 'have not at any period been scarcely so great as at the present time.'[25] 'No one', recalled Glyde's labourer, 'who saw night after night the heavens illuminated by blazing fires will ever forget the fear and anxiety they caused.'[26]

Nightwatchmen were employed and farmers stayed up till past midnight to guard their property. Even among some of the poor the fear took on almost apocalyptic proportions. Two preachers, Winter and Burgis, tramped the countryside warning the people the world was about to end in one great catastrophic fire. These bearers of doom made a very profitable living but they also left in their wake 'consternation and distress' among the poor. The end of the world was fixed for 21 March 1844 but not even a single flame was reported to have occurred on that day. Later in the year another churchman made a religious allusion to the fires in a sermon at Assington, the text of which ran: 'And Abraham got up early in the morning to the place where he stood before the Lord; and he looked towards Sodom and Gomorrah, and toward all the land of the plain, and behold, and lo, the smoke of the country went up as the smoke of a furnace.'[27] While Bury and Ipswich may not have been Sodom and Gomorrah the text was still very apt in the circumstances.

Until the arrival of the national newspaper journalists in late spring 1844 the local press did little more than report the outbreaks of fires, detailing only the date, place, the name of the owner, and the property destroyed; no attempt at editorial comment was made nor instructive suggestions put. However, it was obvious to all that 1844 was an exceptional year; high unemployment was still prevalent, as at Hitcham (S) where two fires occurred in April, and when Campbell Foster visited the town in June he reported that there had been at least three fires in the parish and petty crimes were perpetrated almost nightly; the church had been robbed, the corn mill broken into twice, and many small shops raided.[28]

The epicentre in the spring months lay in the Hartismere, Stow, and Cosford Unions and the payments to insured property holders were

---

25 IESRO, HA 1/HB6/1b/57-8, 60, between May and June 1844.
26 Glyde, 'Autobiography', p. 46. See also Kent, *Remarks*, p. 31; *NS*, 23 Dec. 1843.
27 *NNMPG*, 1 Jan. 1844; *BNP*, 12 June 1844, from Genesis 19: 27-8.
28 *Times*, 14 June 1844.

undertaken mainly by the Suffolk Fire Office, whose secretary Johnson Gedge sent a memo to the Norwich Union on 24 April which suggested an increase in insurance rates. The latter willingly complied and suggested a 1s. per cent increase.[29] Insurance companies were, by this time, showing considerable concern, especially the Suffolk Fire Office whose business was very localized. Gedge reported to the Earl of Stradbroke in May: 'that the losses of this Company by Incendiarism during this period have been at least *four times the amount of the Year's Premiums* on that description of property'.[30] The same office also sent one of its directors, together with Lord Henniker, the Earl of Stradbroke, and the Duke of Norfolk's agent, to the Home Office for a discussion on the state of Suffolk, and sent representatives to meet other insurance companies in London in order to work out a concerted course of action.[31] The Norwich Union was, at first, the main stumbling block to a further rise in the rates, but by July they finally agreed to the following: 'buildings (not thatched) 3s. per cent ... thatched — 5s. farms employing steam threshing machines were charged with an additional 2s. per cent.'[32] The Norwich Union by this time had ceased the offer of rewards and had ordered all their surveyors to inquire into labourers' wages in villages where incendiarism had taken place so that thorough character investigations could be made of the policyholders.[33]

While the insurance companies were reviewing the situation, the landed gentry of Suffolk appeared at last to be shaking themselves out of the lethargy which had gripped them since October 1843. The Home Secretary, Sir James Graham, in answer to their requests, sent Metropolitan detectives to the county but, as later events showed, they were often unsuccessful. On 17 May the Lord Lieutenant met with the leading magistrates at the Angel Inn, Bury, where they discussed practical ways of preventing incendiarism and of discovering incendiaries. Once again associations for the prevention of felons were established and many anti-League organizations assumed the role of anti-incendiaries societies, but in all instances they failed miserably and predictably in their stated purposes.

Twelve fires occurred in the last twelve days of May in Suffolk alone, some of which broke out while normal farm work was in

---

29 NUFO, board mins., 29 Apr. 1844. 1s. per cent increase means the premium was raised by 1s. for every £100 of property insured.
30 IESRO, HA 11/B1/11/7, 4 May 1844.
31 NUFO, board mins., 22 July 1844
32 Ibid.
33 NUFO, board mins., 3 and 17 June 1844.

progress. The 'Lucifer' match and well-lit pipe were no longer the only methods for starting fires. Incendiaries were reported to have constructed 'chemical preparations' which allowed them time to make an escape before the flare-up. Though they were never described in detail, they were probably none other than fireballs which were composed of either smouldering rags encased in pitch and tar, or mixtures of gunpowder and wax. Farmers were puzzled by the fact that the fires were still being lit: 'The supposed motives too have ceased to exist ... The scenes of December and January re-enacted in May a time of the year when field labour is abundant, and the outrages are marked by circumstances which too plainly denote organisation of some sort.'[34] This report coincided with a number of eyewitness accounts of foreigners and strangers actually lighting the fires, or at the very least being in the neighbourhood of them. Many if not all were innocent but xenophobic communities were unwilling to take chances:

> On the days preceeding the fires at Bacton, Gislingham, and Botesdale, respectively, a stranger visited those parishes and made certain inquiries as to the names of the farmers, the wages paid to the labourers etc. We understand that so many suspicious circumstances were considered to attend the track of the individual, that he was apprehended at Botesdale and detained until inquiry had been made at Norwich of a bookseller in whose employment he was, and whose answer was satisfactory that he was discharged.[35]

In June two petitions were sent from Suffolk to Parliament; one requested that the government set up a commission of inquiry into the state of the labourers, while the other called for the return of the death penalty for arson.[36]

With the arrival of the national newsmen there came for the first time detailed reports and investigations, the like of which the region had never experienced before, nor was to experience again until 1874.[37] Foster, in particular, was not averse to publishing unsavoury facts about landowners and it is not surprising to learn that he caused a considerable degree of anger. The *Morning Chronicle* was not as provocative, except in its opposition to *The Times* editorial line, but its

---

34 *The Times*, 25 May 1844.
35 NM, 30 Mar. 1844. For detailed examples of foreigners and gentlemen incendiaries see Ch. 7 on 'The Myth'.
36 Neither petition was successful.
37 Frederick Clifford of *The Times* investigated the 1874 lock-out, see *The Agricultural Lock Out of 1874*.

reports were distinctive for their immediacy and impact. The *Chronicle* reporter traversed the county at great speed, following the fires as they occurred, and his eyewitness accounts of rural life and poverty are unsurpassed for their detail and humanity. Both he and Foster employed new techniques of interviewing the poor in their own homes, in the lanes, or at work, and the replies to some of their questions were remarkable for their candour and depth of bitterness. This is what probably caused the greatest offence to resident landowners who had been under the illusion of 'knowing' their villagers, but in fact the very status of the local squire in a village precluded any meaningful conversation between them and the labourers. Therefore outsiders were the only ones in a position to investigate and interpret the state of the counties.[38]

Foster found that low wages was only one of the many grievances — in some areas he found then to be under 8*s.* a week. Unemployment and underemployment were abnormally high in 1844, and when this was the case, more labourers than usual came into contact with the poor law administration, thus creating more tension. At Rattlesden, near Stowmarket (the greatest number of fires occurred in this area), he found winter wages were still being paid in May, when they were raised from 8*s.* to 9*s.* a week. Three weeks before his visit a farmer had haggled with his men, as he wanted to pay them only 7*s.* a week. A fortnight after this incident the farmer received a warning in the form of a fireball, made of gunpowder, shoemaker's wax, and a box of 'Lucifer' matches lying in the straw.[39] The *Norwich Mercury* also reported this incident and it highlighted the evident bias of local journalists. The *Mercury* reporter wrote:

> How the reporter of the Times will reconcile this attempt (as well as many instances of fires in the neighbourhood of Stowmarket) with his report of the want of employment and lowness of wages being the principal causes of the bad spirit which is abroad, I am utterly at a loss to conjecture, as I can confidently assert, that a more generous master than Mr Manfield, or a kinder man, is rarely to be found, he employs a great number of hands and more than that, he pays them liberally.[40]

Unemployment appeared to be unusually high in this parish: 21 per cent of its inhabitants were receiving parish relief in June, and even then the poor only applied when at the 'last pinch'. When Foster

---

38 *The Times*, 7 June-16 July 1844, and *MC*, 2 July-23 Aug. 1844.
39 *The Times*, 11 June 1844.
40 *NM*, 15 June 1844.

asked a local farmer how the labourers were treated in Rattlesden, he received the candid reply: 'A good straight forward honest labourer is oppressed wonderfully, that is a fact.' It was therefore not surprising to find the talk in the parish threatening, 'that when the harvest is ripe, the fields will be fired'. The *Morning Chronicle* reported that *The Times* annoyed the propertied classes of Rattlesden so much that they met and signed a declaration denying the truth of the statements published in the paper.[41]

Moving to Haverhill the reporter found wages to be generally 7*s.* a week and poverty to be visually striking; at Great Thurlow the cottages were built of mud and the windows were papered up. The labourers were bitter, 'We work hard,' one man told him, 'we till and sow the land till there is an abundance of food, and our reward is starvation.'[42] This was perhaps the bitterest pill the labourer had to swallow — he was surrounded by growing crops, in some cases livestock and game, yet he could hardly afford the humble meals that made up his repetitive diet. The Parliamentary Report, *The Employment of Women and Children in Agriculture, 1843* and *The Times* gave much the same story as regards their diet, which chiefly consisted of bread, potatoes, and cheese, with perhaps very cheap and streaky bacon for the men on Sundays. Their chief beverage was tea either made from burnt crusts of bread, peppermint, or used tea leaves.[43]

It was in this area north of Haverhill that class hatred was found to be most evident, especially in Withersfield where relations between the farmers and the labourers had broken down completely. At one of the two fires in the village the desperation of the people drove them to disregard totally those in authority, including magistrates who were threatened by onlookers while attending the fires.[44] The poor law was undoubtedly unpopular here; one of the threatening letters from Haverhill (two miles from Withersfield) warned, 'If you do not put a stop to the union, we will burn you up, and we will wait till harvest is got in to do it completely.'[45]

In North Suffolk in the Hartismere Union, where at least fifteen fires occurred between January and June, the same hatred for the union existed. One of Lord Thurlow's firemen, who attended most fires in the area, spoke of the general feeling of the onlookers at the fires. He said they threatened to stop the engine and 'that unless

---

41 *MC*, 2 July 1844.
42 *The Times*, 21 June 1844.
43 Ibid., interviews with labourers.
44 Ibid. See also NUFO, board mins., 4 June 1844, for their attitude to Withersfield.
45 *The Times*, 21 June 1844.

something be absolutely done about these unions, the fires will go on'.[46] Foster found a connection between the outbreaks of arson in the Hartismere Union and the position of the farmers who were singled out as targets. He listed sixteen fires, twelve of which had taken place on the property of persons connected with the administration of the poor law. He had no information on the remaining four except that one was a clergyman.[47] To a much lesser extent the same pattern was true of the Thingoe, Newmarket, Mildenhall, and some Norfolk Unions. The Vice-Chairman of the Hartismere Union, the Reverend Day, felt obliged to dispute that such a connection existed and wrote a letter to *The Times* which they declined to print. However, the *Morning Chronicle* supported Day's contention and published his letter. In the newspaper debate which followed it would appear *The Times* had the more reliable information.

During the summer there was some abatement of fires but the scale of incendiarism remained at an unprecedentedly high level. Arson had almost always ceased in June in former years but in Suffolk it continued through the harvest. The weather conditions must have been partly responsible, for 1844 suffered the longest drought in living memory. This had repercussions on employment both before and during haysel and harvest; hoeing weeds proved unnecessary, and the crops were lighter than usual. However, one must keep in mind that some of the fires which were attributed to incendiarism may have been accidental due to the dryness of the season. After the summer assizes, at which a record number of persons were tried for incendiary offences, the fires resumed despite attempts at improving the labourers' lot with allotments, higher wages, more employment, and the formation of societies to ameliorate their condition.[48]

Taking 1843-4 as a whole the concentration of incendiary activity was more pronounced in Suffolk than in Norfolk. In the former county the western poor law unions of Cosford, Mildenhall, Newmarket, Sudbury, Stow, and Thingoe recorded 123 fires; only Bosmere and Hartismere in the eastern division approached similar figures, accounting for a further thirty-four fires. In Norfolk arson was more dispersed, with only the Forehoe and Guiltcross unions reaching double figures of thirteen and twelve respectively.[49] However, like Suffolk, there was a discernible concentration in the southern half of

---

46 *The Times*, 28 June 1844.
47 Ibid.
48 *MC*, 27 Aug. 1844; *The Times*, 21, and 30 Sept. 1844; *NM*, 12 Oct. 1844.
49 These 8 Suffolk unions accounted for 80% of the fires.

the county, and in both cases their epicentres were significantly different from earlier years. Unlike 1822, 1830, and 1835-6, when incendiarism and rioting occurred simultaneously, 1844 experienced little in the way of collective demonstrations. Thus one never senses the fires were going to escalate into larger shows of strength along the lines of Captain Swing. High unemployment, low wages, and the forbidding presence of the workhouse probably forced the labourers to stop short of demonstrating their anger in more overt ways. Only one village, Cavendish, in the heart of the incendiary corner of South-West Suffolk, took the desperate step of coming out on strike when wages were reduced to just 7*s*. a week. An indication of their desperation was apparent when they stated they would 'emigrate rather than submit'.[50] In Norfolk only one significant dispute took place during the year. It began in March and ended in October, though it had been simmering for forty-four years. Snettisham villagers fought with the lord of the manor, Henry Le Strange, over the ownership of a tree plantation. Led by a Primitive Methodist preacher they cut down 300 trees in a single night and were only prevented from further lumberjacking when police armed with 130 cutlasses camped out in Le Strange's hall.[51]

After the dramatic peak of 1844 any subsequent outbreaks of arson appear insignificant in comparison, and this was especially true for Suffolk in 1845. However, that year was interesting for a number of reasons. First, Thingay of West Rudham (N) suffered his eighth fire in twelve years, which made the newspaper's assessment of him as 'an excellent' master seem meaningless. Second, the Norwich Union produced its 1844 report which proved to be the most disastrous on record; their fire losses amounted to over £84,000, which was over twice the average annual loss of the previous twenty-three years. Third, the farmers must have found the experiences of 1844 rather chastening for it was reported that men were more fully employed even though they were 'not actually required'.[52] Finally, as a result of the incendiary explosion the previous year West Suffolk magistrates established a constabulary force, a move which was unpopular and unwelcomed by many in the area. The new police interfered with customary fairs and farmers complained about police surveillance of farmyards because it upset 'the feelings of their labourers'. Police vigilance was, on one occasion, excessive to say the least. Two new

50 *The Times*, 20 June 1844.
51 *NM*, 16 Mar., 25 May, 12 Oct. 1844.
52 *BNP*, 29 Jan. 1845; *NN* 18 Jan. 1845.

constables, Pilbrow and Carlo, were sacked after having been discovered under a table while three suspected incendiaries were being interviewed by a lawyer.[53]

The winter months of 1845/6 saw a resumption of incendiarism in Norfolk which prompted the chief constable in his quarterly report to the magistrates to say that the fires were due to 'the great pressure of the time', a remark which proved to be wholly unacceptable to the assembled gentry who ordered it to be struck off the official records.[54] The concentration of fires now lay to the west in both counties, while in neighbouring Cambridgeshire the two villages of Bottisham and Soham were unaccountably being devastated by repeated attacks. After September Soham was treated by the Norwich Union as a place where only hazardous premiums could be sold.[55]

The price of wheat rose in 1847 to over 100*s.* per quarter in May, before dropping back to half that after harvest. Incendiarism too dropped, although the fires in the first quarter of the year may suggest that wages were not increasing with the rising prices, a fact which was commented on at Norfolk Quarter Sessions. The following year the incidence of incendiarism in the two counties was dissimilar. In Norfolk the heaviest concentration was in November whereas in Suffolk no fires were known to have taken place after late October. The geographical dispersion was also unusual, for thirteen fires occurred in the Ipswich area, whilst in Norfolk no fires were reported in Norwich (in 1847 there had been a number in the area) despite the alterations in the city's poor law administration which had provoked a riot during which a policeman had been killed.[56]

THE MID-CENTURY DEPRESSION 1849-1852

In 1849 a major agricultural depression began which sent wheat prices plummeting to below 38*s.* a quarter and wages fell accordingly. So low did they fall that in Suffolk wages of 6*s.* a week were reported.[57] Incendiarism returned to that county in the autumn on a scale that was reminiscent of 1844. The four Cambridgeshire villages of Cheveley, Isleham, Kirtling, and Soham were also greatly affected, with seventeen fires in these four parishes alone. Indeed, the area west of

53 *BNP*, 30 Apr., 21 May, 25 June 1845.
54 The labourers, the magistrates argued, were particularly well off. *BNP*, 14 Jan. 1846; *NN*, 17 Jan. 1846.
55 *BNP*, 11 Feb. 1846; NUFO, board mins., 21 Sept. 1846.
56 The Norwich riot was extensively reported by *NN*, 24 June 1848; *NM*, 24 June and 1 July 1848.
57 *MC*, 8 Dec. 1849.

Bury was the epicentre of this period of unrest, where six Suffolk villages had at least two fires each.[58] In Norfolk the trend was less clear and the depression did not have as severe an effect as on the neighbouring counties. The *Morning Chronicle* again sent a reporter to this area of England and his visit by chance coincided with the upsurge of incendiary fires. He found in the south-western corner of Suffolk that the wages were lower and unemployment higher than in other parts of the county. Labourers, too, often expressed a deep resentment towards their employers when in conversation with him on the question of incendiary fires. They used expressions such as: 'Oh, sarve him right', 'He was a grinder', 'He was a strict, hard-fisted fellow.'[59]

The *Morning Chronicle* reporter observed that the fires had not occurred in the northern and eastern parts of Suffolk but in 1850 this area too was affected. The fires spread to the Norfolk villages close to the border. Wheat prices fell even further, to 35*s.* a quarter, and many farmers and landowners renewed their protectionist allegiances, believing the repeal of the corn laws had finally begun to take effect. Landowners and rectors reduced rents and tithes by as much as 20 per cent to help farmers, and the latter further economized by lowering wages and dismissing men. Fires occurred with regularity throughout the year in Suffolk, with the months of March, late August, and November especially prominent. In Norfolk the work of Timothy Birch, alias Bowles, made June a notable month for incendiary activity. He lit eight fires on five farms.[60] In general the destruction of property was much greater than in previous years; at Honington, Freckenham, Middleton, Raydon, and Boxted the damage was estimated at between £1,000 and £4,000 on each farm, whilst in the Cambridgeshire village of Cottenham one of the worst rural incendiary fires on record occurred, causing £20,000 of damage to farms and cottages. These large fires became a feature of Cambridgeshire, Hertfordshire, and Bedfordshire, and the Norwich Union was forced to raise premiums in these counties to 10*s.* per cent. Potential customers in Cottenham were, however, refused insurance at any price.[61] Protest in 1850 was not solely restricted to incendiarism, for the workhouses were overcrowded and riot-prone, strikes and parades were seen in other villages, and in Fordham (C) an unusual

---

58 They were Coombs, Cowlinge, Dalham, Denton, Haverhill, and Lawshall.
59 *MC*, 8 Dec. 1849.
60 See *NN*, 3 Aug. 1850.
61 NUFO, board mins., 16 and 18 Sept. 1850.

combination of weapons was employed by protesting labourers. They paraded the streets with banners on which were written, 'Free Trade for Ever', threatening letters were sent, a strike occurred, ploughs were broken, and a farm fired. The events of 1850 finally persuaded the Cambridgeshire magistrates to form a police force.[62]

Incendiarism remained persistent throughout 1851 when wheat prices fell to 35s. 1d. Previously trouble-free areas of Suffolk, for example Copdock and East Bergholt, where seven fires were recorded, were affected but the epicentre still remained to the south of Bury. In Norfolk, too, arson spread to all regions with more than the usual number of fires occurring to the north of Norwich. Furthermore, there was an explosion of serious crime, in fact a 30 per cent increase over 1850 which had been considered a very bad year. High unemployment was universal throughout the region as the poor law returns showed: 103,000 indoor and outdoor paupers in the two counties and six workhouses full to overflowing.[63] To gain some idea of what the slump could do to a village, the atypical parish of Kimberley (a closed village owned by Lord Wodehouse where social conditions were, if anything, better than in open parishes) will be cited. In 1848 there were no recipients of poor relief In 1849 there were two, in 1850 nine were in the workhouse, and by early 1851 fifteen able-bodied were in the house and a further four were receiving relief from a 'common fund'.[64] If this village is any guide then it is possible to conclude that labourers were worst off during periods of low wheat prices rather than the reverse. Men spoke of hunger being 'a sharp thorn' and a threatening letter to Buxhall (S) rectory announced: 'This is to tell you we are all stauving, an if you do not help us we will burn your ould Bones in your Bed.'[65] Even the cold and aloof Sir John Boileau admitted in his diary that 'the feeling of the peasantry [was] bad', and that he had heard 'The Men saying they'd rather toss the farmers into the flames than put out a burning stack.'[66]

Wheat prices remained low and the workhouses full in 1852 but the number of fires fell considerably. However, migration and the resumption of railway building may have eased a desperately bad situation. The three years of depression had left some labourers in complete and utter despair, and others more desperate and violent as the high incidence of poaching affrays testifies.

---

62 NC, 9 Mar. 1850.
63 Glyde, Suffolk, pp. 119 and 125.
64 NN, 1 Mar. 1851.
65 BNP, 23 Apr. 1851.
66 NNRO, Boi 169 1l7X6, 15 and 16 Dec. 1851.

THE ERA OF HIGH FARMING 1853-1870

Those years of depression explain the exodus that began to take place in 1853 from all over rural England; the *Norfolk Chronicle* reported that over 1,000 a day were leaving the British Isles. From Kings Lynn up to seventy men left on the Hull steamer each week. For the first time in many years labourers had collective bargaining power. More strikes were reported in 1853 than in any other year before the arrival of trade unionism in the 1870s. At Marham, Shouldham, and Fincham (N) the strike for increased wages was so effective that the farmers were forced to tend their own flocks at lambing time.[67] Further south the men of Barsham, Mettingham, and Shipmeadow (S) launched a successful strike to raise wages to 9s. a week.[68] Wheat prices were still low, under 44s. a quarter, so their action must be seen as a new step in aggressive wage bargaining. The men here were fortunate in their timing since the Haddiscoe-Halesworth railroad construction was about to commence and a large demand for labour was anticipated. At nearby Harleston the famous 'chap fair' which had been on the verge of extinction only two years before was flooded with labourers demanding and receiving high harvest wages from 'disappointed' farmers.[69]

Events continued to move in the workers' favour when in 1854 the Queen's shilling was a popular enticement for many young farm labourers who left to fight in the Crimea.[70] This war, therefore, had the double effect of relieving population pressure and pushing up wheat prices, thus putting East Anglian farming on a sound footing for a long period of prosperity. Incendiary attacks decreased in number, averaging twenty-nine fires a year during the second half of the decade. Whilst whole tracts of the region remained completely tranquil, incendiarism tended to become less seasonal in character, although autumn tended to register peaks for such activities, reflecting, no doubt, the onset of winter wages. This certainly occurred in the two Suffolk parishes of Haughley and Stowupland where fires broke out a week after wage reductions. In the latter case the *Bury Post* reported the labouring population were 'much exasperated', especially as the reduction coincided with an increase in flour prices.[71] A similar pattern of autumnal wage cuts and increased incendiarism occurred in

---

67 *NC*, 2 Apr. 1853; *NN*, 2 Apr. 1853.
68 *NC*, 23 Apr. 1853; *NN*, 23 Apr. 1853.
69 *NN*, 9 July 1853.
70 *NC*, 23 and 30 Apr. 1853; *NN*, 18 June 1853. See also L. M. Springall, thesis, pp. 91-2.
71 *NC*, 19 Nov. 1859; *BNP*, 22 Nov. 1859.

the two peak years, 1864 and 1868, of the following decade. In the Lawshall beerhouses, where all the talk was of a fire and possible wage reductions, George Armstrong told all who cared to listen: 'They are what I like to see — fires all round — that will coo' them.' Arsonists were, in his opinion, 'good-hearted and plucky men, and if I knew who did it I would treat them with a gallon of beer'.[72] Wage bargaining techniques were, by this time, more varied and less extreme — Haughley's fire was preceded by a strike — and the most popular and safest option for the aggrieved was the simple expedient of leaving service and going in search of a better wage, especially at harvest time. If caught and convicted the worst they could expect was twenty-one days in gaol with hard labour or a 25s. fine.[73]

But returning to the observation relating to this period that incendiarism became less seasonally pronounced, it would appear a number of explanations would account for the flattening of the graph. Winter unemployment was no longer a major cause for discontent but the introduction of new harvest machinery may well have inflated the incidence of arson in the summer months. The most notable change occurred in the social make-up and character of the incendiaries, if the convicted are a representative sample. First, previously convicted arsonists returned from gaol to ply their trade once more. Benjamin Hart is a case in point. He was finally put away in 1856, this being his third conviction for arson in a career stretching back to his childhood when he operated under the name of John Wiley.[74] The cases of Annis, Banks, Crouch, Jackson, and Smith were similar though less dramatic. Such ticket-of-leave men were stigmatized when it came to obtaining employment and their subsequent actions when denied even food only served to fuel public anxieties concerning the end of transportation in the mid-1850s. Here was evidence, if evidence was needed, of the folly of allowing dangerous criminals to roam at large in the mother country on the expiration of their sentences. Long stretches in gaol or overseas institutionalized some like Smith who, on being released from Milbank, wanted to return to gaol at the first opportunity. Others like William Banks, who at 81 years of age was the oldest known incendiary and had a record stretching back to his 1814 transportation, were clearly unrepentant. 'I would have burnt fifty stacks if they had been there,' he told the court, 'and will again, if I get the chance.' This

---

72 *BNP*, 1 Nov. 1864, 28 Mar. 1865.
73 See *NN*, 23 May 1863, 23 July, and 24 Sept. 1864 for examples.
74 *NC*, 13 Mar. 1852 and 8 Nov. 1856; *BNP*, 10 Dec. 1856, when his death was reported.

seemed unlikely in view of his age and the ten-year sentence he received for a fire at Great Barton (S).[75] More common were the sad cases of tramps, beggars, and paupers who, weak from starvation, waited by burning stacks for the police to arrive and arrest them. Their frequent involvement would suggest that arson, as a weapon of protest, was declining in popularity with the bulk of the rural poor, a point borne out by reports of crowd reaction and behaviour at scenes of conflagrations. In all cases, villagers willingly fought the flames, and if anyone appeared less than enthusiastic suspicion immediately fell upon then. Henry Nelson's behaviour of stoking blazing stacks with fuel and knocking other stacks into the path of a fire landed him in court and eventually four years penal servitude. James Jackson was more unusual in that he was actually chased by local labourers for a mile before being arrested.[76] The wandering poor, it would appear, were living very much on the margins of society and were treated with genuine suspicion and contempt even by the indigenous poor.

The 1860s registered larger and more frequent peaks of incendiarism than the preceding seven years; the most notable occurred in 1861, 1864, and 1868. This fact was all the more surprising when one considers that the police and farmers were displaying greater leniency to the very young arsonists who were still causing the insurance companies great concern. The Suffolk Alliance was a case in point, having paid out £1,000 in East Suffolk in two months because of children smoking or playing with matches in the farmyards.[77] Some children were, however, still being brought before the courts. In 1867 the Suffolk Grand Jury requested that legislative restrictions on the sale of matches to small children ought to be considered.[78]

One of the largest peaks of the decade was between November 1867 and March 1868 when thirty-three fires occurred; Suffolk suffered a further fourteen at the end of the year. There came reports in late autumn 1867, both of large numbers of young labourers returning from depressed urban areas and of wages falling behind wheat prices. The weather also played its part, for a long drought ruined the root crop and the corn yield was substantially lower. In Norfolk field work was reportedly completed well before Christmas.[79] The geographical location of protest was similar in character to earlier

---

75 For Annis, *BNP*, 11 Aug. 1868; Banks, *BNP*, 11 Aug. 1863; Crouch, *BNP*, 7 Aug. 1866; Jackson, *BNP*, 6 Apr. 1869; Smith, *BNP*, 27 Mar. 1866.

76 For Nelson, *NC*, 7 Apr. 1860; Jackson, *BNP*, 10 Sept. 1861.

77 *NC*, 5 Oct. 1867.

78 *NC*, 24 Aug. 1867.

79 *NC*, 30 Nov. 1867; *NN*, 26 Oct. and 5 Dec. 1868.

years for the area of greatest unrest was on the Norfolk-Suffolk border.

By the end of the period blazing stacks were still a regular feature of the East Anglian countryside. There were eight fires in November 1870 alone and the troubled villages were identical to those of earlier decades where riot and incendiarism had been most recurrent. Walsham-le-Willows, Rickinghall, Great Barton, Barrow, Dalham, Hundon, Tibbenham, Diss, Harleston, and Attleborough were all traditional hotbeds of social protest and two years later some of them were to be at the forefront of the trade union movement. However, it was the final wave of enclosures which acted as a kind of bridgehead between incendiarism and the trade union movement of the early 1870s. The enclosure movement, which had lost considerable momentum after 1816 when the agrarian sector entered a long-term depression, only re-emerged with the high prices of the 1850s. In Norfolk alone 17,000 acres were enclosed under thirty separate awards between 1853 and 1870.[80] As in earlier decades the poor lost out in the carve-up of the land and this led directly to disputes on an unprecedented scale. The most dramatic of all took place at Fakenham in 1870.[81] These confrontations brought together for the first time all the elements necessary for trade unionism: collective protest, organization, religious leadership and influence, and awareness of legal action.

In April 1870 Fakenham Heath was fired, 'as an expression of abhorrence of what is regarded by some as an act of legal robbery perpetrated by property upon poverty'. After four years of discussion the commons and heath were to be enclosed that year. A month later the allottees began staking out their claims, much to the chagrin of the Fakenham people who went to the heath and uprooted rails and posts. The next day they continued their work and extended their activities to the burning of a stack and the breaking of landowners' windows. Fourteen men were arrested, of whom six were labourers, two fishhawkers, three bricklayers, a shoe-maker, a grocer's porter, and a harness maker. One of them, named Fiddamen, was tried first as a test case but all the witnesses were struck with amnesia or were evasive when questioned.[82] The cases were, however, thrown out as it transpired the landowners had prematurely staked their claims. The situation remained tense because employers began sacking men who

---

80 Mason, *History*, pp. 619-21.
81 *NN*, 30 Apr. 1870.
82 *NN*, 4 June 1870.

they believed had been involved in the dispute. In July Flaxman took up the reins of leadership; he began by holding well-attended meetings, and was soon baiting the authorities by leading a massed body of singing townspeople to the 'back' common which had already been enclosed the year before. After an address he led the crowd back to the town amidst groaning and booing whenever they passed prospective enclosers' homes. Within days Flaxman was arrested and sentenced to eight months for refusing to keep the peace. This turn of events neither slowed the momentum nor harmed the leadership of the cause but, in fact, precipitated a fiercer resolve on the people's part. Protesters broke up into smaller groups and appeared all over the town destroying fences and gates as they went. Armed police arrived to cope with the dispute which was now beginning to escalate, with the appearance of the labourers from outlying villages who had come 'for the express purpose of disturbance and riot'.[83] Flaxman was unexpectedly released from gaol and returned to a hero's welcome at the station where 300 people were singing a popular protest song which began: 'Don't be fidgetty, we shall win our common back again' (Fidgett was one of the enclosers). Night meetings on the common continued, and potato plants were torn up and assaults on police and landowners occurred.[84] Finally, they sent a petition to the House of Commons but to no avail, they had lost the battle. However, all was not completely lost for Flaxman, chairman of the 'Defence of the Poor Association', as his popularity with farm labourers was turned to good effect when he became president of one of the first labourers' trade unions, the Eastern Counties Union, in the spring of 1872.[85] Thus, amidst the meetings, speeches, window breaking, and marches were the flames and smoke on the heath. Incendiarism still remained in the farm workers' arsenal of protest.

Although the 1860s registered a decrease of 100 fires on the previous decade, there were none the less over 300 blazes. Such a figure bears witness both to the persistence of incendiarism and the less than tranquil nature of the East Anglian countryside in the years of prosperity and Victorian orderliness.

Since the inception of the New Poor Law in the mid-1830s the region and its workforce had lived through some of the darkest years of its history, a darkness that was repeatedly illuminated by a red glow on its horizons. This indignation of labour was shortly to be dignified

83 *NN*, 23 July 1870.
84 *NN*, 30 July 1870.
85 *Eastern Weekly Press*, 11 May 1872.

and organized under the banner of trade unionism which injected a moral and religious, one might almost say a millenarian, tone into the rural war. For many in Arch's union the recollection and experience of the previous four decades proved to be a decisive formative period. They were, after all, the generation who had, before the 1850s, no golden age myth on which to draw directly, and when the era of 'high farming' arrived they found its prosperity an illusion. Because of this experience they could only look forward.

This and the previous chapter have outlined the growth, spread, and incidence of incendiarism at a time when arson became synonymous with East Anglia. Why this synonymity should be so was not always entirely clear to contemporaries, especially those living within the two counties, but the following two chapters will, it is hoped, explain and clarify this.

6
Incendiarism: An Analysis

> But that barns and farm-yards, filled with the fruits of the earth,
> should be wantonly set fire to in the dead of night, not here and
> there, and at remote intervals in point of time... — that was a state
> of things so entirely without precedent, that the most skilful in the
> art of disentangling moral problems were unable to account for it;
> while on the masses it produced no other effect than to strike
> them dumb.[1]

This and the following chapter are concerned with the disentangling
of the mass of detail concerning incendiarism, a crime which, as we
have seen, was endemic at the best of times, reaching epidemic
proportions during the worst. Why arson became the foremost
weapon of protest is the problem which concerns us here. What will
become apparent is that no single definitive cause or explanation is
possible. However, arsonists were mostly rational people and rarely
indiscriminate, which means their actions create identifiable patterns,
thus allowing historians to analyse and interpret their crime. The clues
which have remained, the timing and location of fires, and the
ownership and type of property destroyed, will now be examined.

THE LOCATION AND TIMING OF INCENDIARY ATTACKS

Taking the period overall a number of trends are clearly discernible, as
Maps 1 and 2 indicate. First, there were areas of intense incendiary
activity, as for example in Norfolk the city of Norwich experienced
more fires than any other locality, yet immediately to the south of the
city very few occurred. Wymondham also had a large number of fires
and only two neighbouring villages, Hethersett and Great Melton, had
a notable number. To the east there was a marked absence of activity
whilst to the south along the county border a very heavy concentration
occurred in the parishes of North and South Lopham, Garboldisham,
East Harling, Diss, Tibbenham, and, to a lesser extent, Shelfanger and
Banham. Many of the market towns throughout Norfolk suffered,
Redenhall with Harleston, Aylsham, Swaffham, and East Dereham
being clear examples. One other interesting concentration occurred in
the north-west of the county in the Docking area, although Docking
itself was almost completely unaffected. In Suffolk the fire
concentration in market towns was less marked and Ipswich
experienced only half as many arson attacks as Norwich. However,

---

1   Anon., 'Incendiarism', p. 243.

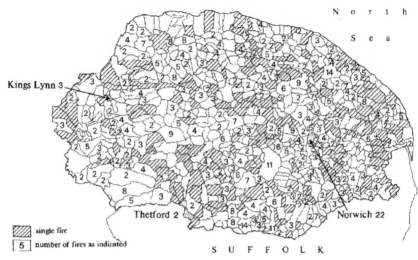

MAP 1. Incendiary Fires in Norfolk 1815-1870

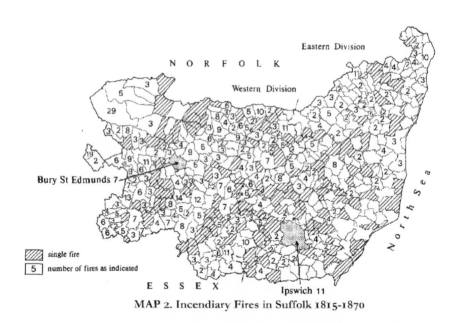

MAP 2. Incendiary Fires in Suffolk 1815-1870

Mildenhall in the extreme and remote west suffered considerably. Within the county were bands or zones of incendiarism, for instance the triangular zone between Wortham and Hopton on the Norfolk border, and south to Great Barton and Bury, or the area to the south and west of Bury where a broad band stretched from the

Cambridgeshire border to Hadleigh and Polstead. In this last-mentioned band were some of Suffolk's most affected villages. The Eastern Division of the county, with a number of exceptions, was remarkably free of incendiary activity.[2]

The relationship between population levels and the incidences of incendiarism in parishes where the crime was common is worthy of consideration. Of the forty-four parishes where arson was most prevalent 60 per cent had populations of well over 1,100 in 1851. This suggests that incendiarism was not wholly restricted to rural 'backwater' villages and that fires had a tendency to occur in places of large populations (large by East Anglian standards). Only three of the parishes had under 500 inhabitants in 1851. It is, however, impossible to conclude that incendiarism was an urban-based crime since many of the fires broke out on farm property. One can only conclude that fires were most likely to be lit in areas of a marginal nature, that is partly rural and partly urban. To emphasize this fact a sample was taken of forty-four parishes, which were close to incendiary-prone villages but where no incendiary fires occurred during the period. Of these parishes only three had populations in excess of 1,000 in 1851 and 64 per cent had populations well below 500. It should, therefore, be emphasized that the larger the village the greater the probability of incendiarism. It was also found that where populations continued to expand between 1831 and 1851 these parishes had an average five fires each during the twenty-year period. In villages which expanded between 1831 and 1841 and then contracted to sizes smaller than their 1831 levels they averaged seven fires each over the same two decades. Despite the reduction in population between 1831 and 1851 it is possible to suggest that these parishes continued to expand until 1845 because migration and emigration in the early 1840s was almost unknown due to the trade depression. Only after 1844 was population pressure relieved. These particular parishes had experienced greater population growth between 1831 and 1841 than the two counties overall.

When incendiarism for the fifty-five-year period is correlated to the Suffolk and Norfolk hundreds a number of interesting features are apparent. First, fire concentration is most pronounced in the Western Division of Suffolk in the hundreds of Babergh, Blackbourn, Hartismere, Lackford, and Risbridge. In fact 68 per cent of the fires in Suffolk occurred in the Western Division. In Norfolk, Clackelose, South Erpingham, and Tunstead Hundreds had the most fires but no

---

2　The exceptions are Bungay, Eye, Framlingham, Ipswich, and Lowestoft.

single hundred stands out as having experienced abnormally high amounts of incendiarism. If the total number of fires is then correlated with the populations of each hundred, we arrive at a ratio of fires to population. This is a more accurate guide to the density of fire occurrence. In Suffolk fire concentration is very pronounced in the south-west of the county, especially in the Risbridge and Thingoe Hundreds. In Norfolk fire concentration is more even but the hundreds of Guiltcross, South Erpingham, Taverham, and West Flegg are noteworthy.

This spatial variation of incendiary activity between the two counties can be partially explained by correlating the fires with areas of probable overpopulation. In Suffolk's case a definite relationship between the two exists in the Hartismere, Risbridge, Stow, and Sudbury unions but in Norfolk the relationship is less pronounced, with only the Flegg and Guiltcross unions appearing to have had large populations and high incidences of arson. One further explanation linking arson to overpopulation concerns the location and the depressed state of the cloth manufacturing industries. The towns and villages of Costessey, Diss, Garboldisham, the Lophams, Norwich, Redenhall with Harleston, and Wymondham in Norfolk, and Bungay, Hadleigh, Long Melford, and Mildenhall in Suffolk, where such economic difficulties existed, were mainly located within the epicentres of incendiarism.

The next question concerns the connection between riots in 1816, 1822, and 1830 and the incidence of incendiarism in particular villages. Most parishes disturbed by riots in 1816 and 1822 were free of fires between 1830 and 1870. Only six towns disturbed by riots in 1816 and 1822 had a large number of fires over the entire period.[3] In the cases of Norwich and Ipswich, and to a lesser extent Diss and Bury, the riots were more the result of their role as important county administrative centres. As many as thirty-four villages where there had been riots in this early period either had one fire only or no fire at all during the entire period. As for the parishes seriously affected by the Swing Riots only nineteen experienced six or more fires between 1815 and 1870, which represents a mere 11 per cent of all villages disturbed during the 1830 troubles.

Furthermore, 52 per cent of the Swing-affected villages experienced only one fire or none at all over the entire period. A similar disjunction between incendiarism and trade union activity was

---

3   Namely, Diss, Norwich, and Wymondham in Norfolk, and Bungay, Eye, and Ipswich in Suffolk.

found.[4] Therefore there would seem to have been little relationship between a village that resorted to collective protest and one that was frequented by incendiary outbreaks. One should not expect a relationship to exist between the two since emigration and migration, particularly of young single men, often followed the ending of riots. The removal of these potential activists thus eased short-term economic social pressures.

To discover at what time of the week fires broke out, a sample of 1,071 fires (55 per cent) was taken. It was found that the daily variability of arson attacks ranged from 18.7 per cent on Saturdays to 12 per cent on Wednesdays. The slight increase at weekends — 35 per cent of fires took place then — coincided with the labourers' brief rest period of Saturday afternoon and all Sunday. This inclined some to believe and argue that drink was largely to blame for both arson and other rural crimes. 'If it were not for this drinking,' Judge Patterson remarked to the jury at the 1844 Norfolk assizes, 'you and I should have nothing to do.'[5] Many of the convicted incendiaries had, it transpired, spent their evenings drinking, gossiping, and singing with their fellow labourers at the beerhouses before setting out to start a 'flare-up'. However, the most that can be said about alcohol and its relationship to arson is that it gave some men the courage to put words into actions, and beerhouses were often the scenes of pre-riot, pre-poaching, pre-incendiary planning.

The character of incendiarism can be more clearly understood from its monthly variability in which the winter months of November, December, and January accounted for 37 per cent of the fires, an average of four fires a month for the entire period, whereas the haysel and harvest months of June to August accounted for only 16 per cent. This seasonal variation in incendiary activity is significant and will be discussed below.

PRICES, WAGES, AND UNEMPLOYMENT

There is a negative correlation between high wheat prices, which to a large extent determined the price of labour, and incendiarism. When wages lagged behind relatively high wheat prices as in 1831 (Norfolk excepted), 1838 to 1841, and 1855, the number of fires was very low. In fact they averaged no more than 17.5 a year. When the equation

---

4   The following parishes were noteworthy for incendiarism and trade union activity:
    Aylsham, Costessey, East Harling, North and South Lopham, Swaffham, and
    Wymondham in Norfolk; and Rickinghall, Walsham-le-Willows, and Wortham in Suffolk.

5   *The Times*, 10 Apr. 1844.

was reversed, high wages in comparison with low wheat prices, as in 1822, 1835, 1848-52, and 1858-60, fires were far more frequent, averaging fifty a year.

The relationship between low wage areas and incendiarism was particularly pronounced in both counties, but more especially in Suffolk, where in four years of intensive incendiarism (1843-4 and 1849-50) two-thirds of the fires took place in the western region. In Norfolk, the Forehoe, Guiltcross, Diss, and Clavering Hundreds were likewise areas of intense incendiary activity and these areas had been identified by Foster as having had lower than average wages, small farms, and a declining weaving industry. Further evidence of this connection between low wages and incendiarism appear in the trials of the convicted and in some of the threatening letters. One of the most explicit came from Grimwade of Polstead who wrote:

> Sir, — This is to inform you that unless your tenant, Mr. Brown of Polstead, pays his men an advance of wages (the present being 8s. per week for twelve hours labour) he will be visited with a blaze, but your timely interference may prevent the calamity.
> A Polstead Labourer[6]

Wages fluctuated annually but there was a tendency for them to rise or fall at two particular times of the year; early November and springtime. These two points of the calendar coincided with the natural cycle of arable farming which also had repercussions on farmers' labour requirements. Therefore it is impossible to separate the two variables of wages and employment in any clear-cut way. However, there was enough evidence to suggest that a relationship between wages and fires existed. The monthly variation of fires indicates an enormous peak in November, and a slight peak in March and April (the number of fires for these two months was not exceeded until October). Obviously the variable factor of employment was reflected in these figures but newspaper evidence suggests that farmers often decided winter and summer wages at these times of the year. At Elm in 1832 two fires occurred in November shortly after farmers had met to discuss wages.[7] Over thirty years later, in late October 1864, the labourers of Lawshall were extremely perturbed by the rumour that wages were about to be reduced to 7s. a week. A very

---

6 The 'Polstead Labourer' was in fact a farmer's son, *MC*, 27 July 1844. Grimwade added a postscript: 'Mr. Brown's 8s. per week and 30s. per week for a policeman will not do; not that an 8s. labourer does not want looking after, for it is impossible for that man to live honestly without getting into debt.'

7 *BNP*, 28 Nov. 1832.

large fire occurred that same evening.[8] Wage reductions were clearly the subject of much angry and bitter pub and field talk between the men. 'Don't you know the reason why these fires are?' asked one young labourer to a maidservant, 'it was because the masters had lowered the wages I should not be surprised to see one here.'[9] Incendiarism, like the strike weapon, was used as a method of wage negotiation, but the choice of tactics depended very much on the level of labour supply. For that reason strikes were almost non-existent between 1834 and 1850 when the level of unemployment was high. Labourers believed fires could halt further wage reductions or in some cases actually force wage rises. In a society where it was impossible for employees to put forward requests for higher wages extreme methods were resorted to.

Until the outbreak of the Crimean War, East Anglian labourers suffered considerably from unemployment and underemployment. These two variables provide the main key to the prevalence of incendiarism, for heavy unemployment, protest, and downturns in the rural economy invariably occurred simultaneously. Arable farming was, and is, geared to the seasons of the year, and as such its labour requirements varied between the extremes of heavy demand during the summer to the very low during the winter months when the fields had been ploughed, and in some cases, drilled, and when threshing by machines had cleared much of the corn. In a broader sense arable farming was also very susceptible to weather conditions, and crop yields moved from scarcity to glut within the space of twelve months. Crop yields affected corn prices, and if the price of corn fell because of a heavy harvest the farmers responded by cutting their costs, the heaviest being labour. The severity of labour cutbacks often depended on the attitude of tithe-owners and landlords who had within their power the decision to reduce tithes and rents.

The year 1844 was an unusual year since wheat prices remained around the 45s. mark, a figure well in excess of depression year prices, but unemployment was well above the norm. Foster estimated that the fall in wheat prices in the preceding two years was comparable to a doubling of rent for farmers. Furthermore tithes had doubled and other farm produce such as cheese and pork had dropped so dramatically in price that many ceased production of these foodstuffs.[10] The farmers also had the additional psychological

---

8   *BNP*, 1 Nov. 1864; see also *BNP*, 22 Nov. 1859, for a similar case.
9   *NN*, 7 May and 8 Aug. 1870.
10 *The Times*, 4 July 1844.

burdens of the propaganda of the Anti-Corn Law League to contend with. Faced with such economic pressures farmers were forced to ignore the peripheral tasks of good husbandry such as ditch clearing, hedge cutting, and drainage schemes, all of which provided a great deal of employment during the winter. The *Morning Chronicle* reported on the general untidiness of the fields while on tours through the region.[11]

Whenever the agrarian sector faced crisis a familiar argument concerning the benefits or hindrances of large and small farms always came to the fore. Generally speaking large areas of Suffolk and eastern and southern Norfolk were on heavy land where small farms predominated. Heavy land produced greater corn yields per acre, required more labour, and rents were proportionately higher than on the light land soils of West Norfolk, where farms were large and labour requirements and rents were lower. The small farmers were generally regarded as the villains of the piece due to their uneducated, prejudiced, and narrow-minded attitudes.[12] Conversely, the substantial farmers, and more especially the large landowners, were praised as enlightened agriculturalists mindful of their employees' well-being. Obviously such generalizations are untenable, for examples of liberal and illiberal employers could be found from both groups. Lord Leicester, for instance, invariably received universal praise from visiting national journalists, but there is much evidence to suggest that his housing was at best moderate, at worst dreadful.[13] He was also responsible, more than others, for the clearing of villages. Large landowners, through engrossment, forced out the smallholders and reduced labour requirements from the usual four men to every 100 acres to one man for every 50-75 acres. Furthermore they introduced machinery more speedily and encroached on traditional rights and customs more completely. However, small farmers were accused by journalists, supporting the landowners, of lacking sufficient capital to withstand downturns in the economy, with the consequent effect of creating greater redundancy among the workers.[14]

Small farmers appear to have been under financial pressure from

---

11 *MC*, 10 July 1844.

12 *The Times*, 10 and 15 June, 4 July 1844; *BNP*, 19 June 1844, letter from a 'Plain Man'; Henslow, 'Suggestions', pp. 1-9; *MC*, 10 July 1844.

13 For reports praising Leicester's estate see *The Times*, 4 July 1844; H. Colman, 'The Agricultural Labourers of England', *Labourers' Friend* (Aug. 1844), 58-63. For a more accurate assessment of the estate cottages see R. A. C. Parker, *Coke of Norfolk: A Financial and Agricultural Study, 1707-1842* (Oxford, 1975).

14 Caird, *English Agriculture in 1850-51*, pp. 145-7.

landlords, especially during periods of depression when their rents were not always reduced because intensive competition and demand from prospective tenants kept market forces in the landlords' favour. In the heavy lands of Suffolk it was reported that farmers were also on very short leases, which meant they were unwilling to sink capital into the land without the guarantee of seeing a return. Farmers in these areas were therefore more likely to withstand economic pressure by saving on labour costs in the form of low wages and redundancy. In some instances they threw land out of cultivation, which also affected labour requirements.[15]

High unemployment was the result of downturns in the economy and this in turn forced labourers to seek aid from the poor law guardians. *The Times* steadfastly maintained that incendiarism and the New Poor Law were directly related. The *Morning Chronicle*, on the other hand, utterly rejected this argument, provoking bitter inter-newspaper rivalries in the process. *The Times* appears to have won the argument on the basis of the accuracy of Campbell Foster. He gave the names of over thirty farmers who had suffered fires and who had been, or who were, connected in some way with the local poor law boards.[16] However, such an argument was not conclusive, for nine-tenths of the guardians were farmers and, as will be seen, direct protest against the poor law could often take very many forms. Therefore it was more likely that labourers' hatred was directed at the farmers because they were employers of labour and not simply because of their associations with the poor law, although the latter would not have enhanced the farmers' position in a rural community.

The evidence which shows conclusive proof of the relationship between incendiarism and unemployment is of a fragmentary nature, since most surviving poor law records are either too general to be of much use or else they simply do not exist. Reliance has necessarily been placed on eyewitness accounts which in 1844 and 1849-50 were substantial. There are, however, two groups of records from the Depwade Union in Norfolk and the Cosford Union in Suffolk which provide detailed records of pauperism in the mid-1840s.[17] The former shows that the number of male able-bodied indoor paupers was proportionally greater in 1844 than in 1843, representing 21 per cent

---

15 BNP, 19 June 1844; *The Times*, 15 June 1844, when Foster reported that between 50 and 120 applied for each farm going vacant.

16 *The Times*, 21 June-16 July 1844; *MC*, 2 July, 5-11 July 1844, when Revd Day entered the argument and effectively ruined the *MC*'s case.

17 NNRO, C/GP3/192, Depwade Union Weekly Returns of Indoor and Outdoor Paupers; the Cosford Union Returns were generously provided by Julian Harber.

of the total indoor paupers and 16 per cent respectively. In addition 13 per cent more people were receiving outdoor relief in the first twenty weeks of 1844 than in 1843. Looking at the Depwade figures from 1842 onward there appears to have been a long and gradual deterioration for male labourers and their families which even encompassed the 1843 harvest. The summer of that year is known to have been disastrous due to a forty-minute hail storm on 9 August which devastated crops over a wide area of East Anglia. This act of nature may have started a rapid and irreversible deterioration since less harvest work meant less harvest earnings, followed by less threshing, and therefore greater winter unemployment. Farmers, too, suffered financially as insurance did not cover their losses, even though over £10,000 was raised in subscriptions in Norfolk towards compensating them.[18] Their financial position was less secure than in previous years and in order to stabilize their economic position costs were reduced. The main sufferer at the end of this chain of events was the labourer. Nature may have contributed to the beginning of this disastrous period, it definitely sustained it because the longest drought in living memory occurred from spring to the summer of 1844. Weeds stopped growing, hoeing proved unnecessary, and hay-making too was retarded with only one hay crop being possible.[19]

The Cosford Union figures were based on poor law expenditure and like the Depwade returns they show a sudden rise in late January 1843, but for the summer months were also considerably higher than in the previous year. The rise continued until a peak in January and February 1844 was reached. The figures also record a significant peak in May 1844, when there were the unprecedented and never-to-be-repeated twenty-eight incendiary fires in Norfolk and Suffolk.

Wages, too, appear to have been disproportionately low in 1843 and 1844. In fact they were the equivalent to the wages of 1822-4, 1834-5, and 1851, when wheat prices were as low as 7s. 3d. a peck and no higher than 7s. 8d. In 1843 and 1844 a peck of wheat fetched between 9s. 6d. and 10s. Clearly the labourers were carrying the weight of the farmers' and landlords' burdens. These two years were unusual due to the unique set of circumstances and pressures which occurred in a train of worsening events. Such a depression was vastly different from those in 1822-3 and 1849-51 when prices tumbled and farmers went

---

18 *BNP*, 16-23 Aug. 1843; *NM*, 12-19 Aug. 1843.

19 *BNP*, 26 June 1844. It should be noted that a drought occurred in 1868 which also coincided with the last peak of incendiarism. The press reported famine conditions, high unemployment, and numerous accidental fires, *NN*, 8 Aug. 1868 and 21 Jan. 1869.

bankrupt. In the mid-1840s farmers over-reacted to a poor harvest which yielded little income since high wheat prices, the usual sign of a poor harvest, never materialized. Economic pressure caused them to reduce wages to an abnormally low level and the weather in turn presented them with the opportunity to reduce their labour forces. The late 1840s and early 1850s were more typical of depression years but protest never reached the heights of 1844. It is not difficult to see why. Depression in the form of low wheat prices was obvious to all, and the labourers were psychologically more prepared for the consequences. Wages, too, held their level better than wheat prices in this latter period, so that labourers in work were still able to afford bread and flour whilst in 1843 and 1844 this had not been the case.[20]

MECHANIZATION AND INCENDIARISM

Of central importance to the unemployment issue was the use of 'intermediate technology' or simple machinery, which provoked large-scale riots and demonstrations up to 1830. Thereafter collective action rarely recurred. This did not mean that hatred for machinery had been dispelled, although a cursory glance at the 1830-70 period could lead one to conclude that this was indeed so. However, a closer investigation of the evidence suggests a strong antipathy against all kinds of machinery and technological change, however simple. For instance, it has been commonly assumed that the scythe had replaced the sickle by 1830 in East Anglia.[21] In Norfolk, though, there is evidence that the cost- and labour-saving scythe had not been fully accepted by this date; as in the case of Tingay of Little Ellingham who caused 'great offence by mowing his wheat for the first time' in 1831. He found threatening letters stuck on sticks in his fields, and later he found his wheat sheaves burnt.[22] In that same year it was further reported that 'in many parts of the county', especially the Tittleshall neighbourhood, farmers were receiving threatening letters during harvest time. One letter left little doubt as to what the grievance was:

---

20 Foster found people at Rattle Row (N) digging up half-ripe potatoes, *The Times*, 16 July, 1844.

21 E. T. J. Collins, 'Harvest Technology and Labour Supply in Britain 1790-1870', Ph.D. thesis (Univ. of Nottingham, 1970), pp. 382 and 329, where he noted the practice of mowing wheat was introduced shortly before 1843, and in heavy land areas of Suffolk it was as late as the 1860s. See also P. J. Roe, 'The Revolution of Norfolk Agriculture in the Nineteenth Century 1815-1911', M.Phil. thesis (Univ. of East Anglia, 1975), p. 38.

22 *EA*, 16 Aug. 1831. It may have been the same Tingay of West Rudham who had the distinction of having had 8 fires in 12 years.

To the Meetner
Rendham — felt Betts
You old half-crown screwing elf is all your hellish, kind pious
intentions to mow and rake the land, and starve the poor — either
to work them to death by these d_____d machines — remark, it is
not the respect the noble general have for you and for your selfish
set that this woeful work is not begun, however, take this for
granted, look into the fields and see by a little what a deal mean,
and be ruled by them that give you good advice, and decline all
these abominations, if not you will repent, and stand a chance of
carrying both your beds and fire at your back — the general now
declares if they will decline he is more ready to do the same, if not
he is resolved to fulfil every promise he has made without fail.
God Save the King.[23]

Another note was also found in a field where sheaves had been
thrown into some water and others heaped up with a pile of matches
and tinder placed by them. It read:

The noble general and his gang are slow to anger, and of tender
mercy — notwithstanding if they have devils to fight against they
must and will play tricks to beat them, and so they will if the
obstinate rogues do not give in, and this instant too — there is no
time to lose — we again say if they will decline the Colonel is
willing to do the same — this composition is not genuine the next
shall be if 'tis wanted; gun-powder and casks filled with brimstone,
pitch and tar, and fireballs, will be in readiness if they are wanted.
This gallant and most noble general fire request only reasonable
and just terms for the poor, and then he will be satisfied and not
without — be not obstinate.[24]

The first of these two letters pointed to another grievance, the use
of rakes. On the face of it, the rake appeared to be a fairly innocuous
implement but it had the effect of minimizing the gleanings of the
poor. This customary right came under increasingly greater pressure
during the next forty years. Thus in these two counties where labour
shortages were not experienced at critical times of the year the
substitution of one implement by another more efficient implement
caused the winter time fear of unemployment to become a possibility
during the summer months.

The greatest hatred was reserved for the threshing machine, which
after 1822 became the initial target for many incendiaries. Similarly it
has been found that farmers using such machines were also singled
out for incendiary attacks on other parts of the farm. The speed with

---

23 *EA*, 30 Aug. 1832.
24 Ibid.

which these machines were reintroduced after the 1830 riots was not clear, but it would seem that in Norfolk they were back in general use as early as 1832. In Suffolk the picture was even less clear since machinery was not so extensively used as in Norfolk before or after 1830.[25] However, by 1844 both counties had resorted or begun to thresh mechanically on a widespread scale. In that year a machine at Rudham was broken and then fired, and at Walter Belchamp on the Suffolk-Essex border farmer Chinery, who was also a machine manufacturer, suffered extensive damage from a fire, as did Heifer the Farnham manufacturer. In the latter case the fire may have been accidental but the bystanders refused to help and celebrated the destruction.[26] Twenty out of every thirty labourers interviewed by the *Morning Chronicle* complained of threshing machines because they had been made redundant by them. Further north the reporter found that Norfolk farmers who used threshers were receiving threatening letters: 'they are continually being sent, all of them complaining of the machines — threatening to damage new crops if machines were used in the coming winter'.[27] One labourer who actually worked a threshing machine was convicted of sending a threatening letter to his employer: 'Farmers we are starvers, we wol not stan this no longer: this 600 and 8. Rather than starve we ar turmint to sit you an fire. You are roges and robbs the pore of there livin by imployan thrashmanssh-ans, this primsas will soone take place fire if you donot olter ...'.[28] Fires occurred from the remaining years of the 1840s up to the early 1860s on premises where threshing machines were used. Other implements too were occasionally singled out, such as ploughs, drills, and dressing machines.[29]

During the mid-1840s another invention began to make its presence felt and that was the mechanical reaper. This presented a greater threat to employment than the thresher. However, its introduction was not ushered in by any riots or protest. This can be explained by the fact that reapers were usually only adopted in areas of Britain where labour shortages occurred at harvest time. Agricultural technology, although advanced in theory, was slow to be adopted for

---

25 *BNP*, 7 Nov. 1832 and 16 Jan. 1833. Roe's claim that the Swing Riots did not significantly affect the widespread use of threshing machines in Norfolk appears to be correct, thesis, p. 38.
26 *NM*, 5 Oct. 1844; *MC*, 10 and 25 July 1844.
27 *MC*, 10 July and 23 Aug. 1844.
28 *The Times*, 27 July 1844.
29 For fires which destroyed machinery see *BNP*, 28 Jan. and 23 Sept. 1846, 2 Oct. and 6 Nov. 1850, 12 Mar. and 22 Oct. 1861; *NC*, 31 Dec. 1853, 1 Mar. and 15 Nov. 1856.

practical purposes because the social consequences of mechanization had greater repercussions on farmers than did machinery on crop yields. In fact, it should be emphasized that rural technology, unlike industrial technology, affected neither the quality nor the quantity of the end product, for those lay with the vagaries of weather and the biological processes. Guano, rather than reapers or threshers, had a profounder effect on production but it did not set in motion a chain of social crises.

The spread of mechanized implements was generally slow in this agriculturally progressive region of England. Norfolk was reported to have had only one steam threshing machine in 1844 and three years later its novelty was such that a local newspaper reported a forthcoming demonstration of one.[30] The protests of earlier years may well have slowed down its introduction since farmers, with a surplus of labourers, would have regarded the benefits of threshing forty-two coombs in four hours as dubious. The reaper too was only gradually introduced to the region, first by experimenters like Mechi, and later by West Norfolk farmers who had suffered from labour shortages at harvest time for over thirty years. By 1858 reapers were fully established in this western area and steam ploughs too were gradually appearing by this time.[31] The introduction of new machinery did not pass without incident — four agricultural implement works were burnt at Chelmsford (E) in 1858, at Diss in 1860, and twice at East Dereham in 1860.[32] Ploughs and hay-making machines were occasionally broken and threshing machines continued to be burnt in the 1860s. It has been possible to deduce from indirect evidence that the introduction of reapers and horse-drawn rakes caused considerable antagonism. The *Norfolk News* implied that protest against machinery had over the years become much more subtle, so subtle that it would be impossible to document anti-reaper protest. Labourers, it claimed, first made the horses nervous of the machines and then broke them 'accidently' by turning too sharply.[33] Even as late as 1871, on the eve of trade unionism, antipathy for agricultural machinery was still evident. At Tottington (N) farmer Welch's new steam chaff-cutting machine was sabotaged when someone put a piece of iron in it. Shortly afterwards a fire destroyed the machine and two stacks. One suspect, an employee, was alleged to have said: 'I should

30 *NN*, I Sept. 1847; Read, 'Recent Improvements', quoting Bacon, p. 280.
31 *NN*, 23 Aug. 1851; *NC*, 7 Aug. 1858; Read, 'Recent Improvements', p. 280; *NN*, 16 May 1857 and 23 Mar. 1861 for steam ploughs.
32 *NC*, 10 Apr. 1858; *NN*, I and 8 Sept. 1860.
33 *NN*, 25 Aug. 1868 and 25 Sept. 1869.

like to see the b...... thing fly into fire, as such things hinder poor men of work when it is wet.'[34]

Thus, whilst setting the pace during the period of 'high farming' through increased use of fertilizers, drainage, and farm building reconstruction, Norfolk and Suffolk lagged behind more backward rural areas in the adoption of machinery. The social aspects of a large and cheap labour force, which had a propensity to protest against mechanization, unemployment, and low wages, weighed heavily on improving farmers who, from the known events, preferred social harmony to more efficient production.

INCENDIARISM AND THE POOR LAWS

The relationship between fires and the harsh administration of the poor laws was in Foster's opinion self-evident. His reports in 1844 dwelt on the 'ticket system', the labourers' bitter denunciation of the workhouse regime, and most important of all he identified many of the victims of incendiarism as being poor law guardians.[35] The evidence appeared to be conclusive. The question is to what extent does his thesis hold good for the period as a whole? Were the poor laws, old and new, responsible for transforming deep-seated resentment into acts of incendiarism?

If the period from 1815 to 1835, the pre-reform period, is examined an interesting picture appears to emerge. In the years leading up to Swing, unemployment and the poor rates rose, suggesting that increased tensions would have sparked off unrest. The surviving evidence shows that, on the contrary, there appeared to be little in the way of poor law related grievance. Of the fires attributable to the poor law, there were three very small ones at Swaffham and Smallburgh workhouses in the 1820s, and four others on property owned by overseers at Terrington, Wiston, Letheringham, and Wells. It would also seem that one other fire may have been directly related to the administration of relief. At Hitcham (S) parsonage in 1820 it was reported a fire occurred when a large number of unemployed had their application for assistance refused.[36] Ten years later the Swing rioters rarely complained of poor law practices, which suggests, as Digby has argued, the labourers were pressing for economic objectives

---

34 *Eastern Daily Press*, 5 Jan. 1872.
35 *The Times*, 21 June-16 July 1844.
36 In the order in which they appear: *NC*, 5 Feb. 1825; *BNP*, 5 Aug. 1829; *NC*, 16 Mar. 1816; *BNP*, 29 May 1822, 19 Nov. 1828, 21 Oct. 1829, 9 Feb. 1820; HO 64/1, letter from Revd Mathews, 10 Feb. 1820.

as workers and not as paupers.[37] While it is impossible to prove this inference the evidence of the 1831-5 period, especially in Norfolk, may in fact suggest that the poor laws only became a significant bone of contention after Swing. During those four years leading up to the Poor Law Amendment Act the laws were undergoing alteration in a manner that has been well described by Marshall in his study of Nottinghamshire.[38] Edgefield, as we have seen, perhaps typified those parishes which experimented with their labour surpluses. Here the unemployed became so demoralized that protest became extensive. In 1832 a major dispute between paupers and the poor committee sparked off a fire because allowances had been cut. The following year G. B. Ballachey, a local landowner, suffered extensive damage, as did another guardian, at the hands of incendiaries, and there was even an attempt to burn down the workhouse in the same week. Later in the same year the deputy overseer lost a barn through fire and finally, eighteen months later, eight desperate young men resorted to the novel tactic of taking over Ballachey's house and refused to leave until an alteration was made.[39] Wymondham (N) too tightened up its poor relief, leading initially to clandestine and open meetings before culminating in two enormous fires on four farms.[40] Elsewhere between 1832 and 1834, two houses of industry were fired and overseers at Cossey, Langham, Great Bircham (three times), Yaxley, Terrington, and Croxton had fires on their property. In two instances the incendiaries were known to have been refused relief.[41] In short, changes were already being made in the years leading up to the Poor Law Amendment Act which were provoking the poor into acts of incendiarism.

In the summer months of 1835 the implementation of the new act brought about Cobbett's 'Rural War', but his prophecy was not fully realized immediately as the war was waged openly in East Anglia for only two years. It re-emerged but as a clandestine war in 1843, by which time the numbers of adult able-bodied receiving outdoor relief

37 Digby, thesis, *passim*. See also Hobsbawm and Rudé, *Captain Swing*, p. 59, who cite the Rural Queries' findings of unemployment, low wages, and beershops as the primary causes of the riots.

38 J. D. Marshall, 'The Nottinghamshire Reformers and their Contribution to the New Poor Law', *Econ. Hist. Rev.* 13 (1961), 382-96.

39 *BNP*, 21 Mar. 1832, 24 Apr. and 8 May 1833; *NC*, 9 Feb. and 3 Aug. 1833, 9 Oct. 1833; PRO, HO 52/26, letter from Leak, 1 July 1835; G. B. Ballachey, *A Letter to the Editor of the Norwich Mercury Respecting a Reduction of Wages in the Parish of Edgefield* (Norwich, 1833).

40 *NC*, 23 Nov. 1833.

41 *EA*, 22 Jan. 1833, 26 June 1832, 24 Jan. 1832, 21 Feb. 1832; *NC*, 10 Aug. 1833, 22 Feb. 1834, 19 Apr. 1834, in the order in which they appear.

was significantly lower than during all the years between 1835 and 1870. In effect they were being offered the workhouse or nothing and many labourers preferred the latter option and lived off their wits, and criminal ones at that. Foster certainly found this to be the case in 1844: 'they will starve to the last pinch rather than enter the workhouse'.[42] At the Thingoe (S) house the only inmates were thirty old men, yet there had been numerous applications for relief from young labourers. In another example, Shipmeadow (S), where the young men did accept the indoor orders, they not only rioted but set fire to the place.[43] It was only after 1853 when agriculture became buoyant once more and the rural workforce began to leave the land in large numbers that we see protest, incendiarism in particular, against the poor law recede. Even after this date, however, institutionalized paupers occasionally resorted to fire. It is possible to conclude that the administration of the poor law undoubtedly led some labourers to fire workhouses and other overseers' and guardians' property but, as we have seen from previous examples, it is impossible to agree wholeheartedly with Foster's argument, which was too narrow and partisan. We cannot determine whether the victim was fired because he was an employer or a guardian, nor is it possible to separate with any ease the poor law system from unemployment because the former only came into play as a result of the latter.

INCENDIARISM AND RURAL CRIME

What relation, if any, did incendiarism have to other rural crimes? In other words, did the setting of fires occur in isolation to whatever else was going on in country districts, and were incendiaries a quite different breed of criminal to the thieves, sheep stealers, and others who made their living through crime? It will be shown in Chapter 7 that some of the convicted incendiaries did have previous convictions for other crimes and that some of them employed arson as a weapon of terror in an escalating war of vengeance against particular individuals. As so few arsonists were caught the question has to be put regarding those fires where no arrests or convictions were made. Circumstantial evidence, which is all we have to go on, is less than satisfactory, but it does appear to be the case that certain people were susceptible to incendiary attacks because of their role in disputes and crimes of a non-incendiary nature. Local magistrates, as one would

---

42 *The Times*, 11 June 1844.
43 PRO, HO 27/74, vol. 3, 1844. Of the 14 arrested 12 were aged between 16 and 22.

expect, were particularly vulnerable if and when they discharged their duties with something approaching enthusiasm. One justice of the peace at Lawshall (S) received a threatening letter which informed him he was 'no justice, and that sholud [*sic*] be the first to suffer'. His property was burnt shortly afterwards. Grigby, the Drinkstone (S) magistrate, played a leading role in the arrest of the 1816 rioters and he too suffered the consequences.[44] Arson in such cases was designed to dampen their legal spirits and presumably pressurize them into greater leniency. The same could be said of farmers who acted as prosecutors in cases of a non-incendiary nature and then suffered the heat of revenge. One Hardingham farmer prosecuted sheep stealers and received a threatening letter and then fire for his troubles. In a similar case Waters of Hardwick (N) successfully prosecuted two sheep stealers but just before the trial he received the following anonymous note:

> Mr. Waters, You had better not go against these men; if you do you will surely be shot, or burnt out of house, home, wife, premises, and all you are worth destroyed. ... Here are sveral more than you expect. We will send you to hell flying, and I will be damned if this be any sham; for I'll go to hell if do not do you.[45]

In other cases it appears that farmers were subject to vendettas for unspecified reasons and fire was just one weapon in escalating wars of retribution; Balls of Lessingham, for example, had his harnesses flung into a pit, his calves strung up, and his farm destroyed by fire. Thieves also attempted to cover their tracks by setting fire to houses when making their escape.[46]

However, the crime most frequently associated with arson was poaching. The game laws, after all, created more tension between the labouring community and the property owners than any other set of laws, with, perhaps, the exception of the poor laws. It therefore comes as no surprise to learn that many of the convicted arsonists were poachers too, and that, in other instances where no conviction was brought, poaching lay at the root of the incendiary attacks. This was particularly the case in the Suffolk villages of Polstead, Stanton, and Withersfield.[47] Thus in many cases incendiarism was employed to restrain prosecutors and magistrates from carrying out their duties or

---

44 *NC*, 17 Aug. 1816; *SC*, 11 May 1816.
45 PRO, HO 64/3, letter from Wodehouse, 221311. 1833; *BNP*, 3 Apr. 1833. See also HO 64/3, letter from Howman, in which he relates how a fire at Mattishall was connected to the arrest of a pea stealer, 9 Feb. 1833.
46 *NC*, 31 Jan. 1818; *NM*, 20 Jan. 1844.
47 See Ch. 9, section on protest and poaching.

at least to compound their behaviour in future cases in all manner of rural crime. We shall never know how successful the incendiaries were in moderating the force of law.

Consideration will be given to other specific reasons assigned to incendiaries' actions which never appeared in the law courts. These grievances were often wide ranging and highlighted other areas of oppression which were not commonly associated with acts of incendiarism. Rural housing was known to be poor and neglected by landlords until the 1860s and tenants' rights were non-existent. At Woodditton (Cambridgeshire-Suffolk border) an enormous fire in 1838 was related to the eviction of some cottagers. At Little Whelnetham (S) the landlord Major Rushbrooke left sorely needed cottages vacant for most of the 1852 summer and these were fired four times.[48] Commons disputes also escalated into fires, and in two other cases the loss of customary rights produced similar consequences. At Wortham (S) farmers reduced the lunchtime break period from two hours to one and this affected the horseman's work. At Haughley (S) the 'principal' parishioners placed 'false notices' (i.e. unofficial notices announcing the cancellation of the fair) on the green at the time of the annual fair, which they believed had had a deleterious effect on the morality of the community. The people burnt the fences surrounding the showground area.[49]

VICTIMS OF INCENDIARISM

Rural incendiary attacks were almost wholly directed at farmers. This clearly is an important characteristic of the crime. Within this amorphous group it was possible to identify various social and economic gradations. Important landowners who were direct victims of incendiary attacks numbered thirty-three. As landlords these men suffered considerably in an indirect way since many of their tenants had fires. In fact nearly every major landowner had at least one fire on his or her property during the period. Only thirty owner-occupiers have been positively identified as having had fires, which is undoubtedly an underestimate. The group which comprised landowners and rich tenant farmers, termed 'esquires' by the press,

---

48 *BNP*, 7 Nov. 1838, 16 June, 28 July, and 4 Aug. 1852.

49 *IJ*, 10 May 1851; *BNP*, 4 Sept, 1860. In East Anglia the work day was known as either 'one journey' or 'two journey' work. In the former case lunch breaks were short and taken in the fields, but the men and horses returned early in the afternoon for the animals' feeding and rub-down. In the latter case horsemen took their teams back to the stables at lunchtime and then returned to the fields afterwards.

accounted for forty-five fires, as did the clergy who were the greatest sufferers of the non-farming group. Interestingly the latter suffered proportionally more in the first twenty years of the period when anti-religious feelings ran higher due to the tithe question and the growth of non-conformity. There were fifteen fires on poor law property, usually workhouses. Overall, a noteworthy change with regard to the sufferers of incendiary attacks took place around the early 1830s. Before that date only 60 per cent of the victims were tenant farmers, the remainder comprising of major landowners, gentry, rectors, poor law officials, and millers. Thereafter farmers were by far and away the chief sufferers. This may reflect both a change in labourers' attitudes towards their social superiors and a realization on their part that rural social relations had indeed altered. The cash nexus, always the foremost relationship between masters and men during the entire period, may well not have been recognized as such until the 1830s. Labourers may have suffered under the delusion that the paternalism of landowners and gentry still operated, until the time of the Swing Riots when redress was sought from the rural leaders, but to no avail. Put simply, the farmers came to be recognized as their enemies because it was they and not the landowners who, to all intents and purposes, controlled and directed the social and economic circumstances of their lives.

Fires on common land, perhaps a surprising target, were infrequent and the damage was often only superficial. In nearly every case, even those where no convictions were made, it was possible to identify the reasons for such attacks. In Bungay, for instance, it was traditional to fire the common on 5 November. This tradition, however, did not meet with the approval of the rural constabulary who vainly tried to stamp out the practice. In time these celebrations altered in character and became anti-police displays.[50] Other commons' fires were related to disputes over the ownership of the land. At Fakenham this was clearly the case, whereas the fires at Mousehold were more complex and related to strained relationships between the Freemen of Pockthorpe and less privileged members of that community.

There was a whole host of other targets: shopkeepers, millers, vets, wheelwrights, a saddler, a postmaster, watchmaker, carpenter, butcher, carrier, cattle dealer, town corporations, bakers, a blacksmith, and six manufacturers. Publicans on ten occasions were targets, although in one case the landlord was himself accused of starting the fire in order

---

50 E. A. Goodwyn, *A Suffolk Town in Mid-Victorian England, Beccles in the 1860s* (Ipswich, n.d.), p. 30.

to hide his embezzlement of labourers' society's funds.[51]

Incendiarism was clearly directed against the landed and propertied classes since in only seven cases were fires begun on cottages or 'hovels' of the poor. If we accept that the majority of fires were begun by labouring people it is possible to conclude that incendiarism was not an intra-class method of exacting retribution. Fighting and 'rough music' were considered more appropriate for such occasions. However, it should be pointed out that many cottages were gutted by flames due to the firemen's inability to halt the spread of the fires. In some villages where cottages nestled up to farmyards many villagers were made homeless. This was particularly true of the Cambridgeshire villages of Bottisham, Cottenham, Over, and Soham, which between them lost in excess of forty cottages and twenty farms. So great was the destruction that the Norwich Union ceased business in Cottenham altogether and refused to take on new business in the whole of Cambridgeshire or re-insure thatched properties. The scale of incendiarism in these villages during the 1840s altered their architecture since replacement dwellings were constructed of brick and tile, a less risky proposition for the insurance companies.[52]

The destruction or firing of property has generally been described as 'burning stacks' or 'flaring ricks'. Undoubtedly stacks were the easiest of targets; they stood away from farms and possible detection by watchmen and guard dogs, they were extremely combustible, especially in winter when few other materials were so dry, and they produced the most spectacular effect for the cost of one 'Lucifer' match. The East Anglian dialect described incendiary fires as 'flare-ups' and one can well understand this descriptive term when one considers the speed with which dry straw burns. Stacks were repeatedly fired, so much so that insurance companies recommended that farmers space them further apart so as to minimize damage.[53] However, this study has brought to light two interesting features concerning the types of property destroyed. First, stacks were the most frequently chosen targets but they were by no means the only targets. Second, there may have been a relationship between the type of target and the intensity of the incendiary's hatred. Just under half of the fires solely destroyed stacks and in over 40 per cent of cases

---

51 John Huff of the Crown Inn, Stoke-by-Nayland, was found head first in a water butt attempting to commit suicide after he had fired some of the inn's outhouses in which the society's book was hidden, *BNP*, 14 Apr. 1863.
52 *BNP*, 11 Feb. 1846, 16 May 1849; *NC*, 13 Apr. 1850, 23 Aug. 1851; NUFO, board mins., 31 Sept. 1846, 16 and 18 Sept. 1850, 15 Sept. 1851.
53 Glyde, 'Suffolk', p. 126; NUFO, board mins, 11 Dec. 1843.

farm buildings and implements along with stacks were burnt. Non-agricultural buildings — gaols, houses, pubs, shops, and workhouses — accounted for a further 7 per cent, and hedging and fencing 3 per cent. Widespread damage to farm property was therefore more extensive than previously thought.

The proximity of fires to either farm houses or farmyards in years of greatest distress is an intriguing point. In the years of least incendiary activity in Suffolk stack fires accounted for 60 per cent of the damage to farmers but in the decade 1843 to 1853 they fell to 40 per cent. During the exceptional year of 1844 damage to buildings represented two-thirds of all fires. It would seem, therefore, that the incendiary's target altered in years of greatest distress. However, the Norfolk findings present a contrary picture in so far as stack fires accounted for 62 per cent in most years and dropped by only 2 per cent in 1844. Are these contradictory findings a statistical aberration signifying nothing, or are there explanations for the divergence in targets? Three possible reasons can be put forward which suggest that differences between the two counties were not merely accidental. Widespread incendiarism occurred in Norfolk first, and in 1830 eighteen of the twenty-two fires destroyed stacks. After this initial outburst came the prolonged and intensive incendiary period of 1831-4 which can be compared with Suffolk's peak of 1843-4. During these four years stack fires represented only 52 per cent of farm-related fires. Second, by 1844 Norfolk had a rural constabulary throughout the county, unlike Suffolk, and this may have forced incendiaries to seek targets away from areas of possible detection. Lastly, in the 1840s despair and hatred in Suffolk was more keenly felt than in Norfolk.

On this last point there does appear to have been a direct correlation between incendiarism and the emotions of hatred, despair, and revenge of the incendiary. As will be seen later, many incendiaries knew the occupiers of the properties they were firing. If they had decided to fire the buildings a degree of detailed knowledge concerning the layouts of the premises was necessary in order to avoid detection and make a quick escape. Firing farm buildings also produced the strongest psychological damage to employers. The fire was no longer only a 'flare-up' but also a 'warming' in its most literal sense. Furthermore, for the majority of local incendiaries their criminal act was not spontaneous but premeditated, if only over a glass of beer. Tramps and vagrants, on the other hand, fired stacks close to highways.

It has been necessary to dwell on this correlation as it partially helps our understanding of the psychological make-up of the incendiary and may also lead us to a fuller understanding of the characteristics of a crime which has never been systematically analysed by historians. It is impossible to draw any definite conclusions until further studies in the rest of the country have been made, but one can conclude in the case of East Anglia that incendiaries' choice of targets was often not without design.

PROTECTION AND DETECTION

Nineteenth-century incendiarism presented totally new problems for law enforcement bodies and insurance companies. Unlike other methods of protest such as riot, incendiarism could not be combated by the usual forms of protection and detection. When confronted with this new weapon the magistrates were completely baffled. A bewildered Duke of Grafton wrote to the foreman of the Suffolk Grand Jury, 'and I acknowledge that I feel at a loss to think of any particular measure which can be deemed efficacious to the great ends of prevention and detection'.[54] With the advent of incendiarism in the early nineteenth century, insurance companies and property holders resorted to traditional policing methods: associations for the protection of property extended their activities, new ones were established — at least seven between 1817 and 1827 — Bow Street officers were called in, larger rewards were offered, patrols were established, and 'addresses' to labourers were printed and distributed. All of these methods proved futile.

The lure of money appears to have been successful in only one case, at Bradfield, and these two informants were forced to leave the country.[55] The silence of the communities was most impressive, especially when the rewards were spectacular by the standards of the day. In 1831 Sir Henry Durrant offered a cottage with two acres. The Earl of Hardwicke continued this misguided and optimistic approach ten years later when he offered £50 plus £40 a year for life to anyone who could offer information that led to a successful conviction. By that time, 1843, nearly every fire had some kind of monetary reward attached to it but the idea began to lose favour a year later. One unfortunate by-product of insurance company and landlord benevolence was the payment of expenses in cash or beer to those

---

54 PRO, HO 52/3, 4 May 1822.
55 *BNP*, 4 June 1845. The Suffolk Fire Office and the parish donated a 'liberal' sum of money which enabled the couple to emigrate to Canada.

who helped to extinguish the flames. There were a number of instances where the helpers became too drunk to render any useful assistance and it was not inconceivable that the payment of beer or money to fire-fighters acted as a further incentive to light more fires.[56]

In the long run insurance companies probably benefited from incendiarism for it brought them more business. If the evidence provided by newspapers is a reliable guide then the number of properties insured in the 1820s was low, but the position was reversed by the mid-1830s when the majority of tenant farmers were covered for their own stock and property. However, the large landowners appear to have been less prudent and many waited until the 1840s before tightening up their financial management. Only then did they take out insurance, usually a response either to a fire in their neighbourhood or on one of their own properties. Lord Ashburnham's indifferent attitude on such matters increasingly alarmed Wright, his steward, who urged him to insure his extensive estate when arson broke out in the vicinity. In the correspondence between the two it transpired that Ashburnham was still under the illusion, in 1842, that the hundred would pay compensation under the Black Act. Once informed of the repeal Ashburnham's parsimony knew no bounds as he instructed Wright to make the tenants pay for the insurance of his buildings. 'I do not however know of any property upon which the occupier pays for insuring the landlord's building,' Wright replied, 'nevertheless ... it may not be too much to require the tenants on this estate to pay the expenses of insuring ...[57]

The other benefit accruing to insurance companies as a result of arson was their increasingly systematic investigation of clients and prospective clients, in which particular emphasis was placed on the reputations of farmers with their employees. The Norwich Union instructed its agents to avoid 'all persons [that] may be unpopular or obnoxious' and 'that on all occasions of going to any parish in consequence of an incendiary fire, the Surveyor makes inquiry as to the scale of wages for the farming labourers, and reports the information he obtains to the office'.[58] A few months later the same company ordered their surveyors to check every policy holder who was due for renewal who had had an incendiary fire. Some farmers were either banned or refused insurance cover, among them were: Raynham of Bildestone, Staples of Exning, Golding of Dalham, Coe

---

56 *BNP*, 4 Apr. 1832.
57 IESRO, HA 1/HB6/rb/24-7, 31.
58 NUFO, board mins., 4 Dec. 1843, 3 June 1844.

of Sedgeford, and every farmer in Withersfield was blacklisted and their renewals suspended.[59] Despite the long-term gains insurance companies suffered considerably in the short term from losses sustained through arson attacks. In 1850 Suffolk magistrates compiled a table (see Table 6.1) of losses sustained by the various companies in Cambridgeshire, Essex, and Suffolk between 1846 and 1849.[60] Not only is this a valuable guide to the amount of damage caused by incendiarism but it is also a useful indicator of the popularity of the different companies in the region. It was estimated that another £90,000 damage was not accounted for because sufferers were either not insured or were insured with other companies. These losses were considerable but the losses of the Suffolk Fire Office and the Norwich Union during years of incendiarism were proportionally much greater due to the local nature of their businesses. The former company, for example, paid out over £54,000 between 1843 and 1851.[61] The Norwich Union, which had one-sixth of the nation's farming insurance by 1858, was a far larger company and thus able to withstand the debacle of 1844. However, its annual report in 1845 was 'disastrous', with losses amounting to £84,000. In the previous twenty years losses had never exceeded £40,000.[62]

In their efforts to protect their financial interests, the insurance companies pressurized local county elites. They met county magistrates and reported on the extent of arson; they issued proclamations in favour of rural constabularies, and in the case of Soham the Norwich Union and the Suffolk Fire Office paid for London policemen to be stationed in the village.[63] The latter company was most influential in establishing a police force in West Suffolk at the end of 1844, when Bevan, a magistrate and director of the company, made a powerful speech winning tenant farmers over to the idea of a rural constabulary in that division of the county. Earlier that year the company had also been active in producing a poster for the attention of farm labourers which informed them of the protection that insurance companies offered to farmers and landlords.[64]

---

59 NUFO, board mins., 17 and 28 June 1844, 4 Jan. and 27 Dec. 1847, 29 Oct. 1849, 11 Nov. 1850.
60 IESRO, HA 11/B1/24/5.
61 IESRO, HA/B1/23/17. I am grateful to David Jones for allowing me to use these figures.
62 *NM*, 18 Jan. 1845; *NN*, 18 Jan. 1845.
63 NUFO, board mins., 21 June 1846.
64 *BNP*, 30 Oct. 1844. The poster was reproduced in the *BNP*, 1 Feb. 1844.

TABLE 6.1 *Insurance company losses in Cambridgeshire, Essex, and Suffolk, 1846-1849*

Company	Losses			Company	Losses		
	£	s.	d.		£	s.	d.
Suffolk Amicable	22,010	2	10	Royal Exchange	12,173	18	4
Phoenix	14,848	13	8	Essex Economic	11,249	3	5
Farmers	14,547	1	0	Atlas	3,683	16	7
Sun	14,478	6	0	Globe	2,898	10	0
Norwich Union	13,386	19	11	Norwich Equitable	1,033	12	6
				TOTAL	110,303	18	3

Source: IESRO, HA 11/B1/24/5.

At the start of this period there was no professional police force in either county, and prevention and detection was either undertaken by interested individuals or by three official though highly disorganized and unpaid bodies: the village constables, the special constables who were sworn in only during times of extreme unrest, and the highly mobile yeomanry which was a quasi-military force comprised of local landowners and their tenant farmers. None of these groups were effective during periods of incendiarism, especially the last two which were mobilized only during periods of riot and open confrontation. The village constables were notoriously ineffective because they neither had the time nor the inclination to investigate their neighbours. An overzealous constable was not a popular local figure, as Rayson of Hardingham found to his cost after successfully discovering the culprits for some barn robberies. His premises were fired. There were other cases of animal maiming and rough music against such men.[65]

Special constables were similarly exposed to intense pressure and threats, which exasperated Kay who witnessed a riot at Semer workhouse. The 'local police', he informed the Poor Law Commission, 'took care not to arrive until the riot was quelled'. Eventually London police were called in to clear this particular disturbance.[66] A number of parishes in both counties employed Metropolitan constables before the establishment of their own local

65 *NC*, 26 Jan. 1833. In 1835 Schomberg wrote to Lord Melbourne that farmers refused to be sworn in as special constables for fear of reprisals, PRO, HO 52/26, 29 July 1835.
66 PRO, MH 32/48, letter to PLC, 27 Dec. 1835.

police forces, and with a great deal of success. The Reverend Wodehouse of the Forehoe Hundred reported that the three men hired by himself 'changed the whole character of the place' within months of their arrival. The Reverend Barton of Blofield also reported similar successes in his union, with the exception of the village of Thorpe which had refused to pay for this service and was thus subject to many depredations.[67]

Although the introduction of the rural constabulary met with strong opposition, Norfolk and East Suffolk established police forces in early 1840, whilst West Suffolk and Cambridgeshire remained unpoliced for another five and ten years respectively. The East Suffolk force was, from its inauguration, more para-militaristic in its approach. No doubt this was a reflection of the experiences of its first chief constable, Captain J. H. Hatton, whose seventeen years in the Royal Irish Constabulary repressing rural disorders and the Ribbonsmen was considered sufficiently relevant and impressive to the county magistrates. Although he resigned at the beginning of 1843, his successor, another John Hatton (no relation), continued the paramilitary tradition by issuing cutlasses — he had originally requested firearms — to his night-duty constables in 1844. Whilst the arming of the East Suffolk force was not directly related to incendiarism, since it arose after the murder of Constable McFadden who was investigating a barn robbery, it does suggest that the night-time beats in rural areas were every bit as dangerous as those in major conurbations. Hatton certainly thought so, and the cutlass order was not rescinded until the mid-1860s.[68] The Norfolk police, under Colonel Oakes, was however more typical of rural constabularies in that they armed themselves with cutlasses only on exceptional occasions, at Snettisham in 1844 for example, but this did not prevent the force earning an unenviable reputation for its brutal treatment of prisoners.[69]

The police's success in dealing with incendiarism was, to say the least, mixed, but it must have been thought sufficient for West Suffolk and Cambridgeshire to follow suit since the establishment of their

---

67 PP 1852-3, XXXVI, Rural Constabulary First Report to the Select Committee, pp. 136-7; PRO, HO 73/6, pts. 1 and 2, for the returns from Hethersett, Houghton, and Burnham.

68 C. Emsley, '"The Thump of Wood on a Swede Turnip": Police Violence in Nineteenth-Century England', *Criminal Justice History*, 6 (1985), 132-4; S. H. Palmer, *Police and Protest in England and Ireland 1780-1850* (Cambridge, 1988), p. 451; C. Prescott, 'The Suffolk Constabulary in the Nineteenth Century', *Suffolk Institute of Archaeology*, 31 (1967-9), 16-36; R. Swift, 'Urban Policing in Early Victorian England, 1835-56: A Reappraisal', *History*, 73 (1988), 218.

69 Palmer, *Police and Protest*, p. 451.

rural constabularies was a direct consequence of the high level of incendiarism found within their borders.[70] West Suffolk also had the beneficial experience of hiring Superintendent English in 1844, a most energetic, dedicated, and effective detective. He must be considered the outstanding policeman of the period. Blyth, years earlier, had written to Melbourne requesting men 'that can descend to the very heart of our society' and this was just what English did. He was the forerunner of the plain-clothes policeman, for he dressed and worked as a labourer in order to gain working people's confidence. He eventually brought to trial George Dye, John Frost, George and Jeremiah Head, and Samuel Stow.[71] Only one other constable, PC Frew, had as good a record; he made five arrests for incendiary acts in two and a half years.[72]

Other members of the rural constabularies had less laudable records. Two named Pilbrow and Carlo resorted to hiding under a table while three suspects were interviewed by their lawyer. Other policemen planted informers, usually convicted petty criminals, in the same cells as incendiary suspects.[73] The police were obviously under considerable pressure to make successful arrests if they had to resort to such tactics. In the majority of cases they only had circumstantial evidence to go on: footprints, gossip in the pub, or reported sightings of shadowy figures near the scene of conflagrations. This lack of hard evidence even brought a reaction in the House of Commons, where Colonel Fox repeated the rhetorical question of the Chairman of the Suffolk Sessions: 'it might be asked why the rural police had not prevented these crimes ... ?' Fox answered himself: 'Even if the whole of the Metropolitan police were sent down to Suffolk it would be impossible to give security against these outrages; unless, indeed, a policeman stood sentry in every homestead all night.'[74] Graham, the Home Secretary, emphasized this point when he replied that members of the Metropolitan force had indeed been sent, 'but as yet no detection had taken place'. Other concerned individuals offered their own advice on detection and prevention, among which were the recommendations of the use of bloodhounds and the reintroduction

---

70 PP 1852-3, XXXVI, 46.
71 *BNP*, 11 Sept. 1844, 9 and 30 Apr. 1845, 8 Oct. 1845. English received over £100 and a watch for his troubles.
72 *BNP*, 9 Aug. 1864.
73 *BNP*, 25 June 1845. See other cases, *BNP*, 16 Aug. 1843, 2 Apr. 1845. Pilbrow knew the infamous Williams and planted him in a cell with the incendiary, Dew. See also Jones, 'Thomas Campbell Foster', p. 17 n. 49.
74 *Hansard*, 22 Mar. 1844, p. 1368.

of capital punishment for arson. Neither were taken too seriously.[75]

One important aspect connected with incendiarism in the pre-1851 period which hindered police detection was the enormous solidarity, and even overt sympathy, of the majority of the working people towards the instigators of the fires. Although incendiarism was essentially a secretive vengeful crime committed by one or two individuals, their identities were often well known to the rest of the community. They were, in the words of one labourer, 'screened by the multitude', who were, added a land agent, 'bound in a bond of secrecy'. Investigators found that 'every mouth' was shut tight whenever enquiries were made. An arsonist was 'encouraged to work out any act of revenge of malice', wrote the Reverend Henslow of Hitcham, 'confident that his neighbours ... will not give evidence against him'.[76] Every village was thus a closed parish to those in authority and few policemen were able to descend to its very heart.

To what degree fear or sympathy were responsible for the silence one cannot judge, though the former must have been powerful when placed in the context of close-knit village communities where blood relations exerted a powerful influence. To inform on a neighbour was considered reprehensible and did not pass without notice. There were several instances of unpaid informers offering evidence against incendiaries. A man named Rye was hanged on the information provided by Watts who turned King's evidence. He was recognized by the crowd at the hanging and was attacked. He eventually left for America after his fellow villagers had shunned him. Effigy burnings and 'rough music' were meted out to others.[77]

Crowd reaction at fires was the best barometer by which to measure the general opinion with regard to incendiarism. Instances of ill-feelings, hatred, and unbridled pleasure are too numerous to mention in detail but some examples are given to show the range of crowd feeling. It could vary from sullen silence at Briston (N), distinct coolness as at Saxthorpe (N) where labourers drinking in the public house only five yards from a fire refused to lend assistance, or stoking the fire with wood. At other villages firemen were shot at, helpers stoned or beaten up, pipes and buckets cut to shreds, and furniture

---

75 On the issue of bloodhounds see NC, 8 Feb. 1834, when it was reported that the Duke of Marlborough had successfully tracked down an incendiary with a bloodhound after a fire at Woodstock. The deployment of mantraps and spring-guns in stackyards was also suggested.

76 Henslow, *Suggestions*, pp. 4-5; Glyde, 'Autobiography', p. 46; IESRO, HA 1/HB6/16/62.

77 BNP, 16 and 30 Apr. 1834. For other examples see *Hansard*, 19 July 1844, p. 1097; *NNMPG*, 1 Jan. 1844.

and drink pilfered. At Wenham onlookers refused monetary inducements to help, which surely signified deep resentment. The *Morning Chronicle* correspondent provided one particularly powerful eyewitness account of a fire in 1844:

> ... they jeered and laughed at the men who worked at the engines or otherwise exerted themselves, and testified their delight in loud shouts of laughter when any part of the building fell in and blazed up. ... Considerable damage was done to the growing crops of barley and wheat by the crowds, who for several hours amused themselves, men chasing women and women chasing men, all rolling together, and shouting, and larking in the smoke and red glare.[78]

Alcoholic beverages were often distributed to helpers but with little success since many became too drunk to help or care. Such reports of crowd misbehaviour provide ample evidence of the people's approval for the fires. Furthermore the scenes of arson attacks provided a platform for perfectly legal demonstrations against employers. Collective community displays of protest were, therefore, evident even though incendiarism was primarily an individual act of hatred and revenge.[79] However, there is a notable contrast between the pre- and post-Swing eras. In the earlier period it appears that labourers did lend their assistance, but after 1830 and the defeat of organized collective action, their attitudes hardened significantly and there are few instances of aid being given to farmers until the 1850s.

This point needs to be emphasized in the context of the Wells-Charlesworth debate. In Wells's opinion covert protest was the significant and enduring feature of social unrest in the English countryside during the first half of the nineteenth century and, by implication, arson replaced overt collective protest when the latter failed as a tactical weapon in the 1790s. This idea — the evolutionary process of one form of protest being replaced by another — is also shared by Charlesworth.[80] However, he regards arson attacks as peripheral to the mainstream of rural protest which was, until 1830, characterized by collective action. Arson, in other words, reached appreciable proportions only after the Swing Riots. This debate raises

---

78 *MC*, 10 July 1844; Briston, *NM*, 13 Nov. 1830; at Saxthorpe drinkers in an adjacent inn refused to help, *BNP*, 2 Jan. 1833; Wenham, *The Times*, 4 Feb. 1844; firemen attacked at Witchingham, *BNP*, 9 Nov. 1831; hoses cut at Bacton, *The Times*, 13 Mar. 1844; looting at Hartest, *NC*, 15 Apr. 1843.

79 *BNP*, 24 May 1843: 800 pints of beer were consumed during and after a fire.

80 Wells, 'Development', pp. 115-39; id., 'Social Conflict', pp. 514-30; Charlesworth, 'Development', pp. 101-11.

many questions. Did arson simply replace collective overt protest? Was one form of protest used exclusively? Was arson the significant and enduring feature of social unrest? The answers to these and other questions are not straightforward but a number of points can be made in the context of this study. Arson did not directly replace the food riot, as Wells has suggested, for as we have seen incendiarism after 1830 did not coincide with high food prices; on the contrary quite the reverse occurred. Second, overt collective protest did not disappear in the aftermath of Swing. Between 1831 and 1834 there were thirty-seven strikes and demonstrations, and an additional twenty-five strikes and demonstrations during the introduction of the New Poor Law in 1835-6 in this region. Thereafter there was a lull in the 1840s when collective unrest receded, only to re-emerge from 1850 when strikes, workhouse and enclosure riots, and charity disputes occurred on an almost annual basis until the formation of the agricultural trade unions.[81] Arson and riot could and did exist alongside one another. Labourers and the rural working class communities in general appear to have been quite selective in their choice of tactics when furthering a dispute; it all depended on what kind of dispute was being furthered. Finally, to return to the original point, arson did give labouring communities the opportunity to transform an act of covert protest into a collective and overt display of hatred against the farmers. As a tactical weapon, then, incendiarism was ideally suited, since perfectly legal (and some not so legal) displays of collective joy and celebration were possible and the authorities were powerless and could do little but condemn the 'unfeeling behaviour' and 'disgraceful scenes' at the fires. The dichotomy between overt and covert protest, therefore, may not be so great when one separates the act of starting a fire from the subsequent reaction the fire engendered.

Further evidence on this point of community reaction abound in observations by reporters and landowners. The supposedly 'slow', 'dull-witted' labourers who were at one moment standing in witness boxes, cap in hand and head bent in deference, were at another genuinely celebrating farmers' misfortunes. The *Morning Chronicle* reported: 'It is a melancholy fact that many people over a great breadth of country speak of the destruction done by this fire [at Farnham] with feelings of high satisfaction.'[82] Campbell Foster heard

---

81 Archer, 'The Wells-Charlesworth Debate', pp. 277-84.
82 *MC*, 8 Dec. 1849. The Farnham fire may not have been started deliberately, as the defendant, Clowe, was acquitted, *MC*, 25 July 1844.

similar sentiments on his journey through East Anglia.[83] Many of these reported phrases have a ring of authenticity about them which contrasts strongly with the reported response at a Gislingham fire. The story ran that when the labourers heard that Lord Henniker was not insured, 'they cried, "Let us do all we can to save his Lordship's property, who has given us employment during the winter, and kept us from the Union-house."'[84] Such language was hardly convincing, but it does raise the point of working people's dual response to the fires. On the one hand, bitterness and joy at the farmers' calamities, but on the other, feverish activity to extinguish the flames. Some farmers like Woods of Coombs were respected and popular with labourers, even a threatening letter said as much, and it was not therefore surprising to find labourers willing to help.[85] Money and drink in other cases were the incentives but one has also to take into account that labourers may have responded and helped in a manner that was expected of them by employers, whatever their feelings towards that particular employer. The case of James Rudland, who was tried and acquitted for a fire at Buxhall (S), amplifies this dual response rather well. He announced to all and sundry during the height of the fires in 1844 that: 'He should like to see all the farmers in the fire roasted on both sides, and he would not try to pull them out; and he should like to have a crome [crooked stick] to turn them over to roast on both sides.' Shortly after a fire in his own village of Buxhall he boasted, 'When he first saw the fire it was the size of a sack and he could have quenched it with three pails of water if he liked.' Yet a few days later, while killing a hog for a farmer's wife, Rudland was reported as saying: 'Missus, I wish the person as did the fire to be served the same as this here hog.'[86]

After 1851 labourers' attitudes dramatically altered and they invariably helped in fighting the fires. This significant development was probably due to a number of factors. Firstly, incendiarism never peaked in any significant way after 1851, suggesting that the emotions of social protest never reached pre-1851 heights. Secondly, unemployment and poverty were not such important trigger mechanisms for incendiary acts and, lastly, many incendiaries no longer came from the agricultural labouring section of the community, but were often tramps and young children. After 1851 the mores of rural society were experiencing considerable changes; education,

83 *The Times*, 7 and 11 June 1844.
84 *NM*, 30 Mar. 1844.
85 *The Times*, 14 June 1844; see also A. Armstrong, *Farmworkers: A Social and Economic History 1770-1980* (London, 1988), p. 86.
86 *The Times*, 29 July 1844.

religion, and respect for law and order were making their socializing effects felt. Incendiarism as a response to injustice was becoming something of an anachronism and the incendiary was fast becoming a figure removed from the mainstream of community opinion.

WHY INCENDIARISM?

East Anglia had a history of social protest prior to 1830 and the combatants involved in the riots, marches, and demonstrations had learnt to their cost that open displays of protest brought in their wake punishments ranging from the death penalty at worst, to imprisonment at best. One has to remember the traumas and the psychological impact that these sentences had on small village communities. In the village of Withersfield, for instance, with a population of 500, it must have been painful to witness the transportation of six labourers, who were later joined by their wives and children.[87] In all, a short-lived riot permanently thinned this small village of well over twenty inhabitants. Many of these open confrontations were also unsuccessful in achieving their desired aims, the riots of 1835-6 especially so. Therefore there was little incentive to organize or protest if the ringleaders were to be singled out and given harsh sentences while points of grievance continued to exist. Open confrontation was also hindered by the increase in population, since employers held the whip hand on the employment market. Thus one major avenue of rural protest was closed up and the alternatives of covert individual terrorist action became a more viable proposition. Practicality was a strong driving force; fear of detection, fear of punishment, fear of association, all created a climate of secretiveness. The army, the yeomanry and the special constables were all powerless against such night-time attacks on property. To this extent Hobsbawm and Rudé were correct to view incendiarism as an active response to defeat.

If incendiarism was, as often argued, so detrimental to the economic interests of labourers, why then did it develop to such an extent before 1850? Farmers before 1830 were probably not insured and the fires would have caused financial hardship, but after that date insurance protected the majority and the fires were not so economically devastating. But was the main purpose of incendiarism to cause financial loss to property holders? The answer was considerably more complex than simple economics. Incendiaries never

---

87   PRO, HO 52/20, letter from Revd Mayd, 8 Feb. 1832.

aimed to kill or injure property holders and their choice of targets was often discriminatory. That much we can be sure of. These acts of protest should be placed into a similar category as 'ceffyl pren' of Wales and the 'rough music' of rural England. It was a psychological weapon with a great deal of impact in the small communities. The sufferer was a target of hatred and he and the rest of the community knew as much. The victim had been singled out for special treatment and the fire was there to publicize the fact that he, more than any other person, had transgressed against someone or some custom. One labourer made the telling remark of an incendiary victim: 'the sooner he's out of the country the better.' In another case, Peck of Congham (N), although insured, claimed another incendiary fire 'would oblige him to relinquish business altogether'.[88]

The publicity factor of incendiarism was important, for some fires were reported to have been visible across forty miles of countryside and they attracted large celebrating crowds, up to 3,000 in one or two cases. It is impossible to quantify the fear of fire but undoubtedly the farmers' fear was considerable. In a letter to Melbourne, the Home Secretary, the Reverend Brett of Congham wrote that 'panic generally prevails' in the county after the large number of fires.[89] Labourers maintained 'nothing scares the farmers like a good fire'. This quite natural dread cannot be emphasized enough as a psychological weapon. Such a 'flash and a scare' provoked a response from employers, often a favourable one, and to that end it has to be considered successful in a limited way.

Labour was adversely affected after a large stack or granary fire, especially if the fire occurred before the threshing season, but the incendiary's hatred transcended such considerations. To him the stacks and barns were symbols of wealth, oppression, and power and the fires were a method of 'getting even'. If this was the case then it was more than likely that fires were lit in a less discriminating fashion during periods of greatest distress, because all employers would have been regarded in a similar way as oppressors of labour. Campbell Foster thought this to be the case in 1844 when he wrote:

> Can we feel surprised that a labourer out of work half the week, and leaving his home, without having broken his fast ... should return a dangerous man, ready to strike a lucifer match and thrust it into the farmer's stack, who will not give him work, or into any stack, because it is the evidence of wealth and comfort, which,

88 *BNP*, 1 Aug. 1832.
89 PRO, HO 64/2, 8 Oct. 1831.

hungered and starving, he hates to see?[90]

While farm work may have been adversely affected by incendiarism on a very localized scale — the individual farms which experienced arson attacks — regionally, employment was created by farmers keen to lessen the possibility of incendiarism in their neighbourhoods. Nightwatchmen were employed extensively during intensive periods of incendiarism. In a number of cases they proved ineffective and in at least two cases nightwatchmen were actually convicted of incendiarism. One labourer reportedly said 'the fires did poor men good, for they now get two shillings a night watching them'. General farm work 'not actually required, that is not immediately beneficial, such as marl and clay carting, cutting down fences, cleaning borders', likewise increased.[91] Arson also halted intended wage reductions and, in some cases, forced them to rise by a shilling or two a week.

Incendiarism was primarily a response by labourers, especially the younger ones, to the oppressive social and economic conditions which they were forced to endure. It is possible to describe the fires as disorganized and uncoordinated acts of protest kindled by a workforce lacking bargaining power and fearful of open confrontation. It is hoped the following chapter will explain the motives of the incendiary more clearly.

90 *The Times*, 11 June 1844.
91 *BNP*, 4 Apr. 1832 and 1 Nov. 1864; *NC*, 19 Nov. 1859; *NM*, 15 Apr. 1845.

7
The Myth and Reality of the Incendiary

INTRODUCTION

East Anglian farmers and gentry were often at a loss when trying to identify incendiaries, especially during the upsurges of arson in 1843-4 and 1849-52. Why this was so is not altogether obvious. The reasoning powers of supposedly responsible and intelligent men appeared, temporarily, to leave them. It would seem their misguided sense of paternalism, with a little prompting from their 'loyal' subjects, led them into making self-delusory remarks regarding the affection of their 'peasantry' towards them and the farmers. In some ways they were the victims of their own rural-idyll propaganda of the well-ordered and hierarchical society. An example of this blinkered reasoning can be discerned in a letter from the Mayor of Ipswich to the Home Secretary, Robert Peel. He wrote that the fires were the work of strangers, there being 'no disorderly spirit existing in the mass of the lower orders'. The year was 1822, a year as we have seen, of riots, demonstrations, fires, and threatening letters. This same letter actually concluded with the observation that the poor were almost totally unemployed.[1] Such stupidity led the farmers to look everywhere, even to the continent, yet they failed or refused to come closer to home, to the very villages in which the fires had taken place, to find the incendiaries.

Another intriguing reaction on the landowners' part, again indicative of their bewilderment, was the belief the fires were all part of one large plan to overthrow them. There was, in their opinion, a 'systematic and carefully planned' campaign against them amounting to revolution. Unlike France of 1789, 'La Grande Peur' in East Anglia's case ran, not through the cottages of the poor, but through the farmhouses and mansions of the wealthy — or, as one *Times* correspondent put it, 'Guerre aux châteaux, paix aux chaumieres'.[2] Such fears were founded on a number of observations, not least the sheer scale of the fires during certain months in certain years. This, to the gentry's way of thinking, surely indicated a secret labourers' organization of some sort. In this, as in so many other explanations, their fears were founded on terror rather than on reality.

The incendiaries, whoever they were, have remained anonymous figures even to this day, although there have been two studies which

---

1   PRO, HO 52/3, 2 Apr. 1822.
2   *The Times*, 20 May 1844.

have extended our knowledge.[3] They have generally escaped the historians' scrutiny largely because they evaded detection by contemporary police forces. Only a minority of incendiaries were ever arrested, let alone found guilty. Foster estimated the arrest rate in 1844 was only one prisoner for every fifteen fires. Later in the year he raised it to one in twenty. His estimates, however, did not correlate with the facts since one person was convicted for every seven fires. Taking the period as a whole 649 people were arrested and tried at the assize courts for the 1,970 fires in the two counties.[4] However, of the 649 committals, only 307 were found guilty. The conviction rate was therefore 47 per cent of those arrested or, expressed in another way, one person was found guilty for every six fires. The figures for arrests and conviction rates for the overall period hide certain trends which are clearly discernible in Tables 7.1 and 7.2.

The figures in the two tables clearly show the police's increasing effectiveness in both arresting the right people and making more successful arrests in relation to the number of fires. Before 1840, when neither county had a professional constabulary force, the parish constables arrested one person for every five fires that occurred. Nor were they successful in arresting the right people since three out of every four of those charged left court as free men. With the introduction of the rural constabulary in 1840 in Norfolk and East Suffolk the arrest rate rose: one arrest for every three fires, and the conviction rate almost doubled. After 1850, when the police were fully established in the region, the arrest and conviction rates continued to improve. The impact of the police was, therefore, significant in the successful detection of incendiaries, but their presence was not the only reason for this improvement. The type of person convicted for incendiarism after 1852 was often quite different in character and motivation from those in the earlier half of the period.

The historian, in his search for the incendiary's identity, is left with only a small proportion of the culprits. Nor can the historian be confident in discovering the motives or grievances of those found guilty of incendiarism. It is quite probable that the convicted incendiaries were not representative as there were a large number of children, vagrants, and mentally subnormal people convicted. And as *The Times* pointed out, 'that the one who is apprehended is normally

---

3   Jones, 'Thomas Campbell Foster', pp. 5-43; id., *Crime, Protest*, pp. 33-61.
4   A complete list of those tried for incendiary offences can be found in Archer, thesis, pp. 667-88, app. iv, table 18.

the one holding the spite and is known to be spiteful'.[5]

TABLE 7.1 *Persons committed and found guilty for incendiary offences in Norfolk and Suffolk, 1815-1870*

	Committals	Guilty	Convictions rate as % of committals
1815-19	17	5	29
1820-9	28	9	32
1830-9	71	18	25
1840-9	202	88	44
1850-9	184	102	55
1860-70	147	85	58
TOTAL	649	307	47

Sources: Local newspapers, 1815-70; *Times*, 1843-4; *Morning Chronicle*, 1844; PRO, ASSI 33/12-14, ASSI 35/276-90, HO 64/1-6; IESRO, HA 11/B1/11/2; NUFO, board minutes 1840-51.

TABLE 7.2 *Number of fires and persons found guilty for incendiary offences in Norfolk and Suffolk, 1815-1870*

	Fires	Fires per incendiary
1815-19	66	13
1820-9	159	18
1830-9	372	21
1840-9	624	7
1850-9	412	4
1860-70	337	4
TOTAL	1,970	6

Sources: As for Table 7.1.

What kind of mercy could the convicted expect from the English courts? The answer, quite simply, was very little. Fire was a powerful and feared weapon and special condemnation was often reserved for incendiarism, a crime considered 'second only to murder', or as one Home Office correspondent put it, 'one of the blackest and most atrocious crimes of which human nature is capable'.[6] Given that the prevailing mood towards incendiarism was so hostile it is hardly

5   *The Times*, 4 July 1844.
6   PRO, HO 52/3, letter from Grafton, 4 May 1822; *The Times*, 8 Apr. and 22 Aug. 1844.

surprising to find judges passing heavy sentences upon the guilty (see Table 7.3).

TABLE 7.3 *Sentences passed on incendiaries in Norfolk and Suffolk, 1815-1870*

Sentence	No.	% of total
Death	26	8.5
Transportation	119	38.8
Gaol	110	35.8
Other (fines, whipping, etc.)	52	16.9
TOTAL	307	100.0

Sources: As for Table 7.1.

All forms of arson remained capital offences until 1837 when the law was repealed. Thereafter arson to a dwelling house remained a hanging offence, whereas other forms of the crime frequently carried a transportation sentence until the mid-1850s when it was replaced by penal servitude. Of the twenty-six capitally convicted, all but one were sentenced before 1838; the exception was the rather unusual case of Sarah Hannible who tried to commit suicide by firing her bedding when in Yarmouth gaol.[7] The sentence was respited. For those convicted in East Anglia before 1838, the majority actually suffered the sentence passed on them and 65 per cent in fact are known to have gone to the gallows. This very high percentage reflects unfavourably with Rudé's findings. He noted that between 1820 and 1833, 55 per cent of all incendiaries in this country had the capital offence carried out. Yet even this figure was high when compared to all other capital convictions. For example, between 1828-34 only one in twenty death sentences was carried out.[8] The hangman was clearly guaranteed more business if incendiaries found themselves convicted at the assizes, especially if they practised their trade in East Anglia. The harsh sentencing of this region may well be a reflection of the fact that the crime was more common and hence more of a problem here than elsewhere.

Transportation to Van Diemen's Land for varying periods, usually for life or fifteen years, became the standard sentence in the 1840s. In some cases, like Birch's, the convicted were keen to go. Others, like Banks, had already been out there and had returned as a ticket-of-

---

7 *NN*, 29 Mar. 1854.
8 Rudé, *Protest and Punishment*, pp. 66-7.

leave.[9] After 1855 sentencing practices changed yet again and distinctions were drawn for the first time between the young and old. Children were sent off to the newly established reformatory schools whereas adults suffered various forms of incarceration, either gaol with hard labour or penal servitude for anything up to twenty years, but more often for a shorter period of between five and ten years. Overall, the sentences moderated during the course of the century, although one wonders how close the government came to reintroducing the death penalty during the explosion of fires in 1843-4. The general public were certainly baying for blood, not for the first or last time, but the government kept its nerve, ignored the petitions, and the danger passed.

The undetected incendiary is obviously the more interesting figure to the historian but his identity must remain a mystery. However, from what we can learn of the convicted and the characteristics of the crime, it is possible to build up a fairly accurate profile of the type of people liable to start fires and their reasons for so doing. Although information on convicted incendiaries remains rather poor between 1815 and 1870, at crucial points during the period particularly full details have remained. This was certainly the case between 1843 and 1845 when public interest was aroused by the frequency of fires in rural England as a whole. The Home Secretary ordered a House of Lords *Return of Ages and Description of Persons Committed for Trial for Incendiary Offences in Norfolk and Suffolk*. This Return was brief but it gave a description of age, sex, occupation, and result of the trial, for all those committed for incendiary offences.[10] Information on convicted incendiaries for other years has been taken from newspaper reports and the few extant assize court records.

THE MYTH

With the advent of widespread and frequent incendiary fires in 1830 contemporaries quickly realized there was a marked difference between Swing the machine breaker and Swing the incendiary. The former, who were identifiable farm labourers, so often reliable, reticent, and deferential, were seen to be marching through the village streets. These men were married, described by their employers as 'steady, quiet, and honest'. Hobsbawm and Rudé found that of the 1,238 prisoners only thirty-two were under the age of 18, and only

---

9   See Ch. 5 n. 75.
10 PP 1844, 258.

thirty-five were over the age of 50. The average age of convicts transported to Tasmania was 29 and those to New South Wales a little over 27.[11]

The incendiary was, by the nature of his crime, very different. He used in most cases the cover of darkness to conceal his presence and escape. The act of incendiarism was anonymous. This gave rise to strange theories concerning his real identity. He was viewed as a sinister devilish figure, an unnatural being shunning the light of day and feeding off the hell-like flames of the black night. The very tool of his trade, the 'Lucifer' match, heightened the devil imagery.[12] He was by definition a coward and most certainly 'unEnglish' in his behaviour. Various theories grew up as to what human form this devil-like figure took. The *Norfolk Chronicle* believed him to be the 'child of the agitating demagogue'. In 1830 some rectors and JPs thought him to be a reader of Cobbett's *Political Register* and even the *Sunday Times*, while others favoured the view that the incendiary was working for political reform or the Charter. In neither county does a relationship between Chartism and incendiarism appear to have existed.[13]

Closely allied to the political doctrine theory was the foreigner and paid agent theory. *The Times* reported that people of some note believed 'that the [Anti-Corn Law] League has paid agents going about the country'.[14] This fear was symptomatic of the almost paranoid and bitter resentment held by farmers at a time when the ACLL was stepping up its propaganda throughout Britain, even in counties such as Norfolk and Suffolk which probably contained some of the most ardent and aggressive protectionists in the country. One further report from a Suffolk newspaper also hinted at the ACLL's involvement. The fires, so the report ran, were the work of miscreants, 'employed by a certain party backed by foreign aid. Foreigners may even exist to ruin our agricultural produce for the hope of finding a market for their own. Those foreigners may be in the disguise of commercial travellers or agents in two or four wheeled carriages.'[15] Only fourteen years before, the English countryside had been teeming with mythical Irishmen, Frenchmen, and Italians buying county maps and travelling

---

11 Hobsbawm and Rudé, *Captain Swing*, p. 209. The average age of Norfolk machine breakers was 27.

12 Anon., 'Incendiarism', p. 244.

13 *NC*, 18 Nov. 1843. However, in Essex a fire broke out in Boreham on the same night as a Chartist meeting, *BNP*, 19 Dec. 1838. Generally speaking, East Anglian Chartists were critical of incendiarism, see Brown, *Chartism*, pp. 75-6.

14 *The Times*, 7 June 1844.

15 *The Times*, 10 June 1844.

in gigs. E. Gibson Wakefield ridiculed this theory in a pamphlet: 'Who is Swing? A well-dressed agent, either of Mark Lane, or of the revolutionary spirit, who travels in a gig, and fires farm yards, either to raise the price of wheat, or to promote reform of parliament. Doubt it not! whispers an electioneering alderman.'[16] The well-dressed agent was seen on more than one occasion in 1844. In one eyewitness account a young woman on her way to Mottesham 'heard a whistle in the direction of the heath, and on looking through a fence she saw a man, dressed, as she says, like a gentleman, stooping down as if in the act of placing something in the furze ... Flames shot up from the whins and the man made off.'[17] In another example two people were walking towards a fire when they met a stranger, 'of respectable appearance', driving a chaise, and they hailed him with 'God bless me Sir, don't you see the fire off there?' The stranger's reply was, 'Yes and a glorious sight it is.'[18]

In one particular case the respectable political agitator hypothesis was turned neatly on its head by the relatively radical *Suffolk Chronicle* which reported the sighting of 'a well-dressed man on horseback', who delivered a threatening letter to a local farm. Was this well-spoken stranger an 'Oliver or Castle', the *Chronicle* wondered aloud, an *agent provocateur* sent by a tyrannical government to discredit the radicals' cause, as they had done only a few years previously?[19]

Another theory grew up, closely associated with the political incendiary theory, which was more vague and threw a sinister light on the whole matter of the fires. Basically it was a belief that some sort of conspiracy existed which was systematically attempting to fire all farmers' property. In effect it was regarded as quasi-revolutionary, but rather than being organized in the Chartist fashion, it was more anarchic in character. Some commentators viewed it as a type of class war in which the incendiary was stalking the length and breadth of the country, stoking up not only the fires but the revolutionary consciousness of the village communities into starting a widespread peasants' revolt. It is difficult to see the incendiary as a vanguard of working-class rebellion, although the incendiary Knockolds may have seen himself in this light.[20] The villagers themselves, in many cases, watched the incendiary fires with pleasure or in silence, which was in effect a seal of approval. So the incendiary was in a sense advertising

16 E. G. Wakefield, *Swing Unmasked* (London, 1830), p. 8.
17 *The Times*, 29 May 1844.
18 *NM*, 30 Mar. 1844.
19 *SC*, 16 Mar, 1822.
20 See Ch. 7 n. 25 for evidence of Knockolds.

their plight, but to believe incendiarism was the touch-paper to general rebellion was clearly untrue. Incendiary fires were, in the main, related to local circumstances and, as such, only took on importance in the immediate neighbourhood. Both counties were experiencing similar attacks on property and their workforce experienced the same social and economic conditions, but that does not alter the fact that all incendiary attacks could not marry, as it were, into one large general uprising.

Some incendiaries and threatening letter writers reinforced the view that a general conspiracy existed, a conspiracy in which all the working people were involved. A threatening letter found at Stowmarket in the spring of 1844 showed how the writer believed himself to be speaking on the behalf of the poor. The writer also implied that he was an outsider who travelled the country making contacts in order to ascertain the local situation. An extract of the letter appears below:

> Gentleman i have thought it proper of wrihting these few words jest to show and let you now how the pore are opressed in this place ... Gentleman i ask you why these pore creatures should be in this state i ask you if there is aney ocasion for it and i as an individual am going through all the villages of Suffolk and Norfolk to hear the starving cryes of the pore, and i as one person unknown to you have been to won or two in this place and they told me that there is plentey of parish property to maintain all the pore in this place ... i shall be in town in a few dayes so that i hope that i shall here that you begin to do sumpthing.[21]

A convicted threatening letter writer, James Friend, adopted a common literary style to suggest to the recipient of the missive that there was an organized body of men against him: 'Farmers we are starvers, we wol not stan this no longer: this 600 and 8.'[22]

Another letter recalled the style of Luddite and Swing notes, the writer warned the farmer that 'I will order so that you have a leaden bullet put through your head'.[23] Letters from the 'General', the 'Colonel', or 'Captain Swing' warned of armies and gangs preparing to attack, not just the farmer to whom the letter was addressed, but all farmers in the area, who were termed in one letter as that 'bloody wheel barrow set'. Farmer Beaker of Knapton received the following note in 1831:

---

21 *The Times*, 14 June, 1844.
22 *The Times*, 26 July 1844.
23 *NC*, 23 July 1853. For a full discussion on threatening letters see E. P. Thompson, 'The Crime of Anonymity', in Hay et al., edd., *Albion's Fatal Tree*, pp. 255-344.

Mr Beaker look out, for on such a tiem [time] your primeses will be on fier, for my eye was on you yesterday, So i thaut as you napton farmers go sporting about with your houns, you ought to look to the pore ... for men vages you have had your vays long a nof, So look out, as you have hung one of our gain [gang], you shall have faiers anow to your heart desier, for we mead just a begining at trunch [a village where an incendiary fire took place], and we men to stir up you napton jentlemen, young robinson for one and Mister Atkson for another, and we shall com upon the round; thear is fifty on us in the gain, and you may catch us if you can.[24]

'[Y]ou have hung one of our gain': Mr Beaker knew what that referred to. It was a reference to Norfolk's most celebrated and admired incendiary of the century, Richard Knockolds. He was a radical, a trade unionist, a weaver, a thief, a self-proclaimed atheist, an organizer of a working-class reading room, a threatening letter writer, and an incendiary. With credentials like these Knockolds deserves to enter the British radicals' hall of fame. Nor is this the end of his remarkable *curriculum vitae*, for it is claimed he had shot one weaving manufacturer and thrown vitriol in the faces of two others during the Norwich weavers' dispute of 1829. He was, according to one newspaper, 'imbued with a bitter hatred against every order of society raised above his own level'. One January night in 1831 he filled his pockets with sixteen fireballs and three threatening letters and took a three-hour walk into the countryside from his home in Pockthorpe, Norwich. He dropped his letters in the lanes and stuffed his fireballs into the stacks of three farmers. Two of his accomplices, to save their own skins, turned King's evidence and he was convicted and later hanged before a vast crowd. His body was on view for three days at a penny a look, and on the day of his funeral the coffin was carried by six men accompanied by six pall bearers along a route lined with thousands of mourners.[25] One small fact does tend to detract from Knockold's altruistic and crusading spirit. He was actually paid expenses by country labourers for his efforts.

Knockolds was unique among those convicted, in that he was a member of a vengeance gang. It is highly unlikely that many of these gangs existed, although one wonders at the presence of a watchmaker from Montgomery, Wales, who was locked up for inciting the labourers to burn property, and the four people from Kent (where

---

24 *EA*, 2 Aug. 1831.
25 *NC*, 16 Apr. 1831; *EA*, 29 Mar. 1831; PRO, HO 40/29, fos. 208-10, NNLHL, N343, the 'last true confession of Knocholds'.

Swing had its origins) who were arrested in the heart of the machine breaking area of Norfolk in 1830 carrying matches, brimstone, and turpentine. And what of the men identified with such certainty by Norfolk's chief magistrate, Sergeant Frere, who told the county sessions that the fires and riots of 1830 were started by strangers first seen at Briston 'with caps of sheepskin on their heads and slops upon their bodies'?[26]

Foreigners, respectable strangers, and political activists vanished into the thin air whence they came, but there was one group of individuals of more substance. Tramps and vagrants travelled the country lanes in sizeable numbers, especially in 1844 when unemployment was a serious problem in East Anglia. Their presence was noted by rich and poor alike and both were equally suspicious of them. It was not therefore surprising to find local communities or individual farm labourers using these men as scapegoats when a fire broke out. It was a usual and effective way for labourers and others to relieve themselves of suspicion. Horatio Balding of Brandon was suspected of starting a fire at Brandon in 1845 but he successfully persuaded his accusers that 'three strangers of shabby appearance' were more feasible suspects. After a fire at Polstead in January 1843 the police went after a tramp who had supposedly passed through the village just before the fire broke out. In another case a farm servant went to a stack to gather kindling, when 'a man suddenly started from the stack and made off by a short cut'. Nine-year-old John Berry was less fortunate. On his arrest for a fire at Debenham he stated that he had seen a stranger, but his story was not believed and he was found guilty.[27] A stranger's very presence in the vicinity of a fire made him an immediate suspect. Farmers and police, at a loss to understand the motives and identity of incendiaries, quickly turned to the first available suspicious person, especially those who were penniless, homeless, and unemployed. It was believed that such people lived by begging and thieving. Very often considerable pressure was placed on such individuals. In one case a suspect was arrested and taken in for questioning after a fire at Ipswich. The authorities could neither extract a confession nor provide enough evidence against him, but all was not lost. He was thrown into gaol as a vagrant in the hope that further evidence could be gained from his own mouth or from others.[28] A former solicitor's clerk from Chester was arrested in 1844

26 *NM*, 4 and 11 Dec. 1830; *NC*, 22 Jan. 1831.
27 *NC*, 30 Sept. 1854; *NM*, 5 Apr. 1845.
28 PRO, HO 52/3, letter from A. H. Steward, 16 Apr. 1822.

while looking for a job in East Anglia — he was later released. At Dereham in 1851 a begging woman was fortunate to be released after being arrested for a fire at an inn where she had been refused water. She was seen by a burning stable, making the evidently satisfied comment, 'they'll want plenty of water now'.[29]

Tramps and vagrants were not the only 'outsiders' in East Anglia to bring suspicion on themselves. The railway navvies were there in large numbers, 1,200 alone were building the Norwich-Cambridge line, whilst those building the Norwich-Yarmouth line put fear and apprehension into the minds of the local respectable inhabitants. A. J. Peacock believes they were probably responsible for more than a little of the unsolved crime in the Eastern Counties.[30] The navvies' presence would have had an adverse effect on the crime rate in the locality where they were working; violent drinking bouts, poaching, and stealing were just three examples of their criminal life-style. Did they, as Peacock believes they might have, become incendiaries too? Five were in fact arrested on suspicion of starting a fire but were later set free. No evidence suggests that they were in any way involved.[31]

The vagrant-tramp theory was strongly maintained by people in high positions; even the Home Secretary, Sir James Graham, adhered to it as late as June 1844 when there had already been the Lent assizes in Norfolk and Suffolk which had shown evidence to the contrary. 'Many of these fires', Graham told the House of Commons, 'were the act of one and the same incendiary probably perambulating the district in question.'[32] The Home Secretary was accused by fellow MPs and journalists of being completely ignorant of the true state of rural England. It is questionable whether anyone was really aware of the situation but Graham clearly indicated that he was less aware than most. When one considers the small fact of over 600 fires breaking out in England in 1843 and 1844, this 'perambulating' incendiary was clearly an energetic figure of notable physical fitness. Graham could have given his argument greater credibility had he mentioned Leech Borley, one of Suffolk's extraordinary fire-raisers. Leech's claim to fame, poaching, incendiarism, and animal maiming apart, for he indulged in all three, lay in his renowned running ability. After his arrest, the Suffolk police's oversight in forgetting to remove his

---

29 *NC*, 19 July 1851.
30 Peacock, 'Village Radicalism', p. 34.
31 Springall, *Labouring Life*, p. 32. She thought navvies were responsible for many of the fires but supplied no evidence to substantiate this assertion.
32 *Hansard*, 12 June 1844, p. 586. For further evidence on tramps see D. J. V. Jones and A. Bainbridge, *Crime in Nineteenth-Century Wales*, SSRC Report (1975), pp. 304-46.

specially made running shoes had amazing consequences. On being found guilty and sentenced to Van Diemen's Land, Leech jumped out of the dock and ran from the courtroom into Bury market-place, never to be seen again.[33] But to return to Graham's point that vagrants were responsible for many of the fires: there was a modicum of truth in his statement as eleven tramps were convicted for incendiarism in the region between 1815 and 1870.

THE REALITY

If we leave aside the various theories and myths and turn now to an investigation of those people actually convicted of incendiary offences, a very different picture of the incendiary's identity emerges. A total of 649 persons were committed to trial at the assizes and sessions, of whom 307 were found guilty. The overall conviction rate was 47 per cent which compared favourably with the national conviction rate of 28 per cent between 1831 and 1843.[34] Of the 307 found guilty, 230 had their ages reported (75 per cent) and 240 had some kind of occupational description attributed to them (78 per cent). Of the defendants found not guilty, one of them was in fact guilty. By some loophole in the law Frederick Borley was acquitted of firing an outhouse which did not come under the terms of the act under which he was charged, but Borley was subsequently found guilty for another fire.[35] Also on more than one occasion defendants were acquitted because the fires which they had kindled were deemed to have been probable accidents.[36]

In all but twenty-six cases the convicted were men. A large proportion of the convicted women were young domestic servants. The list of occupations of the incendiaries, given in Table 7.4, reads like a typical cross-section of an agrarian community, except that people from the upper end of the social scale were under-represented. When the individual occupations are grouped under generic descriptive headings we find that 83 per cent were from the labouring and pauper classes. Craftsmen returned 8 per cent, servants 6 per cent, and the middle class just 3 per cent.

---

33 *BNP*, 10 Apr. 1844; *NC*, 13 Apr. 1844.
34 *Annual Register* (1844), 479; 28 per cent of those tried for incendiary offences in England and Wales in 1831-43 were found guilty.
35 The law was changed in Dec. 1844. to include all types of buildings.
36 e.g. Clowe who was apparently so drunk that he fell asleep with a lighted pipe in his mouth.

TABLE 7.4 *Occupations of persons found guilty of incendiary offences in Norfolk and Suffolk, 1815-1870*

Occupation/status	No. found guilty	Occupation/status	No. found guilty
Agricultural labourers	152	Cooper	1
Domestic servants	12	Coprolite labourer	1
Paupers	11	Factory worker	1
Vagrants	11	Farmer	1
Blacksmiths	6	Farmer's son	1
Boatmen	6	Lighthouse-keeper	1
Brickmakers' labourers and bricklayers	5	Marine store dealer	1
		Miller	1
		Pensioner	1
Shoemakers	4	Postman	1
Unemployed (not specified)	4	Sailor	1
		Schoolboy	1
Carpenters	2	Shepherd	1
Grooms	2	Snuff box maker	1
Hawkers	2	Sweep	1
Shopkeepers	2	Thatcher's Labourer	1
Baker	1	Weaver	1
Cabinet maker	1	Wheelwright	1
Confectioner	1		

Sources: As for Table 7.1; PP 1844, HL 258, *Return of Ages and Descriptions of Persons Committed for Trial for Incendiary Offences in Norfolk and Suffolk, 1844.*

The ages of the convicted appear in Table 7.5. The average age of labourers convicted of incendiarism, 22, was significantly lower than the convicted Swing rioters who were in their late twenties. In fact the age group lying between 9 and 28 years accounted for 78 per cent of those convicted, and those aged between 17 and 21 accounted for 30 per cent. Many of the latter age group were farm labourers. Surprisingly few contemporaries made the connection between the young and incendiarism. One of the few to do so argued in a letter to the *Suffolk Chronicle* that the fires were started by, 'a particular class of farm labourer ... not the old hands, good workers or family men, but single men'.[37]

---

37 *SC*, 13 Apr. 1822.

TABLE 7.5 *Ages of convicted incendiaries in Norfolk and Suffolk, 1815-1870*

Age	No. convicted	Age	No. convicted
under 16*	4	33	2
9	4	34	5
10	6	35	2
11	5	36	1
12	10	37	1
13	9	38	2
14	9	39	1
15	10	40	3
16	10	41	3
17	9	42	1
18	22	43	1
19	12	44	2
20	8	45	4
21	18	46	2
22	7	47	2
23	6	48	1
24	5	51	1
25	7	53	1
26	8	54	1
27	8	56	1
28	6	61	1
29	3	62	1
30	3	70	1
31	4	78	1
32	2	81	1
TOTAL			236

* No other information available on these 4.
Sources: As for Table 7.4.

One theory which gained popular credence among farmers was that fires were mainly the work of children under the age of 14. The figures in Table 7.5 indicate that forty-three children were responsible for a number of fires. It is very likely that most child incendiaries were caught because they were unlikely to make elaborate attempts to hide incriminating evidence but, more importantly, greater pressure could be brought to bear on them by the investigators. Children were often the first suspects, especially crow-scarers in the vicinity of daylight stack fires. The farmer's own children were questioned closely if the fire took place within the farmyard during the hours of daylight. Youngsters were, without a doubt, the easiest to catch and convict. In one case, that of William Wayley (Waley), the prosecution evidence was shown to be fabricated. The judge ordered the case to be stopped when it became apparent to the court that the main witness, a 12-year-old boy, had been offered inducements by Mrs Clarke, wife of the farmer whose outhouse was burnt down.[38] One wonders how many others were not so fortunate as Wayley, especially in the years 1843-4 when the sheer volume of fires built up its own momentum of fear. This in turn would have added momentum to the prosecutors' determination to find the guilty parties. This fact should be remembered when looking at the period 1815-70 as a whole, as children were responsible for most of the accidental fires through incautious play with matches.[39] It is conceivable that children were not given the benefit of the doubt when propertied opinion demanded that persons should not only be caught but be seen to be convicted. Incriminating and circumstantial evidence, such as a box of matches on a 10-year-old boy, took on a new meaning during years of widespread incendiarism. Closely related to this pressure to convict was the pressure on the judges to give harsher sentences. Fourteen-year-old David Jackson found himself in Van Diemen's Land for 15 years in 1844, whereas in 1858 13-year-old John Brand received the fairly mild sentence of three years in a reformatory school and two months in gaol. Brothers James and Stephen Newton, aged 11 and 13 respectively, were sentenced to just seven days with hard labour in 1854.[40] A severe reprimand became standard punishment for the very young who, because of the 'doli capax' principle, were thought incapable of discerning between right and wrong. After 1844 there appeared a general reluctance to prosecute children for incendiary offences. Many reports after that date name children as the perpetrators but they fail to specify whether the fires were of an incendiary type or not. Despite this reluctance, after 1850 when there were fewer fires than in the first thirty-five years of the period, the number of children aged 16 and under convicted for incendiary offences more than doubled. This observation suggests the crime of incendiarism was increasingly becoming a peripheral weapon in the

---

38 *NM*, 13 Apr. 1844.
39 For examples of children causing accidental fires see *BNP*, 24 Jan. 1844, 15 Mar. 1859, 17 Dec. 1861; *NN*, 27 Apr. 1861.
40 *MC*, 5 July 1844; *NC*, 27 Mar. 1858, 4 Mar. 1854.

class war in the post-1850 period.[41]

Why children should turn to incendiarism is not made clear in the available source material. The prevailing motivation of the young incendiary, according to the press, was hooliganism and a vague ill will held by children towards others, that is nowhere defined. To assign a crime to vandalism or hooliganism does not really help the historian. A few cases illustrate the more readily defined reasons for the children's actions, some of which seem to have been devoid of any ill feelings or personal malignity on the part of the child. David Jackson (Jackaman) is just such a case. He confessed to firing a barn at Redlingfield and the police version of his confession given to the *Morning Chronicle* reported: 'He had heard of the great fires in other parts, and had heard people tell of how wonderful large they were. He had never seen a large fire, and thought he would like to see one; so he set fire to Mr Cracknell's farmyard.'[42] Campbell Foster also made the same point, that the power and spirit of imitation was sufficient motive for a child:

> The labourer, half-hungered, will rather rejoice that a farmer had come to trouble, as well as himself, by having his stacks burnt, than express sorrow for it. If he talks of it in his cottage in the presence of his children, he will not condemn the act, and a child may be prompted to set fire to a stack from a love of mischief combined with a notion that it is a 'good job', because all the conversation he has heard has led to that conclusion.[43]

National news too may have had some bearing on children's behaviour. There are two examples, from either end of the period, which show the power and influence of news on the minds of the young. The first is unusual in so far as the boy, 10-year-old Wright, was acquitted. However his actions and the grudge war which developed from his actions led, it would seem, to a more spectacular conflagration. Young Wright, in line with customary practice, lit a fire to celebrate the news of the popular Queen Caroline's acquittal. His employer, Benjamin Barnard of Besthorpe (N), attempted to prosecute him but failed. Undeterred, Barnard fined the lad 6s. for the damage but within days a large stack close to Wright's cottage was completely destroyed. In the second case 13-year-old Webb was arrested for a fire at Ditchingham (N). When asked by the police why he had done it, he replied that he had read about Fenianism, adding

---

41 See pp. 176-7.
42 *MC*, 5 July 1844.
43 *The Times*, 14 June 1844.

'he thought he should like to be a Fenian'.[44]

Consideration has to be given to family rows and parental discipline which sparked off headstrong anger in children and led them to seek revenge. Frederick Cutting was very aggrieved when his father threw him out of the house after an argument. The younger Cutting retaliated by burning down a shed. William Riseborough failed to get his own way when he was refused permission to go to church, and the farmer suffered for ignoring what was, by Victorian standards, a laudable request.

An even more difficult child was 12-year-old Charles Bartrum who burnt down his mother's farm and a neighbour's too. Bartrum was released on account of his poor mental health. The above examples could be categorized under what Peacock has termed 'personal pique'. Personal pique and social grievance are very difficult to define or determine in the case of children who are more irresponsible than adults. It may well be the case that modern psychiatric studies can provide historians with greater insights.[45] One complicating factor which needs to be borne in mind is that children during this period were employed as full-time workers from a very early age. Although they were unlikely to have disputes with farmers over wages or terms of employment, the young still had work-related grievances which they felt compelled to avenge. Brothers Thomas (17) and James Cook (11) registered a protest against their employer because James had been harshly beaten for failing to look after the pigs. Henry Stolliday (14) clearly believed that he had been unfairly made to work on his day off.[46] The farmers of East Anglia were charged by the national and provincial press for being hard task-masters, especially for their grinding practices over young labourers, over whom they had unlimited power. Beatings and whippings for shoddy work were not infrequent. Farmer Viall was, perhaps, the most infamous farmer of the period. It was believed at the time that he had beaten one of his young hands to death. However, at the coroner's inquest Viall was exonerated from all blame for the boy's death. One person felt there had been a travesty of justice as Viall's farm was fired shortly afterwards.[47]

---

44 *NM*, 31 Mar. 1821; *NN*, 18 Apr. 1868.
45 G. H. O'Sullivan and M. J. Kelleher, 'A Study of Firesetters in the South-West of Ireland', *British Journal of Psychiatry*, 151 (1987), 818-23. My thanks to Prof. A. Cox of Univ. of Liverpool for providing me with this information.
46 In the order in which they appear, *BNP*, 21 Oct. 1846, 5 Aug. 1846; *NC*, 18 Sept. 1852; *BNP*, 2 Apr. 1845; *NC*, 29 July 1854.
47 *MC*, 29 July 1844; *BNP*, 3 Jan. 1844; Jones, *Crime, Protest*, p. 41.

Equally difficult to ascertain were the motives of convicted domestic servants who, like the young labourers, not only worked from an early age but were also exposed to the whims of their masters and mistresses. Their youthfulness and inexperience was perhaps more pronounced in East Anglia than anywhere else as the region had a reputation for training up young country girls before sending them up to London. In their early teens they were placed in a farmhouse within the county and once they were proficient the local vicar or squire would find them work in the capital. One of the overriding worries for a newly appointed domestic servant was personal anxiety in the form of homesickness. Away from home for the first time, among new people and in a new village, young girls sometimes went to extraordinary lengths to get themselves sacked.[48] This was usually achieved through shoddy and slow work and general disobedience. But in the case of 15-year-old Ellen Barley it may have become a declared war with her master. Unhappy since she arrived at her new master's house in Thorndon, Ellen was soon voicing her desire to return home to her mother. Her pleas went unanswered and in the space of three months three mysterious fires broke out on the premises. After the third fire a threatening letter was found which, in a circumstantial way, implied that the servant was the guilty party. An extract from the letter read: 'J.P. [John Piper, the master] you shall have another fire if you keep that maid, you shan't have no test while you live at Thorndon if you keep her, for I have threatened this ever ... and catch me if you can.'[49] There was not enough proof to implicate the servant with either the fires or the letter and she was acquitted, but it seems likely that she was involved in some way. Fourteen-year-old Mary Ann Rylett held an equally determined resolution to leave her master at Wormegay (N). 'I did it', she confessed, 'because I did not like the place, and my mother would not let me leave; and so I thought I would burn down the houses.' She had started at least three fires in the village.

Some fires, though, were the result neither of feelings brought about by homesickness nor domestic accidents in which suspicion inevitably fell on servants. Tensions did arise between master and maid over employment, as in the case of teenager Alice Smith who virtually destroyed her master's entire farmyard after an argument with her mistress. The sentiments expressed by another teenager, Hannah Brown, 'that she would as soon be in prison as in service', were

---

48 P. Horn, *The Rise and Fall of the Victorian Servant* (Dublin, 1975), pp. 138-41.
49 *BNP*, 3 Feb. and 31 Mar. 1847.

probably not untypical. She fired her mistress's bedroom after a row and the court duly obliged with a sentence of six months with hard labour.[50] Other women, like Eliza Ward, resorted to arson only after they had been sacked. In this case she received fifteen years transportation for firing her master's outhouse.[51]

Female domestic incendiaries, who tended to fire houses, faced the full might of the English judicial system, more so than male arsonists, especially after 1837 when legal reform dropped capital punishment for most types of incendiarism. Anyone caught and convicted of starting a fire in a dwelling place after this date remained liable to the death penalty, although it was never used. Two servants, Mary Chesnutt and Ann Howard, were sentenced to death before the reform of the law. In the case of Chesnutt, she had been at her new employers for only eleven weeks. Fourteen-year-old Sarah Green was more fortunate as she was acquitted after her employer's furniture and home burst into flames at Flegg Burgh (N). But her troubles did not end there, for Sarah appears to have suffered from that unusual syndrome of spontaneous human combustion. Shortly after her arrest she had the rather alarming experience of bursting into flames herself.[52]

The 'middling classes', farmers, smallholders, and shopkeepers, were not wholly free from guilt when it came to incendiarism. The fires they kindled had little to do with oppression or 'exhausted desperation'. The first point of interest worth noting was that a farmer/lighthouse-keeper and his son were given unconditional discharges despite having been found guilty. Young children excepted, only in one other case, that of a farmer also, was the guilty incendiary given an unconditional discharge. This was perhaps indicative of nineteenth-century justice. Property ownership was considered a sure sign of respectability and responsibility and judges tended to view the actions of incendiary farmers as temporary aberrations of nature. In both cases the convicted parties had attempted to defraud insurance companies. There was money in incendiarism for the middle class. John Knowles, senior, the aforementioned lighthouse-keeper at Happisburgh, had hoped to claim £65 off the Norwich Union for a ramshackle old barn which he burnt down with his son's help.[53] Farmer Walter Symonds of Withersfield had intended to swindle the

---

50 *NC*, 4 Aug. 1860.
51 *BNP*, 13 Dec. 1848; *NN*, 25 July 1846.
52 *NM*, 23 Feb. and 29 Mar. 1828; *NC*, 7 Aug. 1819; *NM*, 1 Apr. 1820.
53 NUFO, board mins., 9 Oct. 1843.

same company out of £400.[54] There is evidence of only two other successful convictions of attempted defraudment; they were the cases of a young jeweller-tobacconist named Jarvis at Yarmouth in 1853 and a miller named Kett.[55] There were several other cases in which defendants were found not guilty, even though the evidence looks quite as strong as that which convicted labourers and paupers. The case of George Turner and Eliza Smith is one such example. Turner, a young journeyman shoemaker, had claimed that Eliza Smith wanted to buy some property which she believed might have been more attainable if it was reduced to a burnt-out shell. She, so Turner claimed, gave him gin and promised money for firing the building.[56] Both were found not guilty. Two other farmers, Gates of Hilgay (N) in 1850 and Thomas Storey of Outwell (N), were also acquitted; in the latter case the court decision was met with rapturous applause from farmers in the public gallery. Storey had taken out an insurance policy a week before the fire.

One is accustomed to reading about the protests of labourers over common land disputes. During this period there were only three examples of a common land dispute which sparked off incendiary fires. In one case the disputing parties were both farmers at Belaugh (N). The common in the village had recently been taken in and farmer Taylor had been allotted more land than many thought fair. The Filby family continued to graze their animals on the land given over to Taylor, and the dispute finally reached a climax when Taylor impounded some of Filby's animals. Filby received fifteen years transportation for firing a wheat stack.[57]

At the other end of the social scale, the paupers, the wandering poor, and the unemployed received little sympathy from the courts. It was commonly believed that vagrants were responsible for many fires and this belief had some basis in fact. The twenty-nine paupers and tramps convicted of incendiary offences represented the second largest descriptive group of incendiaries. However, many of them were in fact local people and their grievances could be related to local social and economic conditions. Very few came from outside the region; the cases of Smith from Kent, a former surveyor from Calcutta, and the Lancastrian Mason were exceptional.[58] Starvation

---

54 *BNP*, 8 Aug. 1849; *NM*, 11 Aug. 1849.
55 *NC*, 19 Mar. 1853; *BNP*, 29 Mar. 1864.
56 *BNP*, 28 Mar. 1849.
57 *NM*, 31 May and 26 July 1845.
58 Smith, *BNP*, 27 Mar. 1866; King, *BNP*, 6 Sept. 1854 and 28 Mar. 1855; Mason, *BNP*, 16 July and 6 Aug. 1861.

and unemployment turned the beggar into an incendiary. Pathetic statements such as that made by Fiddes, 'I done it through despair, melancholy despair', were not infrequently made to police and courts.[59] Many beggars were found standing by burning stacks waiting for the police to arrive. One man, named Timothy Birch, spent an evening in a pub talking to a newly returned ticket-of-leave man, who favourably described the climate, the food, and life in the Antipodes. At closing time Birch, rather the worse for drink, wandered out into the night and started eight separate fires in three villages.[60] Other examples included William Woollard whose request for food was refused by Jannings of Beyton (S), whereupon he became aggressive and threatened to burn down the farm.[61] Woollard was arrested before he could carry out his threat, but in many cases the threats were made and the promises kept. Lewis and Martin, who had only been out of gaol one day, were turned away from Sir Augustus Henniker's residence at Plashwoods where they had gone to beg for food. They retaliated by firing a shed and made off to London where they were finally caught.[62] Some of these cases bring to mind Abbiateci's research on eighteenth-century arson in France where, it appears, 'arson was one of the violent forms of begging'.[63] Cut off from regular employment, shelter, and food the beggars' livelihoods depended on receiving doles from villagers and farmers. To ensure success, in France anyway, they resorted to fire-raising so as to give their threats an added meaning if their requests were met with refusals. As we have seen, blackmail by fire was a feature of nineteenth-century East Anglia.

An important relationship between pauperism and incendiarism was particularly evident in the two counties between 1854 and 1870 when the majority of paupers and tramps were convicted. When this evidence is taken with the similar trend discernible among children — the two groups account for 40 per cent of all convicted incendiaries — it is possible to state with certainty that incendiarism as a crime of protest was radically different in the second half of the period. The crime was becoming a weapon of those who were not directly receiving any of the benefits accruing from the improvements in

---

59 NN, 27 Mar. 1852.
60 Birch, alias Bowles, NN, 3 Aug. 1850.
61 BNP, 14 Jan. 1846.
62 BNP, 7 Jan. and 25 Mar. 1846.
63 A. Abbiateci, 'Arsonists in Eighteenth-Century France: An Essay in the Typology of Crime', in R. Forster and O. Ranum, eds., *Deviants and the Abandoned in French Society: Selections from the Annales*, iv (Baltimore, 1978), p. 166.

wages and employment. Incendiarism, which had been between 1815 and 1851 an accurate gauge of social relations between farmers and labourers, had become a somewhat peripheral indicator of poor social relations within the village community by this later period.

The unemployed, of whom there were over fifty convicted of arson, took their ire out on those unfortunate enough to refuse their requests for work. The most defiant and bitter of all the incendiaries was Robert Dew who had searched unsuccessfully for work. Dew, speaking of his victim, was reported to have said: 'There's old Gapp might employ five or six more on his farm but the old scoundrel has suffered for it, for he has had two fires.' He then added unrepentantly: 'It was the most beautifulest blaze I ever saw. I shall never forget it the longest day that I shall ever draw.' Dew had positively revelled in Gapp's misfortune because on the day after the fire he had gone along to Gapp's farm and jeeringly asked for employment.[64] The want of employment was the commonest motivation for unemployed incendiaries, the more so if there had been a direct confrontation between the unemployed man and the prospective employer. The convicted incendiaries were usually emphatic on this point, Bowles said: 'I should not have done it if they had employed me.' Nathaniel Reader, a blacksmith on tramp, had gone around Feltwell in a vain search for work; he was definitely guilty of starting one fire but was suspected of at least two others.[65] The unemployed were the most desperate and had the least to lose. Benjamin Hart, a name that continually cropped up during this period, said that he had fired a stack at Larlingford in 1852 because 'he had no victuals, no work, no money', and that 'he might be apprehended as he should be better off', a not uncommon sentiment expressed by quite a few unemployed incendiaries. One transportation and four years later, Hart explained after his third fire: 'he had no money nor food and had been out of work for two months.'[66] Many of the confessions of the unemployed men and boys contained pathetic statements: 'I had no food', or 'I wanted a home'. Eleven-year-old George Garrett brought groans of sympathy from the packed public gallery when he explained that he was a homeless orphan and had never owned a pair of shoes in his life.[67] Some of these men had chosen to survive through begging and stealing rather than enter the workhouse. Even then one

64 *BNP*, 2 Apr. 1845. For an example of another man in a similar plight see *SC*, 10, 17, and 31 Aug. 1816.
65 *NC*, 31 July 1852; *NM*, 20 Oct. 1849.
66 *NC*, 8 Nov. 1858.
67 Jones, 'Thomas Campbell Foster', p. 32 n. 123.

could not be certain of relief as John Kerridge found to his misfortune. He applied to enter the workhouse but the relieving officer refused his request. Kerridge felt he had no other options open to him, and so he fired some stacks at Harling. 'I did it that I might be sent away and then I shall have a piece of bread as long as I live.'[68] To men like Coe who 'was glad to do something to get fed', Corder who reckoned he 'could not be worse off', and Kerridge, transportation or penal servitude held no fear, in fact it was a merciful release.[69]

Those who did get an order to enter the 'house' appear to have felt little better off than Kerridge. Several workhouses, Nacton, Shipmeadow, Rollesby, and Smallburgh to name but a few, were fired by unhappy inmates, who believed a transfer to the county gaol was preferable to living in a workhouse. There is little evidence, apart from the threatening letters, to suggest that hatred of the workhouse and the guardians were the overriding factors in motivating country people to start fires. Union houses were burnt, poor law guardians' property was also fired, but in the latter cases very few incendiaries were caught. One can only surmise that, given the high unemployment and underemployment during this period, there was a great deal of hatred towards the 'house' and its administrators. There was obviously a connection between the choice of target and the poverty-stricken condition of Watling in 1849. He had been a long-standing inmate of Smallburgh house, and on his release the first thing he did was to fire the vice-chairman's property. The case of an unemployed wheelwright named Everson was very similar. While he had been staying in the Eye house, a guardian named Nicholls had wandered around the wards haranguing the inmates for their laziness. Everson took great exception to this and fired Nicholls's property.[70] Cattermole likewise found the poor law regime less than satisfactory. He was sent to the parish farm to pick stones, receiving a pittance in wages. He was convicted and hanged for firing the stack of a local overseer.[71] Two other victims of this uncaring and unsympathetic Victorian institution were 78-year-old James Shickles and Malton. Ordered into the workhouse by Allison, the overseer, Shickles requested a lift but was told to walk; consequently he fired Allison's stacks. In the case of Malton, whose application to enter the house was refused, he began by smashing the relieving officer's windows for which he received two

---

68 *NC*, 25 Mar. 1854.
69 *NN*, 8 July 1865; *BNP*, 10 Mar. 1857.
70 *BNP*, 16 May and 1 Aug. 1849, 14 Aug. 1850.
71 *BNP*, 15 and 29 Apr. 1829.

months, and on his release started a fire.[72]

One of the most interesting incendiaries was 30-year-old James Lankester, variously described as vagrant, matchmaker, song-sheet seller, and seller of small trifles. Much detailed evidence has survived concerning Lankester due to the nature of the man and his stated motivation. It seems that, when Lankester had nothing to sell, he along with others tramped around Suffolk exploiting the rural distrust of machinery. He claimed he was a victim of technology, forced out of work by the use of threshing machines. This story brought him food, money, and clothes from sympathizers. Lankester had a sincere hatred for machinery, and this hatred expressed itself in a peculiarly individualized form of philosophy which he expounded to other inmates of a gaol. Lankester's doctrine was conveniently overheard by the overseer who was feigning sleep at the time. The report from the *Morning Chronicle* takes up the story:

> Lankester had not only been able to trace the misery of the present times to the introduction of machinery, he was convinced, and tried to convince others, that cheap corn was the greatest of curses to English labourers. He knew of no means, he said, of raising the wages of labourers, but by raising the price of corn, he knew of no way of raising the price of corn but by making it scarce so readily as to burn the stack yards. He was therefore in favour of burning stacks, though greatly opposed to those who set fire to barns and houses ...[73]

There is no evidence to suggest that other incendiaries were of Lankester's ilk.

Craftsmen were, through their education and independence, the village radicals. They were the leading figures in the Working Men's Associations in rural Suffolk, and one shoemaker named Mills was deeply involved in the anti-poor law demonstrations of 1835 in the Stradbroke area. In only three cases could convicted craftsmen be considered the tribunes of the rural labourers. These were Knockolds the weaver of whom we have already heard, Edmund Botwright, a young blacksmith convicted of incendiarism, animal maiming, and sending a threatening letter, and Robert Grimwade a linen draper, convicted for sending a threatening letter.[74] Of the remaining craftsmen only a little is known: a tailor convicted for two fires in 1856 was insane; a wheelwright was unemployed and in the workhouse; and

---

72 *BNP*, 28 Mar. 1865; *BNP*, 12 Mar. and 29 Oct. 1861.
73 *MC*, 30 July 1844.
74 The letter appears on p. 124.

a cooper had attempted, with his father, to defraud the insurance company.

The majority of known incendiaries were labouring men, usually in farm-related occupations. If we break down the figures of farm labourers, it can be seen that in 44 per cent of the cases the incendiary was working for, or had worked for, the owner of the property where a fire had broken out. Therefore, in almost half the cases the incendiary and the victim knew each other in an employer-employee relationship. The percentage would undoubtedly be higher had more information been available. This may suggest to some that personal and private grievances may have been contributory factors in the ill will between the two parties. The evidence, however, shows that grievances, as well as being personal, were closely related to poor class relations. We have seen that unemployment kindled malevolent feelings within the unemployed incendiary. Farm labourers Robert Dew, Dye, and Medlar referred to lack of employment in 1844 after their arrests. Medlar said his victim 'neither gave him work, nor suffered others to do so'.[75] Whilst unemployment was obviously an important causative factor, a more constant feature of daily life which angered labourers was the manner in which they were treated by their employers. Some farmers were 'personally obnoxious', to borrow the Norwich Union's phrase, especially those on the smaller heavy clayland farms. Parallels were drawn between labourers and slaves; labourers suffered loss of independence, were open to the caprice of employers, were resigned to the docking of pay for poor work or wet weather, and in one case received no wages at all, but instead payment in kind. This caused the *Morning Chronicle* to wonder aloud: 'There are some among the farmers ... who really seem to invite the incendiary to visit their homesteads.'[76] One farmer knocked half a day's wage off a labourer's pay-packet because he turned up late for work after having spent the whole night extinguishing an incendiary fire on a neighbouring farm.

The more enlightened landowners and farmers, despite vociferous opposition, stated what they felt to be the true causes for all the incendiary fires. The chairman of Ipswich Quarter Sessions, Sir Augustus Henniker, told the county JPs that: 'permanent tranquillity was to be obtained by securing to the labourer constant employment, together with the payment of more liberal wages.'[77] These sentiments

75 *BNP*, 24 Dec. 1844.
76 *MC*, 23 Mar. 1844.
77 *The Times*, 22 Mar. 1844.

were also echoed by F. W. Keppell of Lexham Hall, and both men were accused of fanning the flames of discontent.

Unemployment was an issue which made the labourers extremely bitter, especially the young labourers who in the mid-1840s congregated on the village greens during the day and dispersed into the game preserves at night. One threatening letter specifically singled out the lack of opportunity for young men: 'Mr Goose, if you will imploy that out town man i will warm you for I think thear are single men anow in the town if i see him in Norwich with your horses i will birn your primises down stick and stone in a short time then thear will be plenty of work.'[78]

Unfair dismissal or a recent sacking brought immediate suspicion on to a labourer. Many were taken to court but most were able to escape conviction. Wage disputes in the years of low wheat prices were the main causes of friction where convicted incendiaries were involved. Incendiary fires were often timely reminders to farmers to raise wages. The day after pay-day Phillip Hammond burnt his master's farm down, causing £1,400 damage, because his pay had been reduced.[79] There were at least six disputes of a similar nature in 1844. Gill, who was in regular work as a ploughman, only received 6s. a week and had asked for an 'alteration'. The best documented case was that of Samuel Jacob, a shepherd of fifteen years' standing with farmer Boby of Columbine Hall (S). Even the local press was somewhat taken aback at the paucity of Jacob's weekly wage of 6s. a week. At harvest time he received 12-13s. a week, a free dinner on Sundays, and 10s. a week and seven pints a day at lambing time. Jacob had asked for a wage rise but Boby had refused. Boby had two fires, causing damage amounting to £550. The day after Jacob's arrest a further attempt was made to damage Boby's property.[80]

Many of the fires were the outcome of either poor working relations between employer and employee or else their complete breakdown. In both instances they tended to highlight individual tensions. These tensions were, however, common to many in East Anglia. Some incendiaries consciously or unconsciously made wider social criticisms which, at first sight, appear as products of personal pique. John Double was in gainful employment as a nightwatchman and had no known disagreements with his employer. He was found guilty of firing one farm and suspected of starting two other fires on

---

78 *NC*, 29 Nov. 1845, sent by James King.
79 *BNP*, 10 Apr. 1844; *The Times*, 7 June 1844.
80 *MC*, 19 July 1844; *BNP*, 31 July 1844.

neighbouring farms at Capel and Wenham. All three fires were enormous, the damage amounted to nearly £5,000. According to the *Morning Chronicle* Double had very definite ends in mind when he fired the farms. He was attempting to create a situation of fear and panic in farmers who he believed would then employ more labourers as moderately well paid nightwatchmen. The high unemployment and low wages were the crux of Double's reasoning.[81] There was one other incendiary in the early 1850s who regarded incendiarism as a means for creating better and fuller employment.

Many of those innocently charged and many of those convicted of incendiary offences were described as 'bad characters', which often meant they had criminal records. Clow, Botwright, the Head brothers, Snell, Frost, and Stow were all well-known poachers, while Payne, Borley, Williams, Barton, Catchpole, Cattermole, and Micklefield were thieves of some description. Hart had a record as an incendiary and Leech Borley a record for thieving and animal maiming. Some of these men mixed their 'normal' criminal activities with incendiarism, for instance Snell and Frost were stealing pheasant eggs the night they fired a stack. The crime of incendiarism was not, therefore, divorced from other rural criminal activities. This may strengthen the thesis that a large proportion of the fires were motivated through social criticisms rather than personal pique, since the crimes — poaching, maiming, and even thieving — were also crimes of social protest.

Incendiarism differed from many other crimes in that it did not provide direct economic gain for the criminal involved. Two men, John Williams and Frederick Borley, both 'notorious characters', came close to making incendiarism an economically viable crime. Williams, more so than Borley, possessed a great deal of native wit and legal knowledge (he had twenty-three previous convictions) which enabled him to escape conviction in the case of at least two fires. Borley was less fortunate; he escaped conviction in one case but was found guilty, thanks to Williams, in a second trial. Their plan was novel and not without risks, but it very nearly worked and is worth recounting to show that incendiarism could be a crime, not of personal malice nor social grievance, but of economic gain. The *Morning Chronicle* quoted a large part of Borley's confession in which he claimed Williams said:

> Now, Borley you know young Gurt, and can get him to do anything. You get him in a line to set fire to Mr. Canler's premises. Go with him, and let him do it. There will be a large reward offered. I will be in such a way to have seen you and Gurt near

---

81 *MC*, 19 July 1844. See also *BNP*, 29 Mar. 1854, for the trial of William Moore.

Abbot's Hall. I will suspect Gurt, and give information. You will
turn evidence against him; and, not being the actual perpetrator,
you will be admitted witness.[82]

Borley and Gurt, the latter a simpleton who was to be framed, went
to Canler's hopshed, but to Borley's dismay he heard a courting couple
in it and the plan had to be shelved. A week later the same shed was
fired successfully. Williams led the fire-fighting work, for which he
received beer, money, and clothes. A £50 reward was offered and the
next stage of the plan, to claim the reward, went into action. It was
ironical that the law which usually offered so little protection to
labourers came to Gurt's and Borley's rescue. They were both
acquitted on a legal technicality. A hopshed was not a building that
came within the meaning of the statute on which they had been
charged. No reward was collected as no incendiary fire had taken
place. After the trial a second fire broke out at Canler's, causing even
greater damage. On this occasion Borley and Williams used an
accomplice named Durrant, who was also of limited intelligence.
Borley made the mistake of firing the stack himself and was found
guilty and transported for life. Durrant was acquitted and Williams
turned Queen's evidence and was also freed.

Although the evidence is far from conclusive, the incendiary may
have been following a tradition of machine breaking but used very
different methods from the ones employed in 1816, 1822, and 1830.
Threatening letters complained of the continued use of machines and
many incendiary fires destroyed them. But in only one case was an
incendiary convicted of trying to fire one. He was 25-year-old Joseph
Bassett of Rockland St Peter. He said after his arrest: 'I set fire to the
stack but not to injure Mr. Colman [the owner of the stack] but to
burn Smith's machine.'[83]

Finally, there was one small group of incendiaries whose
motivation had no rational explanations. Simple-mindedness and
insanity are commonly associated with rural areas, due among other
things to inter-breeding, and it was therefore not surprising to find
insane or feeble-minded incendiaries amongst the suspects. Nowadays
arsonists automatically receive psychiatric examination because the
medical profession argues that there is a strong correlation between
starting fires and mental disorder. As Abbiateci has stated, 'modern

82 *MC*, 2 July 1844. We know Borley started the second fire because a young boy happened
    to be sitting in a tree overlooking Canler's property and he watched the whole
    proceedings.
83 *NC*, 25 Mar. 1854.

psychiatry has elucidated the psychology of the arsonist and has shown the sexual nature of his tendencies'.[84] In eighteenth-century France he notes 13 per cent of defendants were given a sanity hearing, a procedure quite unknown in this country. However, to believe that East Anglia was peopled by sexually repressed arsonists, although a large number of molested sheep and donkeys might argue otherwise, would be very wide of the mark. The mentally ill and the insane were responsible for only a very small proportion of the fires. An insane tailor named Brightwell was responsible for two fires in 1856, one of which was the cell in which he was imprisoned. Similarly, we find a weak-minded pauper named Mason firing his own bedding in Smallburgh workhouse in 1852. Rumour had it that a simple labourer fired some stacks at Hemsby under orders from a so-called responsible labourer, but it could not be verified. Neither Norfolk nor Suffolk could boast a John Stallan, a pyromaniac who had twelve fires to his credit in Cambridgeshire in 1833, but *The Times* did put out an unsubstantiated story that a simpleton was responsible for six fires at Mildenhall in 1843-4.[85] Modern psychiatric research has indicated a high degree of recidivism among arsonists but this is impossible to verify since many escaped detection, and where they did not, they were sent to the other side of the world.[86] Conceivably, studies on arson in Australia might discover the occasional East Anglian fire raiser.

What makes the study of incendiarism so very difficult and in many ways very different to studies of collective protest is the fact that the crime was committed by individuals. Therefore a variety of trigger mechanisms and individual psychological make-ups made the discontented individual commit 'a crime second only to murder'. As a result of this we cannot hope to find or understand the full story and no amount of quantitative analysis can aid us in our search for a definitive account of this terrorist-type activity. This is especially so in the second quarter of the nineteenth-century when incendiarism peaked, yet conviction rates remained low. The few strands of evidence which remain can only provide fragmentary clues as to the incendiary's identity, and the historian is still left with the stark fact that, for every ten fires which took place, nine incendiaries remained at large.

---

84 Abbiateci, 'Arsonists', p. 160.
85 Peacock, 'Village Radicalism', p. 32; *The Times*, 24 June 1844.
86 O'Sullivan and Kelleher, 'A Study of Firesetters', pp. 818-23. Their study suggests that arson recidivism rates are in the order of 35%.

Despite such drawbacks we can still arrive at a number of conclusions. All the strange theories regarding the incendiary's identity were perhaps wishful thinking, certainly before the 1850s, and only then did the child and vagrant incendiary become a reality. As for the political radicals and activists, the revolutionary outsiders so beloved of those who subscribe to a conspiratorial view of history, they too remained phantoms in the minds of landed proprietors. Although just occasionally a Knockolds or a Lankester would surface to keep the fears alive. Nor were the insane or pyromaniacs, like Stallan in neighbouring Cambridgeshire, very much in evidence. Arson was a rational, though extreme, response by the desperate, the bitter, and the angry.

All the evidence points to more mundane, but no less serious, conclusions. Incendiaries, in general, were local, very often young and single men. Many of them had worked for or were working for the employers on whose properties the fires were lit. Although classed as labourers they were quite different to those men who marched, rioted, and demonstrated in 1816, 1822, and 1830. The latter were often regarded as steady, reliable hands, usually married and approaching thirty years of age. To borrow one local commentator's phrase, the arsonists were 'the loose hands', that is, the casual day labourers who were the lowest paid and the first to be laid off in times of bad weather or falling markets. It comes as no surprise to find low wages and unemployment were the most frequently cited grievances by the guilty. The 'flash and a scare' clearly had the dual purpose of raising wages and providing employment for such men. But we should not simply dismiss the incendiaries as the losers in agrarian capitalist society, for this would overlook one important feature of incendiarism. They may have acted alone under the cover of darkness but their actions were clearly supported by the labouring community as a whole before 1851. The villagers shielded them from the law and gloried in the destruction. The fires were lit on their behalf too and advertised their poverty and bitterness to rich and poor alike, though the former were, on occasions, slow to understand just who was starting up all the fires. The camouflage of deference clearly misled the landed who closed their eyes, if they were ever open, to the rural poverty which surrounded them.

8
Animal Maiming: 'A Fiendish Outrage'?

Contemporaries reserved their greatest moral condemnation for that strange, peculiar, and complex crime, animal maiming. The words 'barbarous', 'fiendish', and 'abominable' invariably prefaced reports of animal killings in the local newspapers. Maiming was, in their opinion, the work of inhuman 'monsters' if not the devil himself. Not surprisingly historians have either shied away from the subject altogether or else have echoed the sentiments of outraged contemporaries. This seems to be a perfectly understandable human reaction, given the perverse and cruel tortures perpetrated on many animals. It takes little imagination on the reader's part to re-enact, let us say, the stabbing of a carthorse with a dung fork. Maiming could be a bloody business, as well as a noisy and tiring one, especially if the maimer was attempting to subdue the struggling animal within earshot of the farmhouse or the proverbial sleeping guard dog. While it is difficult to conceal a sense of outrage when reading of the many and varied tortures the animals had to suffer, moral outrage on the historian's part does not add to our understanding of this crime. It would be best therefore to restrict moral value judgements to an absolute minimum and substitute empathy for sympathy. However, where historians have made a brief reference to this crime they have in the main created a number of misconceptions.[1] The reader is left with the impression that cattle, in the non-legal sense, more than any other animal, were singled out for maiming and, furthermore, that maiming consisted largely of hamstringing or 'hocking' their forelegs. The purpose of this chapter is to examine animal maiming in East Anglia between 1815 and 1870, when the crime was at its peak, in order to identify the different types of animals maimed and the diverse methods employed by the maimers. It may then be possible to put forward some explanations for this universally condemned activity.

There are other reasons which have kept maiming from historical scrutiny. First, the common assumption that rural people have a certain affinity for animals, either of a sentimental nature, or more commonly of a hard practical kind that would ill dispose them to harm or maltreat their own or others' sources of profits. Second, maiming was neither as common as incendiarism nor was it so widely reported in the local newspapers. Where it was recorded the evidence is limited and sketchy to say the least. If there was such a thing as

---

1   Peacock, 'Village Radicalism', p. 45; Hobsbawm and Rudé, *Captain Swing*, p. 56; Rudé, *Protest and Punishment*, pp. 17-18, 149.

submerged crime then animal maiming was the epitome of it. It is possible to state with conviction that the examples cited below formed only a part of what actually took place, how large a part is impossible to tell.[2] Animal maiming remained especially secret because it bore all the semblances of vengeance crime *par excellence*. It was more a personal act of violence by the maimer than any other protest crime. One can view it almost as a form of symbolic murder, and the animal's owner was little inclined to publicize the existence of some private feud. In short, maiming could be an extreme form of psychological terror which could leave the victim appalled and fearful for his own safety.

At this stage it is probably best to define what is meant by the term 'animal maiming'. First, a distinction has to be made between maiming and animal cruelty, a distinction which became important after 1822 with the introduction of 'Humanity' Martin's act, 'to prevent the cruel and improper treatment of cattle', 3 Geo. IV, c. 71, and subsequently consolidated in 1835.[3] It was not simply a question of degree of brutality towards the animal concerned, although it was often the case that maimings were far more brutal than the more mundane acts of cruelty dealt out to horses almost on a daily basis. Before 1822, so far as the law was concerned, animals had no rights, not even to life itself, a point amply portrayed in Hogarth's 'Stages of Cruelty'. Thus the maiming or killing of them was not a crime against the animal but against the owner. In short animals were regarded as property, just as straw stacks or farm implements were pieces of property. The Black Act of the eighteenth century made this point abundantly clear and included animal maiming within its bloody code as a capital offence until it was repealed in 1832. Thereafter, maiming carried a sentence of transportation or imprisonment. The new law of 1822 took not the owner but the animal into account and protected it from cruel or careless handling. Thus maiming was concerned with vindictive and malicious damage which injured the owner, whilst Martin's act protected the animal from carelessness or thoughtlessness. In many cases this distinction between malice and cruelty was clear cut; John Stannard for example was gaoled for twelve months with hard labour, a harsh sentence even by nineteenth-century standards, for hitting and then working his master's horse to death. Another horseman, John

---

2   e.g. some cases of maiming went unreported in the local press but were cited in the returns of the Constabulary Commission, PRO, HO 73.

3   B. Harrison, 'Animals and the State in Nineteenth-Century England', *English Historical Review*, 88 (1973), 788.

Cullum of Waterbeach (C), was adjudged by the court to have acted out of 'wanton levity' in tying string around the tongue of his horse.[4] This incident raises an interesting and potentially fruitful line of enquiry which cultural historians may be better placed to investigate. We are so far removed from this period that it is difficult to assess the relationship between humour and animal brutality, if indeed such a relationship existed. Robert Darnton's *The Great Cat Massacre* brilliantly reconstructs 'the joke', admittedly in a different culture and from an earlier age, but he does point out the universality of cat killing in early modern Europe.[5] At present we have no way of knowing whether Cullum was atypical in possessing, what appears to us, a warped sense of humour, but if we place his attitude into the context of animal baiting, dog- and cock-fighting, then popular amusements clearly hinged on a large degree of animal suffering. Where incidents involved children the distinction between malice and brutality blurs and is complicated by the fact of 'doli capax' and the court's difficulty in assessing the presence of malice in the child's mind towards the owner of the animal. In such circumstances it was usual for the courts to find defendants guilty on the lesser charge and sentence them to a combination of punishments, ranging from a sound whipping, or a fortnight in gaol, to a long spell in a reformatory after the mid-1850s.[6]

The bulk of this chapter is concerned with maiming as defined and understood within the terms of the Black Act. However, there are other grey areas, in addition to the problems of indicting the young, and these were concerned in both instances with theft. First, considerable numbers of sheep were literally hacked to pieces and left to die slow lingering deaths. Where cuts or joints of sheep were taken we must consider this sheep stealing, though in any lay person's language such mutilation was clearly maiming. If the sheep was simply left dead in the field then it has to be considered a case of maiming. Newspaper reports and to a lesser extent assize calendars can be misleading on such incidents since in both instances they were often referred to as sheep killing. Second, the cutting of horses' and oxen's tails, docking in other words, likewise was clearly an act of theft but this has been included in the maiming category because contemporaries often regarded it as an act of vindictive mutilation. Evidence from other counties would appear to confirm the malicious

---

4   *NC*, 7 July 1855; *BNP*, 28 Jan. 1829.
5   R. Darnton, *The Great Cat Massacre and Other Episodes In French Cultural History* (Harmondsworth, 1985), pp. 79-104.
6   e.g. see the cases of Rogers, *BNP*, 19 Mar. 1828; and Ketteringham, *NN*, 13 July 1861.

intent of docking. Lancashire farmers, for example, were loath to lay information against poachers, 'because the next night after they gave information, one of their horses' tails or a cow's tail would be cut off'.[7] In such instances docking was one of the few genuine social protest crimes to provide a financial bonus for the protester.

Despite the obvious difficulties in collecting evidence, a cursory glance at the newspapers, by far the best source material, has shown that nearly every conceivable type of animal, from the domesticated cat to the most important working animal, the horse, was a target. One should not be misled by the phrase 'cattle maiming', for this term was sometimes used in the narrow legal sense to include all kinds of domesticated animals and not simply bulls, cows, heifers, and so forth.[8] Another misconception on the part of historians was that animal maiming was an act of social protest rather like incendiarism. It will be shown that maiming was not always committed by the working class against members of the ruling class. During my research it became evident that in order to understand maiming it was necessary to understand animal care and grooming. Although opposites the two had a close relationship, as will be seen below.

Animal maiming was not a crime peculiar to the nineteenth century; the very fact that it was listed under the Black Act would suggest as much. Furthermore, as far back as 1545 'the devilish act of cutting out the tongues of horses and cattle' was deemed sufficiently common to warrant a statute, 37 Hen. VIII, C.6, S.3.[9] However, the nineteenth century witnessed a large growth in the crime, especially in the years between 1820 and 1850. Whilst it was never a common crime, nowhere near as common as arson for instance, it was certainly not as rare or infrequent as the lack of historical study would imply. Rudé in a brief and general study of indictments, which were only the tip of the iceberg as will be seen, discovered forty-three nationally in 1844. Like arson and poaching, animal maiming was an East Anglian speciality, if we set aside the quite separate question of Ireland where cattle houghing reached epidemic proportions during the nineteenth century. Rudé found the indictments for maiming between 1834-53 were as follows: Norfolk 39, Yorkshire 32, Essex and Staffordshire 25,

---

7   PP 1846, IX, pt. 2, *S .C. on the Game Laws*, pp. 411-12, evidence of William Storey.
8   See the wording of 3 Geo. IV c. 71, 1822, Act to Prevent the Cruel and Improper Treatment of Cattle: 'Whereas it is expedient to prevent the cruel and improper treatment of Horses, Mares, Geldings, Mules, Asses, Cows, Heifers, Steers, Oxen, Sheep and other Cattle'.
9   J. E. G. de Montmorency, 'State Protection of Animals at Home and Abroad', *Law Quarterly Review*, 18 (1902), 33.

TABLE 8.1 *Cases of animal maiming in Norfolk and Suffolk, 1815-1870*

Year	No. of Cases		Total	Year	No. of Cases		Total
	Norfolk	Suffolk			Norfolk	Suffolk	
1815	1	0	1	1843	0	2	2
1816	4	2	6	1844	3	5	8
1817	2	1	3	1845	2	1	3
1818	2	2	4	1846	2	1	3
1819	2	1	3	1847	3	2	5
1820	4	2	6	1848	3	1	4
1821	3	1	4	1849	8	2	10
1822	2	0	2	1850	4	2	6
1823	2	1	3	1851	1	1	2
1824	0	1	1	1852	1	0	1
1825	2	5	7	1853	2	2	4
1826	6	3	9	1854	0	3	3
1827	1	1	2	1855	1	0	1
1828	11	1	12	1856	0	1	1
1829	2	0	2	1857	2	0	2
1830	4	2	6	1858	2	0	2
1831	0	3	3	1859	0	0	0
1832	1	1	2	1860	1	0	1
1833	2	3	5	1861	5	0	2
1834	5	5	10	1862	2	0	2
1835	1	2	3	1863	2	4	6
1836	3	6	9	1864	2	2	4
1837	1	3	4	1865	0	3	3
1838	1	1	2	1866	1	0	1
1839	7	1	8	1867	0	1	1
1840	2	3	5	1868	1	0	1
1841	3	1	4	1869	2	1	3
1842	4	2	6	1870	0	1	1
				Unspecified year	8	0	8
				TOTAL	133	89	222

Sources: Local newspapers 1815-70; PRO, ASSI 33/12-14, ASSI 35/285, HO 27/36, 52, 68, 76, 88, HO 64/2-3. HO 73.

Suffolk 24, Devon and Somerset 22.[10] Presenting statistical returns like this can, in fact, be thoroughly misleading. Recent work on Lincolnshire suggests that there were thirty-one maiming incidents between 1842 and 1850 and yet only three successful convictions.[11] Only further research at county level will reveal the true extent of the crime.

Between 1815 and 1870 there were 133 separate cases in Norfolk and 89 in Suffolk.[12] Reference to Table 8.1 shows that the incidence of the crime followed no immediately obvious pattern, except that in Suffolk it was very much related to the second quarter of the nineteenth century. This is also true of Norfolk but the frequency of attacks was more than double Suffolk's in the years before 1830. Suffolk experienced a more than usual amount of maiming in 1825, during the three-year period 1834-6, and later in 1844 and 1863. Norfolk had four peaks, 1826, 1828, 1839, and 1849; in the last year there were eight trials. If the figures for the two counties are combined we find peaks in 1826, 1828, 1834, 1836, 1839, 1844, and 1849; thereafter the magnitude dropped off considerably until 1863. Some of these peaks coincided with periods of extreme tension and social protest, as in 1834, 1836, 1844, and 1849, when incendiarism and anti-poor law disturbances were frequent. The 1839 peak is misleading to some extent because one individual was responsible for six separate acts of maiming in the village of Buxton, Norfolk.[13] I suggested in a previous article, before research was complete, that animal maiming, along with other forms of individual protest, expanded in the third and fourth decades of the nineteenth century.[14] However, it is now clear that maiming was at a fairly constant level during the three decades between 1820 and 1850, with the 1830s returning the most cases. The original observation, that it was becoming something of an East Anglian speciality in the mid to late 1820s, would appear to be accurate now the research is complete. Evidence from other quarters suggests maiming was becoming sufficiently disturbing for farmers to take action. For many years there had been in existence associations for the prosecution of felons.

10 Rudé, *Protest and Punishment*, p. 18.

11 I am grateful to Tim Baillie for allowing me to quote his findings from his BA dissertation, 'Rural Protest in Lincolnshire 1842-50, (Edge Hill College of Higher Education, 1989).

12 The best sources for maiming cases were the local press, PRO, HO 64/2-3; HO 27/36. 52, 68, 76, 88; HO 73/2, 51; ASSI 33/12-14; ASSI 35/285.

13 See below, nn. 55 and 56.

14 J. E. Archer, '"A Fiendish Outrage"? A Study of Animal Maiming in East Anglia, 1830-70', *Ag. Hist. Rev.* 33 (1985), 147-57.

These self-help societies, made up of farmers and landowners, turned their attention after the mid-1820s to the capture and prosecution of sheep stealers, incendiaries, and animal maimers. Late in 1825 the *Norfolk Chronicle* reported a lot of 'depredations on cattle' in the area to the east of Kings Lynn. A week later an 'association for the protection of property' was established, covering the Norfolk parishes of East Lexham, Kempstone, Litcham, Mileham, Rougham, and Weasenham. The following year, a peak year for maiming, new associations were formed at Swaffham and Aylsham and South Erpingham.[15] Interestingly enough this coincided with a spate of attacks on trees and plantations. Dering lost all his orange and lemon trees at Crow Hall, Miles had an avenue of cedars destroyed at Knapton, and the Reverend Collyer of Gunthorpe had a plantation maliciously damaged. This crime appears peculiar to the years before 1830.[16] In 1834, in the Fakenham area of Norfolk, maiming became such a serious problem that a meeting was called to form an association 'for the mutual assurance against loss by the felonious killing or maiming of Horses and Cattle'. Norfolk's leading landowner, Thomas William Coke, presided over this meeting which had intentions of forming a county-wide association. The newspaper report on the meeting interestingly linked incendiarism and maiming:

> ... and in the actual commission of several similar outrages just ground for apprehending that the Incendiary, finding his diabolical acts fail to inflict individual injury to any extent in consequence of the protection afforded by the offices established for Insurance against Fire, would probably seek to gratify his malignant passions against Individuals engaged in Agriculture by the even more fiendish outrage of killing or Maiming Horses and Cattle ...[17]

A few weeks later all the leading landowners attended another meeting at Fakenham where an association was formed whose subscription was ½d./acre.[18] About fifteen months later in Suffolk another association was called for in the Mildenhall district, after William Poulter of Worlington had two cows and a filly stabbed, a sheep's throat cut, and a donkey maimed, and his farming implements cut to pieces.[19] The geographical location of maiming, on the other hand, sheds little additional light on our understanding of this crime.

---

15 *NC*, 31 Dec. 1825, 10 June and 25 Nov. 1826.
16 *BNP*, 31 May 1826; *NC*, 7 Jan. and 4 Mar. 1826.
17 *NC*, 8 Nov. 1834; Peacock, 'Village Radicalism', p. 45, who also believes the crime increased in the 1830s.
18 *NC*, 29 Nov. 1834.
19 *BNP*, 13 Jan. 1836.

In both counties large tracts of countryside remained trouble-free but concentration was most pronounced in a ten-mile radius of Bury in Suffolk, an area noted for incendiarism. In Norfolk there were minor clusters along the main road between Norwich and Diss, and in the region to the north-east of Swaffham.

TABLE 8.2 *Different methods of maiming and number of animals maimed in Norfolk and Suffolk, 1815-1870*

Method of maiming	Horses	Cattle	Asses	Dogs	Cats	Poultry	TOTAL
Poison	67+	30	-	26+	+	19+	142+
Stabbing & throat slitting	45+	24	7	2	-	-	78+
Tails cut	131+	29	2	-	-	-	162+
Drowning	-	-	-	-	-	-	-
Shooting	8	5	-	2+	-	-	15+
Tongue-Cutting	10	-	1	-	-	-	11
Hamstringing	8+	6	2+	-	-	-	16+
Stick-thrusting	11	1	-	-	-	-	12
Suffocation/ Strangulation	3	4	-	-	-	-	7
Run over	-	-	-	-	-	-	-
Beaten	2	-	-	-	-	-	2
Bones broken	1	-	-	-	-	-	1
Blinding	2	-	-	-	-	-	2
Ears cut off	2	-	3	-	-	-	5
Burnt alive	-	-	-	1	-	-	1
Savaged	-	-	-	-	-	-	-
Decapitation	-	-	-	-	-	4	4
Innards drawn	-	-	-	-	-	-	-
Unspecified	20+	7+	3	1	-	4+	35+
TOTAL	310+	106+	18+	32+	+	27+	493+

continues...

TABLE 8.2 *Different methods of maiming and number of animals maimed in Norfolk and Suffolk, 1815-1870*

Method of maiming	Pigs	Sheep	Game	Fawn	Swans	Unspecified	TOTAL
Poison	84	-	112	-	-	-	196
Stabbing & throat slitting	1	32	-	-	2	-	35
Tails cut	15	-	-	-	-	-	15
Drowning	-	51+	-	-	-	-	51+
Shooting	-	-	-	-	-	-	-
Tongue-Cutting	-	1	-	-	-	-	1
Hamstringing	-	-	-	-	-	-	-
Stick-thrusting	-	1	-	-	-	-	1
Suffocation/ Strangulation	-	1	-	-	-	-	1
Run over	-	28	-	-	-	-	28
Beaten	-	38	-	-	-	-	38
Bones broken	-	3	-	-	-	-	3
Blinding	-	-	-	-	-	-	-
Ears cut off	-	-	-	-	-	-	-
Burnt alive	-	-	-	-	-	-	-
Savaged	-	-	-	1	-	-	1
Decapitation	-	1	-	-	-	-	1
Innards drawn	-	1	-	-	-	-	1
Unspecified	1	26+	-	-	-	47	74+
TOTAL	101	177+	112	1	2	47	440+
						TOTAL	933+

Note: The plus sign denotes an unspecified number.
Sources: As for Table 8.1

Animal maiming is commonly referred to as cattle maiming. This is obviously a misnomer, as Table 8.2 shows. All forms of animals, domestic pets, game, and farm animals, were targets; It should be pointed out that although the killing of game appears high on the table, there were in fact only two cases, one at Denham (S) and the other at South Runcton in Norfolk.[20] As a general rule the smaller the

20 For Denham, *IJ*, 23 Apr. 1842; South Runcton, *BNP*, 14 Dec. 1842, in which 100 pheasants died. Such incidents ignore attempts which failed, e.g. Lord Walsingham's keepers discovered poisoned beans scattered in a plantation at Tottington, *BNP*, 9 May

animal the easier it was to maim in larger quantities at a single stroke, as in the cases of sheep, pigs, and poultry. The larger animals, such as horses, cattle, and donkeys, were rarely maimed in large numbers, unless a specific method of maiming was employed.[21]

The method employed by the maimer was as diverse as the number and type of animals he chose to focus his attention on. Again a misconception has grown up that hamstringing was the most frequent form of injuring animals. This was far from the truth as Table 8.2 shows. Without wishing to go into unpleasant detail some examples of each method would be both helpful, as they can throw light on motives, and explanatory of the terms used in Table 8.2. In the first category, stabbing, a colt belonging to Holl of New Buckenham (N) was found on the common with a 10½ inch piece of a rat catcher's spear in its side, to the depth of eight inches. The animal died two days later. In a similar case at Denston (S) in 1848 a pony was seen wandering with its entrails hanging from its belly and dragging along the ground. Sheep were often killed by having their throats cut, as in the case of four owned by King of Gazeley (S) in 1844.[22] Horse poisoning will be dealt with in greater detail shortly but one example taken from 1847 is representative of its type. Three horses were found dead at Rattlesden (S) after eating their bean meal which had been impregnated with arsenic. In other cases of poisoning, cattle, pigs, dogs, cats, and game were found dead.[23] The third category, of tail and mane cutting, was not as serious as it sounds, in fact it was the only form of maiming which did not seriously injure the animals. Furthermore it could be argued that tail cutting was not maiming at all but theft. In these cases the hairs from the tails and manes of horses and cattle were drawn or cut. Apart from giving the animals a slightly unusual appearance no other damage resulted. The hair was presumably sold by the maimer. This activity was carried out on a large scale, for example at Kilverstone (N) in 1830 farmer Wright had the tails and manes of nineteen of his horses cut. In that year Gilding of Tuddenham (N) had the same done to sixteen of his horses and bullocks.[24] Docking tends to appear in clusters, both in geographical and temporal terms, which suggests that gangs of thieves were responsible. This was particularly evident between 1815 and 1830

1827.

21 Mane cutting and hair drawing were the exceptions.
22 *NC*, 17 July 1841; *NM*, 27 May 1848; *BNP*, 6 Mar. 1844.
23 *BNP*, 3 Mar. 1847, 3 June 1862, 8 Feb. 1863.
24 *NM*, 20 Feb. 1830; *EA*, 26 Oct. 1830. This type of theft virtually disappeared in the 1830s.

when 80 per cent of all cases were reported. Why this crime should virtually disappear after 1830 cannot be fully explained, although one supposition can be put forward. Between November and December 1828 there were seven separate incidents in the Antingham, Norwich, and Scole areas of Norfolk, when it was also reported that not only was unemployment 'rising daily' but the differential between high food prices and low wages was widening.[25] This suggests docking was a poverty-based crime related to crises of traditional subsistence. However, not all tail cutting was theft, as fifteen pigs found to their cost and pain in 1857.[26]

The shooting of animals was far less ambiguous. In 1839 at Buxton (N) animals belonging to five leading landowners and farmers were shot during three summer months. The Norwich police had to be called in to investigate.[27] Sheep were deliberately drowned in the Fens by being driven into the many ditches, pits, and dykes found in that area.[28] Suffocation of animals required rather more personal attention from the maimer than did shooting or drowning since the perpetrator of such acts had to stuff wool down the throats of the sheep, or block the windpipes with large stones, or construct a complex series of nooses in the stalls which would eventually hang the beasts.[29] Horses were invariably the victims of tongue-cutting, which was carried out in a number of ways. It varied from the slitting of tongues up the middle, or the cutting of the tongues in half, to the even more painful wrenching out of the complete tongue, as occurred at Stowe (N) in 1866.[30] Moving further down the anatomy we come to hamstringing, or houghing, the most common method of maiming in nineteenth-century Ireland, which was, as the name suggests, the cutting of the leg muscles of horses and cattle so as to make them lame. Three horses were cut at Sporle (N) in 1841 in this manner, and again, a year later, Aldous of Redenhall had two bullocks mutilated in this fashion.[31] A horse and a number of sheep had leg and neck bones broken, whereas donkeys were maimed in rather a peculiar manner. Their ears were cut off at the base where they met the head.[32] An example of this occurred in 1838 at Lavenham (S) where two donkeys

25 *BNP*, 17 Dec. 1828; *NM*, 29 Nov., 6-20 Dec. 1828.
26 *NN*, 20 June 1857. The pigs belonged to Fyson of Sculthorpe (N).
27 *NC*, 18 May and 24 Aug. 1839.
28 *NC*, 23 Feb. 1839.
29 *BNP*, 10 Jan. 1844; *NN*, 8 May 1869; *NM*, 8 June 1844.
30 *NN*, 20 Jan. 1866; see also *BNP*, 13 Nov. 1850; *NM*, 16 Oct. 1830, for similar cases.
31 *NC*, 1 Jan. and 31 Dec. 1842.
32 *NC*, 18 Nov. 1837; *BNP*, 6 Mar. 1844.

were stolen and later found at Harling mutilated in this manner. In another case a donkey's ears were slit in two from the top to the base.[33]

We come now to those acts of mutilation that outraged people's sensibilities more than any other form of maiming. The anatomical region of horses and cattle which held a strange fascination for maimers, who in these instances may have been in need of psychiatric attention, were the genital organs. Maimers resorted to the use of two-foot knotted sticks, in the case of mares, which they then thrust into the animal's womb and proceeded vigorously to rend it out. A 9-year-old boy was found guilty of such a crime at Nayland in 1842. The same occurred at Bodney (N) in 1845.[34] At Bressingham (N) in 1840 labourer John Long entered the stable with a knife where he cut the penises of a carthorse and donkey and then the 'bearing' of a mare. He was transported for fifteen years.[35] In one other case it is difficult to escape an emotive term to describe the form of maiming. The only descriptive term to come to mind is 'savage'. It involved labourer Robert Key of Reydon (S) who tore out a sheep's entrails with his bare hands from the hind parts of the animal. He was severely dealt with by the court and was transported for ten years.[36] This suggests that harsh sentences reflected the amount of suffering endured by an animal.

In most of the examples briefly outlined above the maimers played an active part in the maiming or destruction of animals. There was, however, an example where the maimer played a slightly more passive role. Near the Fenland town of Downham someone drove 107 sheep onto a railway line, hurdled them in, and left the train to do the rest. Twenty-two were run over.[37] Yet mass killings where blood ran freely were rare. Maiming was, on the whole, fairly bloodless, unless attention was focused on one particular animal, but exceptions to this observation can be found. At Bungay (S) five sheep were found dead and a further eight 'mangled' in 1819.[38]

---

33 NC, 8 Dec. 1838 and 23 May 1818.
34 BNP, 7 Sept. and 2 Nov. 1842; NC, 26 July 1845. An interesting case came to light in 1983 at Dunstable, Beds., in which 9 horses suffered similar attacks, Observer, 8 May 1983. A psychiatrist was called in to help the police investigations. Such cases bring to mind Peter Shaffer's play Equus.
35 NC, 11 Apr. 1840. See also NM, 19 Dec. 1829, when 6 horses died after their intestines had been lacerated by sticks pushed up their rectums.
36 NN, 6 Aug. 1853.
37 BNP, 24 July 1850.
38 SC, 30 Oct. 1819. One of the bloodiest examples occurred at Worlington S) where a filly and two cows were stabbed, a sheep's throat cut, and a donkey injured (by unknown method), BNP, 13 Jan. 1836.

The method of maiming, the choice of target, and the ownership of the animals, all provide valuable clues as to the interpretation and nature of this little known and little understood crime. Peacock has argued emphatically that animal maiming was a crime of protest. There was, he said, 'no other way of explaining some of the dreadful incidents that occurred'.[39] He has, however, failed to note a number of important features. In the case of donkeys and asses it should be remembered that they were commonly owned by working men. It is therefore not surprising to find the majority of owners of maimed donkeys were labourers and craftsmen. We find examples of blacksmiths, a cordwainer, a butcher, and labourers who suffered such depredations.[40] The fact that such cases existed would seem to suggest the maimings were due to personal feuds between members of the same social class. The poisoning of cats and dogs usually indicated that farmers and gamekeepers were clashing over the rearing of game birds. Farmer Sewell of Caldecote (N) told the 1846 Select Committee on the Game Laws that he had had his dogs shot twice in one year. He presumed the gamekeeper was to blame.[41] The same occurred but on a greater scale in the Cambridgeshire villages of Cheveley, Stetchworth, and Woodditton for a number of years. Rewards were offered by farmers but to no avail. The fact that these three villages lay on one of England's most famous game estates, owned by the Duke of Rutland, may have been more than mere coincidence.[42] There were other examples which appeared to be devoid of class hatred and social protest. At Beccles (S) two men killed a horse and then went to its owner and asked for the job of flaying the carcass.[43] And again at Harling (N) a horsekeeper lost his patience with a restive horse and cut its tongue out in a fit of temper.[44]

In a sizeable number of horse maiming cases, around sixty-five cases, there may not have been any ill will intended. The animals' deaths may have been the result of accidents. East Anglia, being an arable region, had an enormous number of horses on the farms, the care and grooming of which were in the hands of the most skilled and highest paid labourers, the teamsmen or horsekeepers. George Ewart

---

39 Peacock, 'Village Radicalism', p. 45.
40 For blacksmiths, *BNP*, 17 Oct. 1849; *NN*, 7 Apr. 1849; cordwainer, *NC*, 1 Aug. 1835; butcher, *NM*, 27 May 1848; labourers, *NN*, 23 Oct. 1852, *BNP*, 24 June 1846.
41 PP 1846, IX, pt. I, p. 440.
42 *BNP*, 24 Sept. 1861, 3 June 1862.
43 *NC*, 1 Aug. 1840. In London gangs killed animals with the view to buying the carcasses for dog meat, PRO, HO 64/6, letter from Atlas Assurance Office, 9 Mar. 1836.
44 *NM*, 28 June 1845.

Evans, in his oral history studies based on a more recent period, has recorded the skills of such men whose pride in their work and the turn-out of their teams was a byword in dedication.[45] These men may have been members of secret societies which kept from the uninitiated the mysteries of 'horse-magic' and recipes to make the horses' coats shine. Horsemen risked gaol in order to keep their horses up to a high standard of turn-out, a standard forced on them not by their employers but through competition with other teamsmen. Lord Leicester's entire workforce of teamsmen was gaoled in 1863 for stealing corn to feed the horses. And the local newspapers were filled with other examples of gaoled teamsmen who were overindulgent at their masters' expense.[46] Later in 1893 William Little in his *Royal Commission Report on Labour* wrote: 'The regard for his horses and his pride in their appearance leads the horsekeeper into trouble, by tempting him to steal corn or oilcake for his favourites among them. In his code of ethics there is no immorality in taking the master's corn ...'.[47] We have therefore on the one hand evidence to suggest that teamsmen pampered their horses to such a degree that gaol could be the result, whilst on the other hand we have the simple fact that over 310 horses seemingly were killed or were severely maimed.

There would appear to be a contradiction. The answer may lie in the fact that many of the maimed horses were poisoned to death. One aspect of the teamsman's job was grooming. The end result of grooming was a 'bloom' or shine on the horse's coat. In order to create a good 'bloom' he needed more than mere brushing. Secret recipes or prescriptions were handed down from father to son, head teamsman to junior teamsman, which obtained a good shine on the horse's coat. The trouble with the secret recipes was that they often contained poisonous concoctions which, taken in small amounts, may not have seriously harmed the horses, but if the measurements were wrong death could result. Among the poisonous ingredients three stand out: arsenic, hellebore, and brake root. Hellebore is derived from the Greek word *helleboros* — *helein* (to injure) and *bora* (food) — which indicates the extremely poisonous qualities of this plant. It could cause slow agonizing death during which a horse would foam at the mouth, shake and tremble, and suffer 'ebullitions in the throat and stomach'.[48] Three died in this manner at Kempstone (N) whilst another three

---

45 See books by G. E. Evans, especially *The Horse in the Furrow* (London, 1960).

46 Five teamsmen were gaoled for 6 weeks for stealing oats and peas, *NN*, 21 Feb. 1863.

47 PP 1893-4, XXXV, *The Royal Commission on Labour*, general report from the Senior Assistant Agricultural Commissioner, W. C. Little, p. 37.

48 S. Bunney, ed., *The Illustrated Book of Herbs* (London, 1984), p. 115.

survived this ordeal in neighbouring Litcham. In the latter case the horseman was fortunate to escape with only a ticking off.[49] The last mentioned root was put into the horses' litter by Robert Hewes of Market Weston (S). Hewes and others were imprisoned or fined for these accidents under the law, 39 Vict. 13.s.[50] This would explain those cases where horsekeepers left suddenly after the deaths of their teams. A gaol sentence awaited them, whether or not the deaths were the results of accidents.[51] Contemporaries were very much aware of the dangers of such ingredients and the practices of their employees. The *Bury Post* advised:

> Anything which relates to the preservation of that valuable part of a farmer's stock, his team of horses, must be of use, and we therefore readily give a place to a suggestion that the master should frequently examine the contents of the manger, many instances having recently occurred of blindness, illness, and even death, from the administering of drugs to improve the appearance of the animals.[52]

Nor was the problem confined to Norfolk and Suffolk. It was reported from Godalming (Surrey), where a horse died because of an obstruction in its throat: 'It is too well known that the country fellows, particularly farmers' servants, have ever been addicted to give their horses eggs and a number of other far less harmless articles with the silly view of making their coats finer than can be obtained from good corn and good rubbing.'[53] In this particular case the obstruction was caused by an unbroken egg. We must therefore treat some of the cases of horse maiming with extreme caution for they may have been the result of misplaced care and affection. There was, however, little doubt where mares had their wombs ripped out, or stallions their penises cut off, or where tongues were slit or cut in two. These acts either signified a serious breakdown in social relations between farmers and workers, or else were the result of some private vengeance feud of a more personal nature.

It is almost impossible to discover the motivation of animal maimers because over the whole period only sixty-four of them were found guilty, or 27 per cent of all known cases. A conviction rate of this order is remarkably high when compared with the 10 per cent rate in Lincolnshire in the 1840s. Their occupations, where known, are

---

49 *NC*, 30 Nov. 1816.
50 *BNP*, 8 and 22 Apr. 1835; *NC*, 7 July 1855; *NN*, 3 May 1862.
51 *NC*, 9 Dec. 1837; *NM*, 7 Mar. 1846.
52 *BNP*, 14 Nov. 1829.
53 *BNP*, 18 June 1823.

listed in Table 8.3. Although in only twenty-eight cases — all male — the ages of those convicted are known, interestingly, the average age was 18. This is remarkably similar to the age grouping of the convicted incendiaries.[54] The most notable feature of Table 8.3 is that farm-work-oriented occupations provided the majority of those convicted maimers. Returning to the question of motivation one has an impossible task since the court cases were never reported in any great detail. However, significant statements in the press did appear which may lead us to certain conclusions. Only on one occasion did a convicted animal maimer actually state his reasons for committing the crime, and he did this in a defiant manner in the open court room. The case involved William Watts, who on receiving a sentence of transportation (he had already served seven years in the Antipodes) spoke from the dock that:

> he was perfectly satisfied with his sentence but to such a state had they brought the poor of this country by oppressing them with taxes, poor rates, and other things, that it was impossible for a poor man to live by honest means, and all this was to support big-gutted relieving officers, and other folks connected with them and the unions.[55]

Watts had shot six horses and cattle in Buxton in the summer of 1839.[56]

TABLE 8.3 *Occupations of convicted animal maimers in Norfolk and Suffolk, 1815-1870*

Occupation	No. convicted
Labourers	16
Horsekeepers	8
Blacksmith	1
Builder's labourer	1
Farmer	1
Hawker	1
Shoemaker	1

Sources: As for Table 8.1

---

54 The average age of farm workers convicted of incendiary offences was 22 and over one-third of this occupational group were aged between 17 and 21.
55 *NC*, 19 Oct. 1839.
56 *NC*, 18 May and 24 Aug. 1839.

In the following cases the motives were, to some extent, obscure, but their actions were the result of real grievances. The first example involved the only farmer suspected of maiming, Thomas Wilson of Cookley (S), who had been evicted from his farm at Michaelmas 1835. He sought his revenge on the incoming tenant, a Mr Foulsham, by poisoning and killing seven horses. Wilson, however, skipped bail and fled to America.[57] Others in official positions of authority in village life were obvious targets. Holmes, a constable at Monks Eleigh (S), had some animals maimed in 1831, as did an assessor at Wicken (C) in 1859.[58] The rector and a preacher of Field Dalling (N) had one horse stabbed to death and another stolen in 1848.[59] The majority of cases, as with incendiarism, were disputes between employers and employees. 'Norfolk Jack' was held responsible for the death of seven horses in the Norfolk-Lincolnshire border village of Elm in 1848. He had been given the sack a few weeks earlier.[60] Likewise Samuel Bolton Junior wounded his former master's horse after being given the sack.[61] Others felt aggrieved for a variety of reasons. David Norfolk's master had issued a warrant against him for poor work. Charles Winn's grievance was of much longer duration. After killing a lamb he confessed that Fowl (the owner of the lamb) 'had ill-treated him when a boy, and he had now only repaid a portion of the injuries he formerly received'.[62]

In only one case did a convicted animal maimer leave behind some kind of written statement. Edmund Botwright, a farming blacksmith, left the following note to Watling, his employer, after he had hanged two bullocks:

> Mr. Watlin Sir, — This comes as a wornin for you and the police it is the entenshun [intention] if an alteration is not made verry quick you shall have a tutch of Carlton [a village where an incendiary fire had recently taken place], for wee have prepared ourselves for you all. I understand you have got a wheat hoe and wee have got a life hoe prepared for you and not you alone, but will the first if you do not make an altershun [alteration], we will make an exampel of you enstead of you making an exampel for the pore to be kept alive, your Exampel is, to have them all starved to deth you damd raskell. You bluddy farmer could not live it was not for the poore, tis them that kepe you bluddy raskells alive, but their will be a slauter made amongst you verry soone. I shood

---

57 *NM*, 16 Jan. 1836.
58 *BNP*, 13 July 1831; *NC*, 6 Aug. 1859.
59 *NN*, 15 July 1848.
60 *NN*, 28 Oct. 1848.
61 *BNP*, 1 Aug. 1849.
62 *NN*, 28 July 1849; *BNP*, 5 Aug. 1846; *NN*, 1 June 1850.

verry well like to hang you the same as I hanged your beastes You bluddy rogue I will lite up a little fire for you this first opertunity that I can make, and I shood lik to have their at the present time. If the pore be not employed different to what they have bin, it shall bee as the promos is made.[63]

The basic grievance of Botwright's powerful letter was Watling's latest piece of machinery, a scuffling plough, referred to as a 'wheat hoe', which had replaced the labour intensive work of hand hoeing. Botwright was as good as his word, for two days later the barn, stables, and four animals were burnt.

Animal maiming was a secretive method of protest. The larger animals were difficult to steal but easy to destroy, and maiming thus had the added bonus of creating financial hardship for the owners. A good horse was worth anything up to 150 guineas and they were not insured as often as farm buildings were against destruction. Animals should also be regarded as property, farmers' property, and as such they were legitimate targets for protesters. It would be wrong to assume that country people had any sentimental attachments towards animals (generally speaking this is a nostalgic urban view of rural life) because the purpose of animals was to create or make profit for the farmers. E. P. Thompson suggested in his essay, 'Crimes of Anonymity', that animals were 'rarely' burnt in incendiary fires.[64] The evidence would suggest that this was far from the truth. In some accounts the incendiary went out of his way to work as much havoc and damage among the farming stock as possible. At Stonham Aspal (S) in July 1844 the incendiary locked up six carthorses in a stable and then fired the building. And the events at Little Cornard (S) in the same year emphasized the country people's lack of regard for livestock. The incendiary in this case fired a sheep pen where 120 sheep were burnt. The newspaper report went on: 'A number of labourers after the flames had nearly subsided, were seen cutting off the hind quarters of those less damaged, and afterwards carrying them away for their families to eat, but they were at length prevented from repeating so disgraceful an act.'[65]

Concern for animal life came in every case but one from the middle class, whose sentimentality was later to be depicted in Landseer's paintings. One anonymous farmer when writing to the Home Secretary in 1844 was presumably hoping to move the latter to action

---

63 *NM*, 8 June 1844.
64 Hay *et al.*, ed., *Albion's Fatal Tree*, p. 278.
65 *MC*, 25 July 1844; *The Times*, 17 Apr. 1844.

when he wrote: 'I am sure sir if you had been the spectator of some fires as I have your heart would have been melted to hear the cry and groans of the dying animals burning by inches. I am a small farmer but I darst not put my horse in the stable at night not knowing how soon the hand of the incendiary may visit me.'[66] Sir James Graham was, however, made of stronger stuff and remained unmoved by the events or the descriptions. There may well have been a close relationship between maiming and incendiarism as the above examples indicate. There were also four trials where defendants were tried for both incendiary and maiming offences. In the first, it was reported that Aaron Wright had declared to his friends that he was going to 'stick' a sheep, but eventually decided on firing a haulm stack, much to their amusement. The second case involved three labourers who successfully evaded conviction for a fire at Winfarthing Lodge (N). The newspaper reported one of them as having confessed to the intention of wanting to cut the throats of twenty-three horses that same night.[67] David Waites, a teamsman, was the prime suspect for a fire at Yelverton (N) because he had been sacked earlier for injuring a horse, but was acquitted for lack of additional evidence. John Brown was not so fortunate, as it transpired in court that he had cut a horse's tongue before firing an outhouse at Hockwold (N).[68] However, unlike incendiarism, maiming was neither a public nor a well-publicized act of terror. There was an element of intimacy between victim and perpetrator that neither required nor sought the involvement of others. On only one occasion was the maimer's identity widely known. Henry Green, described by the press as 'an inhuman monster', was eventually brought to trial for horse strangulation by his colleagues who had withheld the information for six months.[69]

Maiming was also carried out in conjunction with other crimes of social protest, especially harness cutting. This occurred at Lessingham (N) in 1818 where farmer Balls had his harnesses flung into a pit, his calves suspended by their necks from a beam, and finally much of his farmyard destroyed by fire. Farmer Dade of Naughton (S) discovered four hens decapitated and strung up after a

66 PRO, HO 40/59, letter from a 'farmer', 19 June 1844. The exception concerns a convicted incendiary named Wodehouse who expressed sorrow at having burnt some pigs, *NC*, 24 July 1858.
67 *CC*, 26 July 1851. Wright's friends gave him some matches and asked him not to fire their homes. See also *EA*, 22 May 1832.
68 *NN*, 31 Mar. 1855; *NC*, 24 July 1858.
69 *NN*, 8 May 1869.

fire had destroyed all his farm buildings in 1824.[70] Other examples of harness cutting in conjunction with maiming occurred at Woodbridge (S) in 1832, Lavenham (S) in 1835, and Wacton (N) and Worlington (S) in 1836.[71] Thieves would occasionally resort to maiming: at Chedburgh (S) robbers poisoned two yard dogs and all the fowl in 1818; in 1826 at Wicklewood (N) a dog's throat was cut by poultry thieves, and in 1821 at Hempnall (N) thieves stealing clothes 'knocked' a horse's eye out.[72] In four threatening letters reference was also made to the killing of the stock if the writers' wishes were not carried out. The general tone of letters ran along the following lines:

> ... and mind we dont poison your Warter and make ind of you and your stock.
> ... you are trettened to be burned and as shure as it is spoke it will be done and very soon By your corn or Cattle and there is a fresh plan laid to distroye your sheep ...
> My intention is to kill your poney and to do you all the mischef I can ...[73]

It is difficult to know where animal maiming lies in the hierarchy of protest crimes, if indeed a hierarchy existed. However, in some instances maiming could have been the response to the most serious breakdown in personal relations between master and men. This was especially true of horsekeepers.[74] Maiming may therefore have been the nadir of social relations. This point can be further emphasized by interpreting maiming as a kind of symbolic murder of the farmer; Botwright had written, 'I shood verry well like to hang you the same as I hanged your beastes', and the anonymous writer threatened Green he would 'make ind of you and your stock'. Whether or not the maimer could actually bring himself to commit murder is not really the point. The farmer, when confronted with the carcasses of his dead stock in the early morning, probably did not question the subtleties of the maimer's motives and ultimate objectives. Dead animals meant an act of killing had occurred and it was only a question of time and degree before the maimer turned on him or his family. Maiming as an act of transferred or symbolic murder and as a weapon of

---

70 *NC*, 31 Jan. 1818 and 15 May 1824.
71 *NC*, 27 Aug. 1836; *BNP*, 16 Sept. 1835, 13 Jan. 1836, 27 June 1832.
72 *NC*, 4 Apr. 1818 and 17 Nov. 1821; *BNP*, 13 Sept. 1826.
73 PRO, HO 40/29, letter to Green of Walpole St Peter (N), 1831; PRO, HO 40/29, sent to Oldroyde of the same parish in 1831; PRO, HO 52/10, sent to Smythe of Brandon (S), 1830.
74 No horsekeepers were convicted of incendiarism in the region. Shepherds, too, had a propensity to steal sheep rather than start fires.

psychological terror was, one has to admit, a powerful, effective, and unequivocal statement.

Although no examples were found in East Anglia future research in other regions may discover a parallel with Luddism. Hobsbawm once described machine breaking as 'bargaining by riot', and it is not inconceivable that bargaining by animal maiming, or animal luddism if such a term can be employed, was not resorted to by disgruntled farm workers. Botwright's case, cited above, is unusual but even here there is little sense of actual bargaining taking place. He had, after all, killed the animals prior to the sending of the letter and the burning of the property, which suggests that Watling would have stared at the dead beasts with a sense of blank incomprehension. The sequence of events might imply that the maimings were fulfilling one of two functions, either it was a spontaneous reaction on Botwright's part when he discovered the scuffling plough, or it was intended, in some premeditated way, to serve as an example of his sincerity of intent once the letter had been received by the farmer. This could conceivably be described as bargaining, but maiming in this instance served more as a back-up pressure to his ultimate sanction of fire. Incendiarism, it will be recalled, was deployed for all manner of reasons: to improve wages and employment opportunities, to halt the spread of machinery, even to bring the perpetrators themselves to gaol or transportation, as well as being acts of personal vindictiveness. Maiming, from the little evidence which has survived, suggests a narrower range of objectives on the maimers' part. Although historians cannot enter their minds — in some cases they were almost certainly deranged — maimers seemed to have taken up their cudgels, sticks, and knives only after some disagreement had taken place. In that sense it was a retrospective response which did not necessarily intend to put right a wrong or restore the *status quo*. It was thus both a vindictive act of revenge and terror in the most literal sense and a sudden release of pent-up aggression that had either been simmering for years or had been triggered off immediately after some dispute. Either way the maimers gained some sense of satisfaction from the acts of maiming, this being an end in itself. This is borne out by what must be considered the epitome of all crimes of social protest, the destruction of small disposable and consumable animals such as poultry and sheep. This was the supreme act of hatred and revenge in which an element of self-sacrifice (the leaving of the dead meat) was involved. In only one form of maiming was there any profit accruing to the maimer and that was the cutting of horses' tails, for horse hair was at this time a valuable and saleable commodity.[75]

In considering animal maiming we need finally to return to the notion of the farmyard hierarchy alluded to in Chapter 2. However unskilled the labourers were, they were not, as Keith Thomas has observed, at the absolute bottom of animal creation, since they were able to rule over the domesticated beasts which formed a 'sort of inferior class' — though the ruling class did display, on occasions, a tendency to merge the men and the draught animals into a position of equality.[76] Animals, after all, were symbols of their wealth and property ownership. The labourers, however, regarded themselves as being superior and were thus able to relieve their anger or frustrations on them. Moreover, what must have been particularly galling to workers was the fact that animals were guaranteed some level of care and a consistent amount of food, whatever the price of corn, and hence the animals' conditions were, in relative terms, perceptibly superior to their own. Maiming was, therefore, the transference of ill will and latent hostility down the line of the farmyard hierarchy, and the bottom line was the horse or cow. It was a testament of man's inhumanity to man but, ironically, the animal came out worst in this chain of domination and oppression.

To conclude, then, animal maiming while never as common as incendiarism displayed some similarities, but it has to be emphasized that it was not always, as is usually thought, an expression of social or class hatred. In the case of horses, misplaced care and attention could often result in death. In other examples the grievances could be of a more personal and private nature. But where grievances existed maiming was, perhaps, a more successful method of protest in narrow economic terms than incendiarism as animals were rarely insured against such attacks. It also had the added force of appearing much more evil and sinister, since it involved the killing of living creatures, and not, as in many cases of incendiarism, the destruction of inanimate objects. Historians must not lose sight of this fact and they should dwell for a second or two on the outraged sensibilities of Victorian farmers who experienced a mixture of horror and disbelief. The sufferer may also have thought that the death, often by very violent means, of his stock symbolized in some way a death or murder-wish directed at himself. Furthermore, before historians

---

75 However see n. 43 above which suggests animal killing in urban areas could have been connected to the dog meat trade.

76 K. Thomas, *Man and the Natural World: Changing Attitudes in England 1500-1800* (London, 1983), p. 50.

shudder at these violent deaths of animals and pass moral judgements on the maimers, they should remember that the maimers often had grievances and that the death of an animal was, perhaps, preferable to the murder of a human being.

9
The Poaching War: 'The Great Attraction'?

INTRODUCTION

In East Anglia the pheasant, that rather stupid and ill-adapted bird of flight, was the principal object around which was fought the region's longest running rural war. Protected by a 'thicket' of complex game laws it was responsible for social disharmony, unrest, and bloodshed between all social classes. It was 'the great attraction' which brought the labouring poor to the woods and tied many of the landed gentry to their estates in the autumn and winter months. The gentry were so jealous of their privileges that they not only erected considerable legal barriers but also ensured that their monopoly was well protected by virtue of their roles as prosecutor, judge, and jury in game law cases through their role as magistrates. As one game preserver, the Duke of Grafton, openly admitted, 'the game law has always been executed with extreme justice'. They were in Blackstone's phrase, 'little Nimrods', 'wholly unfit to try game law cases'.[1]

Poaching stands out as being different from arson and animal maiming for a number of reasons. First, poaching, whether by the hungry lone labourer or professional gang, had an economic or at the very least an obvious material gain for the criminal. One recent historian has gone so far as to describe it as an industry.[2] Second, it could be a group activity; in fact with the passing of the 1816 Night Poaching Act, which made armed night poaching a transportable offence, the violence and bitterness between poachers and keepers escalated. The former were now more determined than ever not to be caught and for them security lay in numbers when they went out on their nightly jaunts. Although the severity of the law lessened with time, the poachers' collective spirit did not, so that even as late as the 1870s the local newspapers still carried accounts of 'dreadful affrays'. Poaching was, then, the long, bitter and persistent war of the nineteenth century. Third, the majority of country people, both farmers and labourers, never accepted the game laws and the exclusive nature of the rural sport of shooting. No armies of keepers, no statute book of laws, no mantraps, and certainly no titled gentleman, could dissuade them from their belief that poaching was not a crime. Game, in their opinion, was made for the poor as well as for the rich, a view justified in the Bible. God put man 'in command of the fishes in

---

1   Quoted in Hammonds, *Village Labourer*, p. 163.
2   Jones, *Crime, Protest*, p. 63.

the sea, and all that flies through the air...'[3] Thus to be caught poaching
was considered 'a hard case' to which no moral stigma was attached.
Little wonder that poachers held both the law and its institutions in
contempt. This is amply borne out in the trial of Waller, Green, and
Chapman who were caught in the Gurney plantations at
Hempstead (N). One of the defence witnesses, Wright, told the court
how he had received 'a severe blow of a heavy bludgeon'. Green
interjected, 'How dare you say it was with a heavy bludgeon. I hit
you (loud laughter); you lie, it was with a little wattle. (laughter).'
Another keeper was brought forward for the prosecution and he
claimed he was kicked severely. Again Green interrupted, 'How dare
you say I kicked you severely; I only gave you one kick, you
varmint. (great laughter).' In their defence Waller argued that they had
run into the plantation in order to avoid a party of men who were
pursuing them because Chapman had struck their dog which 'had
made an imitation to bite him'. The 'ingeniously contrived defence'
was further embroidered by Chapman who said somebody in the
plantation had struck him on the head with a stone. 'That', he said,
'was his defence — (laughter) — and a very good defence it
was. (great laughter).' To which the judge replied, 'That's no defence at
all'. Waller and Green were transported for seven years and Chapman
imprisoned for twelve months with hard labour.[4]

Humour, however, rarely found a place in the covers and
plantations, especially in the first half of the nineteenth century when
the poaching war was at its height despite the growing relaxation in
the laws. In 1827, for example, mantraps and spring-guns were banned
mainly because they were singularly unsuccessful in deterring those
people for whom they were designed. On all but one occasion they
maimed, shot, or killed the innocent — old women out nut gathering,
a plant-collecting curate, three sons of Admiral Wilson, himself a keen
preserver, and keepers.[5] Two Suffolk estates, Moseley's at Rushbrooke
and Pettiward's at Stowmarket, had appalling records, having claimed
five and four innocent victims respectively in the mid-1820s. The
game laws were reformed in 1831 in order to allow a substantially
larger group of people to enjoy the privileges of shooting, but in
reality neither farmers nor labourers benefited from this purely
cosmetic exercise in reform.

---

3   Genesis, I: 20-6.
4   *NM*, 6 Apr. 1844.
5   For examples of these accidents see H. Hopkins, *The Lang Affray: The Poaching Wars 1760-1914* (London, 1985), p. 170; *BNP*, 16 Jan. 1822, 18 Feb. and 27 Oct. 1824, 4 Jan. and 24 May 1826.

Two opposing moral standpoints, game regarded as belonging to a propertied minority and legitimized by law, and game as 'fera naturae', brought a great deal of tension and open conflict to rural areas. Had the game laws not existed the history of crime in rural England would have been a very different story. Poaching was the most constant and common method employed by the poor of snubbing the tenets of the wealthier classes.

The questions concerning the scale and movement of poaching and the poachers' identity can be approached from two directions: from the statistics, and from contemporary observations and opinion. Both are, to a large extent, unsatisfactory, the former because no complete or consistent runs of figures exist for the nineteenth century, when the laws were frequently altered and when minor infractions of the game laws — the most common — usually escaped documentation altogether until 1856. The historian is thus left with the problem of matching one set of incomplete returns against another. The latter's drawbacks are the bias and subjectivity of contemporary qualitative opinion which was invariably written by hostile game preservers. Above all else, neither approach can even begin to estimate the numbers who were never caught. The dark figure for poaching was truly enormous and it was a dark figure in more ways than one. Conviction figures suggest poaching was a daytime activity — in 1869, for example, 90 per cent of all game law convictions were for trespass in pursuit of game during the day — and yet contemporaries were overwhelmingly worried about night-time attacks. This was reflected in the stringent laws of 1816, 1817, 1828, and 1862, which were designed to eradicate poaching between the hours of sunset and sunrise. However, the conviction rate for night poaching remained low throughout the period.

Despite the evident drawbacks some valid observations and conclusions can be drawn from the statistical material. Prisoners committed to the Norfolk and Suffolk gaols for game law offences peaked just before the Captain Swing Riots; 121 (November 1829-February 1830) falling to 75 (November 1830-February 1831).[6] But once the trials and riots were over, game law incarcerations renewed their upward trend; 123 (November 1831-February 1832) to 388 (November 1832-November 1833).[7] Thereafter the picture is less

---

6   PP 1831-2, XXXIII, *Number of Persons now Confined in the Gaols of England and Wales, Scotland and Ireland for Offences Against the Game Laws*, pp. 183 and 187.

7   PP 1833, XXIX, *Return of Number of Commitments under the Game Laws in England and Wales*; PP 1834, XLVII, with the same title.

clear, as the gaol returns' presentation altered. However, if the evidence from Bury gaol, which housed 75 per cent of Suffolk poachers, is any indication, then game law imprisonment dropped rapidly after 1835 and continued at a relatively low level during the brief agrarian boom of the late 1830s and early 1840s.[8] The figures in Table 9.1 show a buildup, especially rapid in Norfolk, from the relatively crime-free year of 1839 to the eve of the incendiary upsurge of 1843-4. Over this period poaching increased nationally by 67 per cent, in Norfolk the increase was 150 per cent, and yet in Suffolk it was only 29 per cent. The figures also suggest that in Suffolk poaching accounted for a larger proportion of crime, so much so that it had more game law convictions than any other county in England and Wales in 1839-40. By 1843 Suffolk had slipped to sixth place, whereas Norfolk fell from eighth to eleventh place between 1839 and 1843.

TABLE 9.1 *Poaching convictions and poaching as a percentage of all male convictions, 1839-1844*

| Year | Norfolk | | Suffolk | |
	Poaching	% of all convictions	Poaching	% of all convictions
1839	69	6.7	148	17.6
1840	97	8.9	155	20.4
1841	111	8.6	136	22.2
1842	146	10.3	140	19.0
1843	177	12.9	196	21.1
1844	-	-	176	-

Source: PP 1846, IX, *Select Committee on the Game Laws*, pt. I, p. 265. The national average was 7.5%.

Further evidence through the 1840s indicates a decline in poaching convictions (1843 excepted) until 1847, when the figures began to climb with the advent of depression and incendiarism in the mid-century years.[9] This overall pattern is confirmed when one examines the figures for more serious offences, such as assaults on gamekeepers,

8 PP 1836, XLI, *Return of Number of Commitments, Prosecutions, etc. under the Game Laws in England and Wales*, pp. 371-3, 394-5.
9 PP 1846, XXXIV, *Returns of all Inquests in England and Wales upon the Bodies of Gamekeepers; the Verdicts of the Juries. Returns of Number of Persons Convicted under the Game Laws*, p. 609 onwards.

in Table 9.2. One feature which emerges from these figures is that serious poaching offences increased substantially in 1843. This should have warned the ruling elite that all was not well in the rural districts. Poaching convictions, therefore, may act as a useful index to determine the social and economic plight of farm labourers. Hobsbawm and Rudé found this to be the case shortly before the 1830 riots.[10] Another point to emerge from Table 9.2 is the general decline in violence. Newspaper reports from the 1820s and early 1830s indicate that violent affrays were at a much higher level, reflecting the much harsher sentences meted out to night poachers, the increase in game preservation, and the determined violence of the preservers themselves, who until 1827 set mantraps and spring-guns for the unwary.

TABLE 9.2 *Numbers tried and convicted for serious poaching offences in Norfolk and Suffolk, 1834-1851*

	Norfolk		Suffolk		
Year	Tried	Guilty	Tried	Guilty	GUILTY TOTAL
1834	27	24	16	12	36
1835	10	10	11	2	12
1836	23	16	15	8	24
1837	13	12	7	6	18
1838	3	3	5	5	8
1839	10	10	6	5	15
1840	7	7	6	3	10
1841	8	3	5	2	5
1842	2	2	2	2	4
1843	16	11	7	7	18
1844	14	4	6	6	10
1845	0	0	3	3	3
1846	3	1	9	9	10
1847	7	7	5	3	10
1848	8	7	4	4	11
1849	0	0	11	10	10
1850	17	15	0	0	15
1851	10	8	11	6	14

Sources: Compiled from PP 1835-52, *Criminal Returns and Statistics.*

10 Hobsbawm and Rudé, *Captain Swing*, p. 57.

TABLE 9.3 *Convictions under night poaching and 1862 Acts in Norfolk, 1860-1870*

Night Poaching Act		1862 Act	
Year	Convicted	Year	Convicted
1860	22		
1861	24		
1862	30		
1863	17	1863	13
1864	15	1864	19
1865	11	1865	16
1866	25	1866	14
1867	11	1867	25
1868	7	1868	11
1869	10	1869	-
1870	7	1870	20

Source: PP 1872, X, *Select Committee on the Game Laws*, pp. 9-11.

Although much of the 1850s are a statistical desert, surviving evidence is contradictory. The parliamentary returns suggest poaching dropped substantially during the decade after 1852, with the exception of a small peak in 1859 when half of the forty-four defendants on the Norfolk assize calendar were charged with game law offences.[11] Whereas the Norfolk return for first and second offences for night poaching (see Table 9.5) suggests that, although there was a decline in convictions after 1852, the decade had a far higher number of prosecutions than any other between 1830 and 1870. The 1860s are interesting for the introduction of the 1862 Poaching Prevention Act, which Joseph Arch regarded as a notorious milestone in the history of the farm labourers. The most detailed returns, again from Norfolk, cite two separate acts. The first two columns in Table 9.3 show an overall decrease in night poaching, which Colonel Black, the chief constable, thought was due to the 1862 act. But if the columns are added together, a valid exercise given the purpose of the Poaching Prevention Act, then a rather different picture emerges. No overall decline is apparent and furthermore, as with earlier trends, a small peak is apparent immediately preceding the final outbreak of

---

11 PP 1864, XLIX, *Return of Prosecutions in England and Wales under the Game Laws, 1857-62*; *NC*, 9 Apr. 1859.

incendiarism in 1868. The total number of game law convictions in the county between 1863 and 1870 were as follows:[12]

Year	1863	1864	1865	1866	1867	1868	1869	1870
Convictions	240	280	232	241	250	221	258	236

The most complete set of returns has been left to the end and these are concerned with first and second offenders against night poaching between 1829 and 1870 in Norfolk.[13] In all, 623 were convicted, of whom only twelve were second offenders, a surprisingly low figure. As the return is concerned with new offenders it is probable that many were young labourers and for that reason it is possible to draw tentative conclusions relating to rural protest in the region. Table 9.4 displays large fluctuations with deep troughs occurring in years of incendiarism, as in 1831, 1844, and 1845, and the years of agricultural boom at the end of the 1830s. The overall decrease after 1862 may well be related to the Poaching Prevention Act. On the other hand, some peaks coincide with periods of known distress: 1835-6 when the New Poor Law was implemented, 1843 when incendiarism was on the increase, 1846 when the potato blight ravaged the labourers' staple food crop, and the long peak of 1849-53, which was a period of depression and incendiarism. Overall, these and the earlier figures suggest not only that poaching convictions tend to rise before periods of social tension and economic distress; they also indicate the continuing popularity of poaching well into the 1850s when all other indications suggest it should have declined. In addition, when the figures for 1860 to 1870 in Table 9.4 are correlated with the convictions for night poaching in Table 9.3, a general indication can be gained of the numbers prosecuted who were both new to the courts and, no doubt, reasonably inexperienced in the sport. During this decade 75 per cent of those prosecuted for night poaching were either first or second offenders. This suggests that not only was a new generation entering the poaching war but it also confirms the continued and widespread popularity of the crime. However, the motivational factors driving men to poach were not solely related to poverty, job insecurity, and the like. We would be foolish to underestimate the thrill and excitement of the sport experienced by the hunter.

---

12 PP 1872, X, *Select Committee on the Game Laws*, pp. 11-12.
13 NNRO, C/S6/1, *Norfolk Return for First and Second Offences against Night Poaching 1829-70*.

TABLE 9.4 *Norfolk return for first and second offences against night poaching, 1829-1870*

Year	Convicted	Year	Convicted
1829	14	1850	29
1830	8	1851	36
1831	1	1852	36
1832	8	1853	32
1833	13	1854	12
1834	15	1855	12
1835	18	1856	16
1836	21	1857	19
1837	11	1858	18
1838	10	1859	19
1839	7	1860	5
1840	8	1861	21
1841	15	1862	24
1842	12	1863	11
1843	33	1864	14
1844	9	1865	9
1845	8	1866	13
1846	28	1867	9
1847	13	1868	11
1848	5	1869	6
1849	28	1870	11

Source: NNRO, C/S6/1.

THE POACHER

Norfolk was the nation's game larder and the region generally was one enormous game preserve. The most densely preserved estates occurred around Holt and Norwich in Norfolk and throughout the Eastern Division of Suffolk.[14] Convictions against the game laws were high here too. These two facts of demography, a high game population and a high poaching density, were not unconnected. *Battues* by day and battles by night disturbed the peace of autumn and winter with depressing regularity. This war between privilege and poverty remained the most notable feature of East Anglia between 1815 and 1870. And yet the poacher is not an easy person to identify or

---

14 Archer, thesis, pp. 346-8, and figs. 1 and 2, pp. 699-703.

categorize, though hundreds if not thousands came before the courts during the nineteenth century. In the 1820s between 25 and 30 per cent of all criminals housed in the county gaols had transgressed the game laws.[15] Such figures did not diminish; over 2,000 poachers were fined or imprisoned between 1863 and 1871 in Norfolk alone, and 649 were convicted under the Night Poaching Act for a first or second offence between 1829 and 1870 in the same county. If, as Joseph Arch claimed, 'every other man you met was a poacher', then the criminal statistics represent only the tip of an immense iceberg.[16] The poacher's very ordinariness brought little comment from the local press and this makes the historians' task of identification that much harder. Just occasionally unusual episodes made national news, as in the unique case of Charles Smith with his twin headstones in a country graveyard, which offer up clues and information concerning the truth buried six feet under.[17]

Who were the poachers of East Anglia? Were they village 'Hampdens' and folk-heroes, conscious of community rights and traditions, who fought the privileged on the community's behalf? Or were they, as the Duke of Grafton claimed in the 1840s, 'half the labouring population of Suffolk'. Or were they, as one recent historian claimed, 'usually drawn from the dregs of rural society'.[18] Thus the poacher has been represented as the village radical, the ordinary man, or a member of the criminal class. In reality the answer is much more complex, their social composition being as varied as the diverse motivations which drove them into the woods and covers. On three matters we can be sure: they were invariably male, they hailed from the county in which they poached, and in 80 per cent of cases they were agricultural labourers. Given the large numbers who were caught and convicted it is possible to categorize them under four headings: gentlemen, children, professionals, and farm labourers, although considerable overlap between the last two groups was evident in years of distress.

Of the four, the gentlemen, or 'sportsmen' as they were euphemistically termed, were the least important, although this does

---

15 *NM*, 11 Oct. 1828; *BNP*, 27 Feb. 1822.

16 The best modern studies are by D. J. V. Jones, *Crime, Protest*, pp. 62-84; id., 'The Poacher: A Study in Victorian Crime and Protest', *Historical Journal*, 22 (1979), 825-60; Hopkins, *The Lang Affray*; P. B. Munsche, *Gentlemen and Poachers: The English Game Laws 1671-1831* (Cambridge, 1981). There has been no major study based on detailed statistical analysis of court records, which suggests the enormity of such an undertaking.

17 Hopkins, *The Long Affray, passim*.

18 E. W. Bovill, *English Country Life* (London, 1962), 185; for Grafton see PP 1846, IX, pt. 1, p. 784.

highlight the fact that all classes bore a considerable antipathy towards the game laws. Tenant farmers in particular tended to side with their workforce on this issue, partly because of their own social pretensions which had risen during the Napoleonic Wars, but more importantly they became victims to the voracious appetites for the ever-increasing game. On the first matter, the 1831 reform, which theoretically overturned the very narrow class-privileged rights of 'qualified' persons dating back to Charles II's time, brought no benefits whatsoever to farmers. Clauses within their tenancy agreements ensured shooting remained quite literally the preserve of the wealthy landowners. As a result farmers could do one of two things. They could and did go out and poach themselves and run the risk of eviction, or they could turn a blind eye to the sporting instincts of their employees. More often than not, farmers caught poaching were doing so more through necessity than excitement. In warm dry springs the game population exploded. At Beechamwell (N) the annual numbers of hares killed normally averaged 500 but in 1844 2,000 were slaughtered. In such circumstances farmers like Lock of Barton Bendish (N) resorted to cullings in an attempt to save their crops.[19] The majority, however, suffered in silence, although in East Norfolk they scored a notable success in the general elections of 1865 when they voted into Parliament a fellow tenant farmer and fierce critic of the game 'nuisance', Clare Sewell Read. This 'bloodless revolution', as Read termed it, did nothing to stem the rising game population so assiduously cultivated by the likes of the Prince of Wales at Sandringham (N) and the Maharaja Duleep Singh at Elvedon (S).[20] One should not overlook the very considerable fact, backed up with evidence from professional poachers, that many notable and titled preservers were themselves tainted with poaching. Since their social status partly rested on the size of the game bags they directly or indirectly forced their own keepers to buy eggs and store birds which were themselves poached, and prior to 1831 they were implicated in the black market of selling game to the dealers. Herein lies the very real hypocrisy of the game laws.[21]

---

19 PP 1846, IX, pt. 1, pp. 390-4. Damage to his crops was estimated at £250.

20 *NN*, 22 July 1865. In the 1860s East Anglian farmers would boo and jeer at agricultural association meetings whenever references were made to the game laws. They also petitioned the Prince of Wales who, on a visit to Holkham, dispatched 2 tons 19 cwt of game to eternity and Leadenhall Market, *NN*, 12 Jan. 1867. For an account of Singh's exploits see D. Johnson, *Victorian Shooting Days: East Anglia 1810-1910* (Ipswich, 1981), p. 113.

21 The most damning evidence was provided by Frederick Gowing to the 1846 *S. C. on the Game Laws*, pt. 1, where he claimed that he had stocked many of Essex's large game

Poaching was a skilled craft requiring years of experience and, as with all crafts, an apprenticeship had to be served. Children were introduced to it very early, in fact the very nature of their agricultural work was an ideal training-ground. Crow-scaring gave bored children the time and experience to trap and snare. One prison inspector noted that Walsingham gaol (N), unlike other gaols, housed many 11-13-year-olds, placed there for snaring. George Edwards, the trade union leader, recalled how he had begun poaching in this fashion in the 1860s. Others who became professionals clearly recalled their first catch; the self-styled 'King of the Norfolk Poachers' trapped his first hare at 9 and was in Norwich gaol by the age of 12. Frederick Gowing was legitimately introduced to the sport as a young rabbit killer on the Marquis of Hertford's estate. In one other area children excelled — egg stealing, or more properly egg collecting, and through this they were provided with their first introductions to the elaborate local networks of the black market. A lifetime's practice thus arose from their work experience as young labourers.[22] But the initiations into the craft took place over a period of years. After egg collecting they progressed to the snaring of wild birds and then on to day poaching. Those who either became addicted to the sport, or simply needed the money on which to subsist, were introduced to night poaching 'by older hands' in their late teens or early twenties.[23] Nor should the role of women be overlooked, even though they rarely participated in the actual trapping or snaring of game. Their involvement was restricted to the carrying and selling on the black market and more commonly, egg collecting. Hoeing fields at nesting time meant that field girls, perhaps more than any other group of workers, were fully aware of the whereabouts of nests. This knowledge provided women with an extra source of income, either from the poacher or the gamekeeper, but in one case they were prosecuted for destroying nests because they no longer received traditional bounty payments for finding game eggs.[24]

It could be argued that the dividing line between the professionalism of the full-time poacher and the casual opportunism of farm labourers is at best blurred, at worst arbitrary. Certainly some labourers, temporarily unemployed, could legitimately be described as semi-professional poachers, whilst other novices teamed up with

---

estates, p. 481.

22 The governor of Norwich gaol reported many of his charges were 'young lads, who have been unfortunately initiated by older hands', PP 1831-2, XXXIII, 183.
23 *BNP*, 4 May and 8 June 1858.
24 *BNP*, 23 June 1868.

professionals. Charles Zipfell, for example, took to poaching 'through sheer want' and was caught with Daniel Mann, an old offender, of whom it was said, 'that for several years ... he has not slept in bed but only in gaol'.[25] However, at the extremes, these two groups were quite distinct; the former made their entire living from it while the latter 'poached for the pot' and, in the words of the Hammonds, 'rehabilitated their economic plight'.[26] The very obvious fluctuations in poaching indictments imply that there are distinctions to be made, especially when, as we have seen, poaching rose immediately prior to years of widespread rural protest. In such circumstances casual poaching was both an act of hunger or economic necessity and a statement of defiance. The contemporary authorities, not normally sympathetic to poaching in any shape or form, spoke of its commonness among the labouring class in general. Both the chief constable of Suffolk and the Duke of Grafton believed that most poaching was committed by labourers who, in normal circumstances, were completely law-abiding, but had through either want of food or love of sport taken it up. Employers spoke of 'industrious' and 'very respectable' labourers who were likewise 'capital' poachers.[27] Lord Suffield, a local game preserver of note, put the matter more bluntly when he informed that citadel of game preserving, the House of Lords:

> The recipe to make a poacher will be found to contain a very few and simple ingredients, which may be met within every game county in England. Search out (and you need not go far) a poor man with a large family, or a poor man single, having his natural sense of right and wrong ... give him little more than a natural disinclination to go to work, let him exist in the midst of lands where the game is preserved, keep him cool in the winter, by allowing him insufficient wages to purchase fuel; let him feel hungry upon the small pittance of parish relief, and if he be not a poacher; it will be only by the blessings of God.[28]

To the majority game was 'fera naturae', the possession of which lay in the person who took it, a point amply illustrated by William Garman, tried for snaring a hare. 'He saw it as he passed,' Garman

---

25 *BNP*, 20 Jan 1857.
26 Hammonds, *Village Labourer*, p. 162.
27 PP 1846, IX, pts. 1-11, evidence of East Anglian residents; Revd R. Cobbold, *Parochial Features of Wortham 1828-70*. Some respectable labourers who were caught poaching suffered deep remorse, see e.g. Robert Collins, who committed suicide, *BNP*, 4 Dec. 1852.
28 Quoted in M. J. Carter, *Peasants and Poachers* (Woodbridge, 1980), pp. 9-10.

told the court, 'he thought he might as well have it as anyone else.'[29]

In years of economic distress and unemployment, the distinction between the casual amateur and the professional became blurred. This is hardly surprising when one considers that even in the best of times the game season coincided with the low point of the farming year when the harvest had been brought in and the men laid off. The depressed state of the textile industries likewise led to increases in poaching convictions. In 1828 at Lavenham (S), where unemployment was high because of the 'decay' of the wool trade, six poachers were arrested and subsequently rescued by fifteen others after a violent fight.[30] The unemployed 'would be sure in the season' to poach since alternative wages, often in excess of a labourer's, could be earned. In such circumstances they would approach full-time professionals like Gowing and voluntarily join his payroll, selling him their hauls and in return he would lend out airguns, traps, snares, and nets. Most of those who sought out Gowing were married family men who willingly risked imprisonment rather than enter the workhouse, because in gaol 'they cannot hear the cries and screams of their children, nor the complaints of their wives, that is what vexes them'. Gowing, likewise, forced on them rules of professional conduct, namely to work only in small parties and not to go armed with bludgeons.[31]

In direct contrast to this form of organization were the notorious gangs who had become a regular feature of East Anglian winter nights up to the early 1850s. These part-timers displayed a desperation and a violent streak not usually associated with rural communities. Although the majority were young farm labourers — unmarried, 'vile, loose characters', according to the chaplain of Walsingham gaol — others like the Bridge gang were composed of a cross-section of rural occupations: Ling was a drover, Gromett a farmer's son, Filby a bricklayer's labourer, and Goodman a farm labourer.[32] Others through sheer strength of numbers defied police and keepers, like the forty railway navvies who poached unmolested with sticks, dogs, and guns in the Risby and Saxham (S) areas.[33] Nor should we overlook the fact that, although East Anglia was a rural region, poaching was frequently a pastime of urban dwellers. Costessey, a weaving suburb of Norwich,

---

29 *NM*, 27 Jan. 1844.
30 *BNP*, 23 Jan. 1828.
31 PP 1846, XX, pt. 1, pp. 629-35. He claims that up to 100 labourers from 15 villages sought him out after harvest when they had been laid off.
32 For poaching gangs see *NC*, 4 Feb. 1843, 2 Feb. 1856; *NN*, 1 Jan. 1870. The average age of those belonging to the most violent gangs in 1823-50 ranged between 23 and 25.
33 *NC*, 10 Sept. 1853.

was a notorious poaching centre, as was the city itself; 'bands of marauders', known as the North Sea Pirates, sailed down the Yare in boats rigged for fast sailing for month-long excursions along the Broads. Under the pretence of fishing they poached and plundered the grounds adjoining the banks.[34] At Beccles (S) many men mixed herring fishing with agricultural labour but if the former failed then they took to poaching to provide a source of income. One classic gang of thirty years' standing, the Westleton Gang (S), known as the 'farmers' friends' because of the care they took in safeguarding farmers' property, were sheep-dippers and fishermen.[35] Thus in all instances these men made poaching a part-time or literal 'moonlighting' occupation during slack periods of employment.

What marked them out from the true professionals was their violence and willingness to confront keepers.[36] Professionals, after all, depended on poaching for their living and were thus prepared to regard fines as an occupational hazard. Staying free of gaol was the uppermost consideration in their minds and so they were little inclined to stand their ground and fight. Immediately after Waterloo the *Suffolk Chronicle* noted how the gangs, composed of demobilized soldiers, drew up in 'battle array':

> Accustomed to a species of discipline, and controlled by the power of coercion, they have accomplished that duty which their situation demanded, whereas now, being let loose from those restraints, and not having, as yet, settled themselves to a course of industry, they yield to the temptation of associates who know the bye ways of the localities, and form a body, not to be dispersed without force; which they, in their turn, resist, without hesitation or dismay.[37]

Their confidence and daring brought them to the very doors of their enemy. At Filby (N) they 'knocked up' the keeper and forced him on pain of death to walk around the preserves springing all the traps and guns. At West Harling and Letton (N) gangs attacked keepers' cottages and forced them to remain indoors whilst they cleared the woods of game.[38] These men were largely responsible for the

---

34 *NC*, 4 Feb. 1843.
35 PP 1846, IX, pt. 1, p. 312; PP 1873, XIII, *S. C. on the Game Laws*, evidence of Howard and Smith.
36 At Crimplesham one poacher told another, 'shoot the bugger [i.e. Roberts, the keeper], blow his bloody brains out', *NC*, 5 Apr. 1856.
37 *SC*, 27 Apr, 1816.
38 For Filby, *NC*, 24 Jan. 1818; West Harling, *BNP*, 15 Jan. 1823; Letton, *NC*, 13 Dec. 1851; *NN*, 20 Mar. 1852. This gang shot Supt. Parker in the face.

'desperate affrays' in which over fifty keepers were seriously injured between 1815 and 1870 and a further five murdered — acts of self-defence in the poachers' view — at Hintlesham (S) 1834, Hilgay (N) 1835, Methwold (N) 1836, Elvedon (S) 1850, and Eriswell (S) 1870.[39] Controversy surrounded the trials for two of these murders. In the Hintlesham case, which provided one of the gravest miscarriages of justice, only one defendant, Edward Chalker, was found guilty and hanged. His protestations of innocence to the very end brought him enormous sympathy from spectators at the scaffold and gave rise to a folk-song which commemorated his martyrdom. It was still being sung ten years later when William Towns, a soldier in the East Indies, finally confessed to the murder.[40] In the other trial, that of the five Methwold defendants, the jury were reluctant to return a guilty verdict on the murder charge but were prepared to offer a decision on the lesser charge of manslaughter, which the judge rejected. He sentenced them to death.[41] Generally speaking, violent affrays declined rapidly after 1851 when the economy, and hence employment, began to improve. The young underemployed, who had been the most desperate and violent element in the countryside, no longer posed quite the same threat as they had done in the first half of the nineteenth century.

The full-time professionals were often a different breed. The majority worked alone with a well-trained lurcher dog or at most with one or two 'pals'. The 'King of the Norfolk Poachers', unusually, worked with his wife. However, there were highly organized gangs operating in the region; the Ixworth gang, hailing from that village in Suffolk, was thirty strong and established its headquarters at the Chequers Inn, Thetford (N).[42] They possessed a bank account, treasurer, an armourer, and transport facilities. So effective were they in West Suffolk in 1851-2 that preservers hired a detective or 'game spy', Ben Knights, who was ordered to infiltrate the group and bring about its downfall. Knights, whose real name was Robert Bougen, hung around the bar at the Chequers and was eventually welcomed into the gang. But his desire to see justice done may in the end have affected his judgement since his actions caused a minor scandal in the region. Many, including the judge at a subsequent trial, regarded him as an *agent provocateur* because he finally booked the gang for fowl

---

39 For Hintlesham, *BNP*, 10 Dec. 1834; Hilgay, *NC*, 12 Dec. 1835; Methwold, *NC*, 9 Apr. 1836; Elvedon, *NM*, 4 and 11 Jan. 1851; Eriswell, *NN*, 8 Jan. 1870, *BNP*, 4 Jan. 1870.

40 *NC*, 25 May 1844; J. H. Kent, *On the Physical and Moral Condition of the Agricultural Labourers* (Bury St Edmunds, 1844), p. 57.

41 *NC*, 9 Apr. 1836.

42 *NC*, 31 Jan. 1852; *NN*, 7 and 10 Feb. 1852; *BNP*, 4 Feb., 24 and 31 Mar. 1852.

stealing at Ingham (S), an expedition which he not only planned but led. The judge expressed 'his strong disapprobation of the conduct of Bougen, which was most illegal and highly culpable. He was sent down here very properly to detect crime, instead of which he had become a leader of *banditti*, and he had no doubt but that he partook of the plunder and planned the expeditions.' Knights was extremely fortunate not to be tried.

The true professionals like Gowing and Burton of Swaffham abhorred violence and chose to pay fines if caught; in both cases they paid out over £200 during their careers.[43] The former even employed a solicitor until he was poached by the preservers and turned on Gowing himself. Their annual income was substantial; a good night's work could net 100 birds, which fetched up to £12 10s. Though seasonal their occupation was guaranteed all the year round because the black market, even after 1831 when the buying and selling of game became legal under licensed dealers, was lucrative. Dead game during the season was sold to carriers like Ringer of Hepworth (S) who was fined £305 on one occasion after being caught with sixty-one head of game, or Wales of Ixworth (S) who met a similar misfortune.[44] They in turn passed it on to the local dealers or the London markets at Leadenhall or Newgate. Later in the century the railways not only eased the problems of dispersal but also opened up a wider market in Sheffield and Manchester.[45] Once the shooting season was over the professionals received orders for live partridge and pheasant for breeding purposes from game preservers wanting to restock their depleted game numbers. The end of April to mid-June was egg picking time and in June leverets were taken. If the professional had a low point of the year then it was in the summer months of July and early August, but even then he would be able to turn his hand to rabbiting.

One of the chief issues, if not scandals, of the professional's work which the 1846 Select Committee highlighted was that the preservers and keepers themselves were deeply implicated in the commercialism of poaching. Their predilection for *battue* shooting meant their appetite for game rose accordingly and could only be assuaged by buying eggs and store birds from the very men whom they tried and prosecuted. The whole area of the game law and its administration

---

43 Burton, *NN*, 12 Nov. 1864. Gowing, in common with other professionals, held a licence.
44 *BNP*, 7 and 21 Sept. 1831. It should be noted that poached game often fetched a higher price at market because it did not contain lead shot, PP 1846, IX, pt. 1, p. 479.
45 See the case of Adams, *NC*, 10 Jan. 1857.

was riddled with injustice and double standards, and for that reason gamekeepers have to be regarded as professional poachers. They 'were in the habit of driving game from each other's covers a few days previous to the season coming in', bought and sold birds and eggs, or shared the profits of poached game with poachers.[46] Local opinion believed the suicide of two of Lord Stradbroke's keepers in August 1844 was connected with their illegal dealings with poachers.[47] Some were even transported, for example, Luke Cutting, keeper for Sheppard at Campsey Ash (S), and in another case William Thwaites, who was sent overseas for fifteen years after a violent affray in 1842.[48] This was hardly surprising as many preservers actually preferred to employ 'ex-poachers' in the hope that 'it takes a thief to catch a thief'. Maulden of Glevering Hall (S), Whitmore of Weasenham (N), and Jennings of Topcroft (N) were all notorious and had strings of convictions to their names.[49]

POLICING AND DETECTION

The job of protecting the game fell to an army of keepers, underkeepers, assistants, and watchers. Lord Suffield employed three full-time keepers, each with an assistant, and could call upon seventy estate workers if the situation warranted it. Just occasionally these labourers and dependent tenants of closed village properties showed remarkable independence. One night in January 1862 a group of armed men were seen entering the Duke of Grafton's estate at Euston (S). The keepers, easily outnumbered, rushed off to the village to raise support for the coming affray and hammered on cottage doors but to no avail. The people of Euston remained in their beds and refused to lift a finger to help. They were fortunate on this occasion as they were only 'carpeted' the following morning.[50]

The keepers' unpopularity was compounded by their physical and social isolation within communities, since they lived out in the wilds, close to the covers and pheasantries, and were never accepted as equals by either labourers or farmers. They spent their days 'sneaking about', watching the community at work, shooting dogs and cats, and occasionally damaging farm property and beating up labourers whom

---

46 PP 1846, IX, pt. 1, p. 632.
47 *BNP*, 3 July 1844. It is thought they had encouraged poaching and had taken a share of the profits, in this case too big a share, and had left the estate depleted of game.
48 PP 1846, IX, pt. 1, pp. 631-2; Glyde, 'Autobiography', p. 48.
49 *NC*, 30 Oct. 1852; *NN*, 5 July 1845; *BNP*, 8 Dec. 1857.
50 *NN*, 25 Jan. 1862.

they suspected of poaching.[51] In many respects they were a law unto themselves, even though the law gave them not only very considerable powers but also protection. Assaults on keepers carried far harsher penalties than assaults on police constables, a significant indication of where rural magistrates' priorities lay.

With the introduction of the rural constabularies in 1839-40 in Norfolk and East Suffolk and in 1845 in West Suffolk one would have expected the protection of game preserves to have been greatly strengthened. Half of the 160 strictest preservers in the region were, after all, magistrates, and in this role they acted as employers of the police. Even before the establishment of the Norfolk police the area around Wymondham experimented with full-time constables. 'The great landowner and game preserver', reported the Reverend William Wodehouse, '... will, I am certain, bear ample testimony to the efficient assistance which they afforded him in protection of his game'.[52] For this reason rates-conscious farmers were opposed to the formation of police forces, as James Baldry bemoaned when he explained the failure to establish a permanent police force in his Wickham Market (S) parish:

> The landlords were favourable, the farmers refused to join. It was the old cause — the latter thought the gentry ought to subscribe largely and that the farmers would benefit and therefore [?] were enough on their part and so the matter fell to the ground. This neighbourhood abounds in pheasant covers strictly preserved — the gentry consider their keepers as a kind of police. The farmers thought that the gentry would soon be able to discharge some of the keepers and thus benefit at their expense.[53]

Although the rural police were voted in by game-preserving magistrates, the chief constables of Norfolk and East Suffolk approached the game laws quite differently. John Hatton, the first chief constable of East Suffolk, told the 1846 Select Committee: 'I at first strictly prohibited the rural police from interfering in the game laws in any way, as I found there was a very strong feeling on the subject, particularly amongst the landed proprietors, who were extremely jealous, and fancied the police would be used for that purpose.'[54] But within a year Hatton changed his stance, ostensibly because he believed most crimes were committed by poachers.

---

51 PP 1846, IX, pt. 1, pp. 440 and 632; *NN* 5 Dec. 1857; *NM*, 18 Nov. 1820.
52 PP 1839, XIX, 136.
53 PRO, HO 48/36, Box 1, quoted in Harber, thesis, p. 48.
54 PP 1846, IX, pt. 1, pp. 497-8.

Henceforth he 'thought it would be desirable to check night poaching ... and gave orders to the police to interfere'. He confronted the problem by setting up a police station in Snape, the poaching headquarters of East Suffolk. Despite great opposition from poachers and warnings that his men would be shot, two constables moved in. A wave of prosecutions soon followed and peace was eventually restored.[55] In Norfolk, Colonel Black was a far less enthusiastic magistrates' pawn, preferring to gain the public's trust and not the gentry's thanks. His men were instructed to follow section 32 of the Standing Orders which read: 'Constables are positively forbidden to assist in watching game preserves or to lie in wait for poachers'. They were also ordered not to interfere if, on their rounds, they heard shooting, other than to notify the keeper. With the passing of the 1862 Poaching Prevention Act, a rural 'sus' law, Black's men were legally bound to enter the front line of the poaching war and stop and search 'any person whom they may have good cause to suspect of coming from any land where he shall have been unlawfully in search or pursuit of game'. The police were, in the words of Joseph Arch, like 'Jacks-in-the-box' who sprang out 'on the labourer from hedge and ditch'. But Black was still reluctant to become involved and reminded his force of section 32 of the Standing Orders.[56] In Suffolk the new law was enforced more thoroughly; a local attorney complained that 'police very frequently stop and search without reasonable and probable cause to suspect'.[57]

The contrasting attitudes of Hatton and Black could well be more apparent than real because the latter allowed his operational officers considerable leeway in combating crime. Superintendent Parker of Norfolk, for example, was shot in the face by the Letton gang in 1852 when leading a *posse* of twelve constables, three of whom were armed with guns. Police involvement in this particular case brought complaints from both the defence counsel and the judge at the subsequent trial, but the police justified their presence by arguing that there had been many robberies in the neighbourhood.[58] However, Hatton did subscribe to the local proverb that poaching was 'the root of all evil', the first step on the road to a criminal career leading to thieving, sheep stealing, and arson. Poachers, it was argued, turned night into day and became idle and demoralized men who shared the

---

55 Ibid.
56 PP 1872, X, *S. C. on the Game Laws*, pp. 12-15; Arch, quoted in Hopkins, *The Long Affray*, p. 239.
57 *BNP*, 21 Oct. 1862.
58 *NN*, 20 Mar. 1852.

same haunts as other criminals.[59] This attitude may partly account for the greater violence shown towards the police in Suffolk. George Swan, for example, attempted to evade arrest for poaching by emptying his double-barrelled shotgun into a police sergeant. Furthermore, shortly after the 1862 Poaching Prevention Act became law another Suffolk constable was murdered. The bitterness of this war was reflected in the fact that night-duty policemen were armed as a matter of course in this county between 1840 and 1865.[60] Chief constables from other counties, most notably Bennett from Gloucestershire and Harris from Worcestershire, were of similar mind to Hatton when accounting for the original source of rural crime. Of the 110 Gloucestershire poachers, ninety-one had, according to Bennett, committed larceny, sheep stealing, highway robbery, and housebreaking. Such damning and incontrovertible evidence should, however, be treated with extreme caution, for Harris presented a similar statistical argument for his county, but he got himself into a total muddle and was virtually accused of doctoring the figures by the 1846 Select Committee.[61]

There was, on the other hand, a contrasting opinion not only held by professional poachers but also by some magistrates as well. 'Poachers were not thieves' since they had both their livelihoods and their reputations to consider. 'Many people would be friends with a poacher but would not like to be friends with a man convicted of felony', reported an inmate of a Suffolk gaol.[62] Furthermore the penalties for poaching, despite many present-day misconceptions on the subject, usually carried relatively small monetary fines. John Glyde clearly subscribed to the view that no positive correlation existed between crime and poaching when he quoted, approvingly, a letter from a Suffolk gentleman:

> I may say safely, that poaching is a great source of evil, and, no doubt, greatly conducive to crime; though it is an extraordinary fact that many practise that offence without committing more serious breaches of the law. There are in this district, annual, biennial and triennial visitants to the gaol for poaching, some of whom have been as many as a dozen times for offences against the Game Laws, yet never convicted of felony, and more than one

---

59 PP 1846, IX, pt. 1, evidence of Grafton and Hatton.
60 *BNP*, 12 Jan. 1853. Another Suffolk policeman was murdered at Halesworth, *BNP*, 2 Dec. 1862.
61 PP 1846, IX, pt. 2, pp. 251 and 332.
62 Glyde, *Suffolk*, pp. 154-5.

whom I should not think likely to commit a larceny.[63]

Both points of view carry an element of truth; it all depends which kind of poacher one is considering. Certainly the economically vulnerable gangs of young unemployed farm labourers were inclined towards the more serious offences of barn robbing, and fowl and sheep stealing, whereas the older married men were likely to be completely law-abiding in every respect other than poaching.

PROTEST AND POACHING

The game laws and their resulting convictions gave rise to considerable tensions in the countryside. William Cobbett's stricture that it 'is nonsense to talk of peace and harmony in the country as long as that law [i.e. the game law] should remain in existence' was based solidly on fact.[64] Protest crime of a vindictive and vengeful nature often resulted. Gates and fences were destroyed in the parks of the Reverend Keppel and the Marquis of Cholmondeley, keepers' houses were attacked, pheasants poisoned, eggs smashed, and ploughs broken. Poacher Isaac Johnson declared war on Holmes, a parish constable, and Sir Robert Pocklington when they took away his hunting dogs. He bought arsenic and poisoned pheasants and five horses.[65] He was further found guilty of stealing four saddles and was suspected of pig and wheat stealing. Rough music, effigy burnings, and attempted assassinations were likewise meted out to prosecutors and their witnesses. Gotterson was shot in the face and chest, whereas Brackenbury was fortunate in having only his bedroom window shattered by a gunshot after acting as a witness.[66]

What, if any, was the relationship between poaching and the more explicit crimes of protest like riot and arson? Poachers certainly have a distinguished tradition as radicals; the story of James Hawker, the Nottinghamshire poacher who waged war against 'the Class', is too well known to need recounting.[67] Evidence from East Anglia bears out their roles as vanguards and tribunes of the labouring communities. Their independence and superior intelligence often marked them out as natural leaders. Protest against the New Poor Law at

---

63 Ibid. 155.

64 Quoted in Hopkins, *The Long Affray*, p. 154.

65 For Keppel and Cholmondley see *NC*, 20 Mar. 1841; *NN*, 1 Feb. 1851; Holmes, *BNP*, 29 June, 6 and 13 July 1831.

66 *NC*, 3 Apr. 1841; *NN*, 6 Feb. 1869. At Clippesby witness John Mumford watched his effigy being burnt. He was accused of being 'No Friend to a poor man', *NN*, 29 Feb. 1868.

67 G. Christian, ed., *James Hawker's Journal: A Victorian Poacher* (Oxford, 1978), *passim*.

Kenninghall (N) was led by poacher William Carman and at Snape (S) many in the crowd were armed with guns of all descriptions. The Swing Riots at Docking were similarly led by the three Goodson brothers, all single farm labourers, one of whom was arrested four years later for attacking a gamekeeper's house at Stanhoe (N).[68] Later in the century 'the King of the Norfolk Poachers' led the fight for local charities in his village, but the man who attained national prominence was William Doughty. The dispute was strictly speaking not concerned with poaching but with commons rights, especially the tradition of digging for rabbits on the Lows at Holt (N).[69] A sporting newcomer, named Barker, bought the rights to shoot rabbits from the trustees of the land and immediately placed his keeper on the common to prevent any further digging. At this point Doughty stepped forward and exercised his rights, an action which brought him imprisonment. And so, in the words of the press, 'Doughty found himself suddenly a village Hampden — the champion of the Lows — the defender of the people's right to the people's rabbits.' Others followed his example and were gaoled and their families installed in the workhouse. This sparked a mass dig by the inhabitants which the Norfolk police were reluctant to interrupt. The Holt rabbit case attracted national notoriety, not least because of the injustice and the attitudes and behaviour of the game-preserving magistracy who handled the trials in the lower courts. Among their number was the hot-headed Lord Hastings, who appeared to have all the intelligence and bearing of a caricature eighteenth-century noble. Not only did he threaten to 'inflict personal violence' on Tillett, editor of the *Norfolk News*, if he published anything contrary to his views on the subject, which the editor immediately did, but he also challenged him to a duel. The two combatants finally met in a classic courtroom encounter — 'Warren' Hastings sitting in the chair and Tillett now acting for the defence — in yet another round of Holt prosecutions. The former won this battle by refusing to stand down.[70] The actual outcome of this commons dispute was still unresolved ten years later when further court appearances were recorded.

With the upsurge of incendiarism in the 1840s, game preservation and poaching became firmly associated with arson. John Bright of the Anti-Corn Law League more than anyone else brought the

---

68 For Kenninghall, *NC*, 12 Feb. 1836; Docking, *BNP*, 5 Feb. 1834; Snape, PRO, MH 32/48, Dec. 1835 and June 1836.

69 For the Holt case, *NN*, 8 and 29 Mar., 29 Nov., 6-27 Dec. 1856, 17 Jan., 7 Feb., 7 Mar. 1857, 20 and 27 Jan., 11 Aug. 1866.

70 *NN*, 27 Dec. 1856.

relationship to the public's attention and parliamentary scrutiny. 'I have noticed', he said, 'where game is most tenaciously preserved, in that neighbourhood have been most incendiary fires.'[71] His campaign smacked of political opportunism and one is left with the overriding impression that his attack on the game laws was done only to restore the flagging cause of the League. By launching the attack he hoped to divide and undermine the rural alliance between farmers and landlords, who were for the most part antagonistic towards the idea of abolishing the corn laws. The fires had brought universal opprobrium to the farmers from the national press, who condemned them for their exploitative and unfeeling behaviour towards their workers. The farmers, for their part and on the defensive, accused game-preserving landlords of causing high unemployment. The game, they claimed, either ruined crops or made it economically impossible for tenants to farm profitably. The game laws, therefore, provided the ACLL with the perfect opportunity to split the tenant farmers from their landlords. Bright called for their total abolition but was more than satisfied when his campaign led to the establishment of a parliamentary Select Committee and a Home Office circular ordering magistrates to lessen sentences in game law cases, after numerous examples of illegal convictions had come to the Home Secretary's attention.[72] Once the corn laws were repealed the anti-game law campaign died, although the original equation of game preservation producing incendiarism did not. Whether arson shared a natural affinity with poaching is hard to judge. Undoubtedly some areas were notorious for poaching; the labourers of Hadleigh, Polstead, and Stoke-by-Nayland (S) swarmed into the preserves of Sir Joshua Rowley and Mr Tyrell, and both Polstead and Hadleigh were equally infamous for the number of incendiary fires and the poor state of social relations within their boundaries. One famous Polstead incendiary, poacher Samuel Stow, wrote a threatening letter to Tyrell and the police after they had successfully curtailed his hunting activities.[73] At Stoke, in 1842, farmer Blencowe had a barn fired because he had discovered local poachers had been using his dog for their nightly activities and had had the dog shot.[74]

---

71 *Mark Lane Express*, 3 Mar. 1845. See also C. Kirby, 'The Attack on the English Game Laws in the Forties', *Journal of Modern History*, 4 (1932), 18-37.

72 *MC*, 8 Aug. 1844. Some short-term gains were made in so far as game preservers drastically reduced hares and rabbits in order to placate their tenant farmers, but this was only temporary.

73 *Morning Advertiser*, 27 Aug. 1844.

74 *IJ*, 30 Apr. 1842.

Other incendiaries had previous convictions for poaching: Snell, Frost, the Head brothers, and Leech Borley to name but a few. The Heads, the night before they started a fire, had been out taking hares which they had then sold to the landlord of the Lamb, who stopped 1s. 9d. for beer and tobacco.[75] At Bradfield (S) Michael Snell and John Frost were egg hunting the very same day they fired some stacks. George Head on the day of his incendiary attack was to have gone to gaol for a poaching offence but announced, 'he would not go in for nothing. We are going to coop tomorrow, but we'll have a damned flare up before we go.' His brother Jeremiah added, 'If Squire Mills (preserver) sends me to gaol, through such a false fellow as Coachey, I will burn down every place the old b..... has got, when I come out.'[76]

In Stanton (S), another arson-prone village, three of five fires in the 1840s were supposed to have been lit as a result of prosecutions and squabbles arising out of the game laws. Labourers here were described by one farmer as the 'most confirmed poachers in the whole county'. The Duke of Grafton informed the 1846 Select Committee that he had heard of two or three cases where incendiary fires were traceable to poaching, and that he himself had suffered at the hands of the famous poacher, animal maimer, incendiary, and cross-country runner, Leech Borley.[77] Game law prosecutions must have been the overwhelming cause for at least one fire in another trouble spot, the parish of Withersfield (S). Here, early one morning, three men were taken from their beds by the police and escorted to the Great Wratting court where they were prosecuted. The villagers, when they got wind of these proceedings, had set off to the court and returned 'intoxicated' that evening. That same night a fire broke out in the farmyard of the prosecutor Robert Chinerey. The village's main preserver and magistrate, the Reverend Mayd, likewise lost a barn through fire after he had sent six men to gaol for poaching offences.[78] One other poaching conviction led directly to a case of incendiarism and this involved Ann Manning, who was suffering severe hardship because her landlord had sold her furniture to pay for overdue rent as her husband was in gaol. As a protest she fired her cottage before moving herself and her five children to the workhouse.[79]

These few examples serve to show how poachers were not necessarily averse to starting fires, but there is evidence, on the other

75 *BNP*, 9 Apr. 1845.
76 Ibid.
77 Kent, *On the Physical*, p. 58; PP 1846, IX, pt. 1, p. 465.
78 *BNP*, 20 Jan. and 29 Dec. 1847.
79 *The Times*, 26 July 1844.

hand, which suggests that the relationship between incendiarism and poaching may have been fairly tenuous. East Suffolk had some of the largest preserves in the country yet incendiarism was relatively unknown there. One particular feature of game preserving could make the supposed relationship unlikely as game was often preserved in the smaller closed villages which were relatively free of social protest in general. There is, however, a complicating factor, since game preserves attracted labourers and poachers from far and wide, but this can be countered by the fact that the majority of fires were started in villages of the incendiary's domicile. Poachers rarely lived in closed parishes but 'spring up in parishes where the freeholds are divided; that is, where they can be located without being removed from their habitations by some large landowner, as in the case of Mr Benyon'. Benyon owned the villages around Stanton where all the poachers lived. The same was true of Snape in East Suffolk whence men would travel many miles with their nets and snares.[80]

There were a number of parishes where incendiary fires occurred more frequently than average which were either in close proximity to game preserves or else had them within their own boundaries. In Norfolk the following incendiary-prone villages — defined as experiencing seven or more fires in 1815-70 — had a game preserve within the parish boundary: Costessey, East Harling, Feltwell, North Walsham, Swaffham, Tibbenham, and Wymondham. And in Suffolk villages in a similar situation were Barrow, Cowlinge, Dalham, Framlingham, Glemsford, Hadleigh, Lawshall, Long Melford, Mildenhall, Polstead, and Walsham-le-Willows. The game laws may have just been one of many factors which turned these villages, especially in Suffolk, into seed-beds of discontent. Samuel Lock of Barton Bendish (N) felt sure that 'wherever there is a populous place within three or four miles of a game preserve, those people are sure to be injured in their moral character'.[81] A picture does, however, begin to emerge, especially when the Swing parishes are taken into consideration. Large open parishes where game preserving was extensive were also centres of social discontent. This can be partially cross-checked with the known abodes of poachers, using the Police Commission questionnaire returns, the Norfolk returns 1829-70, criminal statistics, and hearsay evidence. For Suffolk, only Barrow and Polstead were centres of discontent in which poachers and game

---

80 PP 1846, IX, pt. 1, p. 475.
81 Ibid. p. 395. He also thought that inhabitants of small towns or large villages were more tempted by game than residents of parishes where the game was actually preserved.

preserves were found (see Table 9.5), whereas for Norfolk there is considerable confluence, with Costessey, East Harling, Feltwell, North Walsham, Swaffham, and Wymondham providing refuges for pheasants, poachers, and protesters. Some of these Norfolk parishes can be designated urban by the standards of the time and it seems that not only was it an act of optimism and faith on the preservers' part to locate their covers so close to concentrations of working people, but also that the very preserves themselves did much to poison social relations in their immediate vicinity.

In conclusion one can qualify David Jones's view that some poachers 'waged social war in every way they knew'.[82] Certainly men like Stow, Borley, and Doughty were heroes in their own communities but one is left with the overwhelming impression that poaching was a commonplace crime committed by ordinary men. Its very ordinariness gives poaching its peculiar place in the history of rural crime. It was the social crime of the countryside before the 1870s and in that respect all the laws, mantraps, keepers, police, and preservers were not able to break down the long established belief of communities that poaching was not a crime. Rudé's suggestion that it was ceasing to have the popular legitimacy of an earlier and bloodier age would seem in terms of chronology to be premature.[83] Although the desperate affrays of the 1815-50 period had largely disappeared, along with the gangs of young unemployed labourers, there still remained a substantial body of casual poachers, alongside the true professionals.

---

82 Jones, *Crime, Protest*, p. 82.
83 Rudé, *Criminal and Victim*, p. 85.

TABLE 9.5 *Known abodes of poachers and incendiarism in Norfolk and Suffolk parishes, 1815-1870*

Norfolk	No. of fires	Suffolk	No. of fires
Aylsham	9	Barrow*	11
Banham	5	Bradfield	4
Briston	1	Brandon	3
Cawston	6	Eye	11
Costessey*	9	Great Saxham	3
East Harling*	8	Horningsheath	0
Edgefield*	5	Snape	2
Feltwell*	7	Polstead*	11
Garboldisham	8	Stanton	9
Great		Tunstall	1
Massingham	1	Woodbridge	4
Hickling	1		
North Walsham*	14		
Norwich	22		
Shipdham	5		
Southrepps	0		
Swaffham*	9		
West Tofts	0		
Wymondham	11		

*Signifies game preserve within parish boundary.
Sources: Local newspapers 1815-70; PP 1815-70; PRO, HO 73; NNRO, C/S6/1.

10

Conclusion

One critical question may still be legitimately posed in a conclusion to a study of this kind. Does rural protest really warrant detailed scrutiny, especially when, as was the case, the majority of East Anglian farmers were never woken prematurely from their sleep by the sounds of crackling timber and straw or the screams of animals in their death-throes? Without entering the broader issue of 'why study history', specific answers can be put forward. Our culture, primarily urban and industrialized, draws its popular images and collective memory from the well of the rural England myth. The nostalgic memory of country childhoods, long hot summers, and rolling fields of wheat, which afflicts each succeeding generation, needs to be qualified if not buried altogether. Ironically, this study has shown how long hot summers presaged crises of unemployment and falling wages which led to heat of a different kind — arson. But the nation's awareness of its own history needs to be heightened with the realization that in some areas of the country our rural society was created out of oppression and terror in equal measure.

Academics, aware of the distortions of popular mythology, have nevertheless tended to introduce their own. They have displayed a remarkable proclivity for the milestones which line the route the farmworkers took towards trade unionism. Thus such episodes as 'Bread or Blood', Swing, Tolpuddle, the New Poor Law riots, and finally Joseph Arch's National Agricultural Labourers' Union have all attracted disproportionate attention. These overt collective demonstrations of strength, and one might add weakness, have dominated the texts, with one or two notable exceptions. The years from Swing to Arch have, to all intents and purposes, been treated as a kind of parenthesis which have been impatiently passed over in a single sentence or paragraph. Yet covert protest and social crime, arson and poaching in particular, were constantly and persistently employed for much of the nineteenth century. Moreover, not only were they endemic but they also came in a variety of forms to which this book could not possibly do justice. Although many historians are aware that arson, for example, became more pronounced after the defeat of Swing and rose to a terrifying crescendo in 1844, this remains only a part of the truth in East Anglia. This region was to experience a further 412 fires in the 1850s and 250 in the 1860s when the period of high farming, migration, and rising living standards were meant to have ushered in a new era of social harmony. Further research in other areas (the South-West looks a promising region) would probably repay the time-consuming efforts of an historian. Poaching, likewise, may have become less bloody after 1830, but in no way did it lose either its popularity or its premier position as the social crime of the countryside.

The dichotomy between overt collective disturbances and covert terrorist action has in recent years been the subject of a fairly intensive debate between Roger Wells and Andrew Charlesworth. Both the protagonists appear to accept implicitly the progressive development of protest in a linear manner towards the formation of class consciousness and organized trade unionism. In many ways they accept the Tilly approach to protest, from 'reactive' pre-industrial to 'modern' forms of action. This study, which almost wholly concentrates on the covert and individual methods will, it is hoped, add something to our knowledge and understanding of not only protest but the social relations within rural society that generated such bitterness and recrimination. The evidence would seem to suggest that crimes like arson were considered by contemporaries to be new and disturbing expressions of grievance, especially after the Napoleonic Wars. Certainly incendiarism and maiming had existed for centuries before this period but contemporaries believed the sheer scale of such crimes made them qualitatively and quantitatively different to the occasional incidents which had occurred earlier. Moreover the volume of incendiary attacks rose dramatically after 1830, surely no coincidence with the repression of Swing and, one might add, the invention of the 'strike-anywhere' match. It is perhaps worth repeating that Norfolk and Suffolk experienced 250 fires in the 1860s — a decade of supposed tranquillity — and yet the 1820s, which experienced a major agrarian depression, could only muster 159 fires. Thus it would appear that the claim of Hobsbawm, Rudé, and Charlesworth that arson became popular only after 1830 has some credence. But our collective ignorance of what actually took place both before and after 1830 in terms of rural protest on a national scale does not yet allow for definitive conclusions. In East Anglia collective protest as a tactic neither disappeared temporarily nor completely; it could run concurrently with covert terrorism within the same dispute, as in the case of the implementation of the New Poor Law or enclosure, as at Fakenham. It could also run concurrently in temporal terms, as in the years 1831-4 when fires and strikes were common, in 1844 during an enclosure dispute at Snettisham when one might have expected arson attacks, and during the mid-century depression when there were numerous fires and workhouse riots. All this ignores the other observation made earlier that incendiary attacks between 1830 and 1851 were frequently the meeting points for large displays of collective protest and celebration when hoses were cut, firemen stoned, and flames stoked by onlookers. In such circumstances the individual arsonist was not simply settling a personal score, he was acting for the whole community. One wonders, therefore, whether we can equate methods of protest with class consciousness. More productive may be an approach which considers the levels of community consciousness and equates that to the types of dispute being fought and the tactics employed. Charity, enclosure, and poor law disputes invariably set off collective anger, whereas unemployment was more selective in whom it affected, though its dangers were not lost on the entire parish.

If we accept that covert action became the significant and enduring feature of rural protest during the second quarter of the nineteenth century in East Anglia, we then need to examine the meaning and significance of the aphorism 'pre-industrial', so commonly ascribed to such crimes. Objectively the region was one of the most advanced agrarian societies in Britain, if not the world, and its social structure was well established, albeit constantly changing. It was not a society in absolute transition but one that was based on a market economy which served an industrializing and increasingly urbanized nation. It was not, in the context of the period, a pre-industrial society. The term, in some ways, is meaningless unless it is being employed to denote a traditional and non-industrial society. Was the tactic of arson a symbol, a flare even, denoting the backwardness or lack of an organized working-class movement? A good case could be made for affirming such an interpretation but this may well overlook a general and, to some extent, timeless facet of the crime. One did not need to look very far in Britain of the 1980s to find arson being deployed as a weapon of social and political conflict — it does not belong to the museum of social warfare. Why should supporters of one of the country's most militant, organized, and class-conscious unions, the miners, restore the crime to the arsenal of class war? Why have some elements of Welsh nationalism resorted to the burning of second homes, about one hundred between 1980 and 1985? This number is, despite widespread media coverage, meagre in terms of volume and damage when compared with nineteenth-century East Anglia. Arsonists in the late twentieth century are not only vindictive children venting their hatred on school buildings or the mentally disturbed whom psychiatrists brand as sexually inadequate, but are, on occasions, the politically motivated. Certainly fire is a primeval weapon: so easy to light, so destructive in its simplicity, and so consuming in its effect as to burn away incriminating evidence. But this has always been the case.

If we place nineteenth-century arson in its historical context one matter becomes clear: it did mark a stage in the development of the rural war. The collective disturbances of 1816, 1822, and 1830 were no longer acceptable modes of behaviour to the ruling elites. Thompson's 'moral economy of the crowd' had become immoral and illegal and the law courts, yeomanry, special constables, poor law, and employers saw to that. What other means, then, did the poor, dispossessed, unemployed, and underpaid have at their disposal? There were no arbitration boards, no parliamentary committees, no binding contracts, few public-spirited and paternalistically minded landowners. There were, in short, no avenues of discussion and conciliation open to them. Negotiation for rights, wages, and work was by conflict and confrontation, by fire and fear in other words. Whilst history does not repeat itself general trends in social circumstances and political ideology can parallel past events. We now live, some would argue, in a new age of unemployment and increasing authoritarianism which, though paying lip-service to the values of egalitarianism and concern for the underprivileged, values the virtues of negotiation and compromise with decreasing enthusiasm. When the point is reached where political and social consensus breaks down, sadly, the lighted match, and nowadays the cigarette lighter and blow-torch, cannot be far behind. Arson is simultaneously an act of defiance and desperation. It is also a witness to the weak bargaining position of the protester. We should not, therefore, give the incendiaries an uncritical place in the working class hall of fame. They were not, as Thompson and others have warned, necessarily 'nice' criminals perpetrating 'nice' social crimes. Frequently they were desperate men committing particularly unpleasant deeds in desperate circumstances and there is little honour or dignity in that. Nor should we dismiss them as pitiful broken men; they did after all fight back, and in fighting back brought attention to their plight and that of their fellows. In time the more able and astute among them left the land altogether whilst a few remaining men braved their employers to form the unions of the 1870s. Arson thus stoked two generations of class conflict and kept alive the East Anglian tradition of protest. In such circumstances incendiarism was both barn-razing and consciousness-raising, though not always in the meaning Marx might have assigned to the term. Many became conscious of the fact that, beyond the flat horizons, there was a brighter prospect than the glow of burning stacks.

Returning to the original question, from which we have moved some distance, we should not overlook the importance of these crimes to contemporaries. Maiming was considered the most horrific, poaching the most common, whilst arson remained 'second only to murder', in both the literal and metaphorical sense. Of all the property crimes covered by the Black Act incendiarism remained on the statute book far longer and the majority of the convicted before 1837 were hanged as a consequence. The panic and terror it engendered among property owners was impressive. Therefore the fact that only a minority of farmers experienced a 'flash' should not lead one to underestimate it, since the 'scare' was felt not only in the immediate vicinity but in the neighbouring parishes for miles around, as Ernest Selley observed, 'The flaming ricks and smouldering barns were beacon fires flashing messages.'[1] It is hoped this study has served to fill a lacuna and, although the evidence and findings lack the excitement of the massed ranks of rioting labourers, an examination of these crimes brings to light the mundane and prosaic nature of the permanent tensions and conflicts within rural society.

Finally, it is worth summarizing the impact and effectiveness of these crimes of the night. Poaching remained the running sore which created tensions between all classes of rural society for much of the nineteenth century. Game preservation was one of the few areas which brought masters and men together, but it remained an implicit, unspoken alliance, with no more than a blind eye from the former towards the activities of the latter. Indeed, it would have been surprising had their viewpoints converged in an organized anti-game lobby since the antipathy of the respective classes was based on separate and antagonistic premisses. For the labourers' part, poaching challenged the very basis of rural society, the rights and inviolability of property ownership, in so far as game was 'fera naturae' and the property of the finder — hardly an attitude which found sympathy with their masters. Farmers' hostility was, for the most part, grounded on their enthusiasm for market-oriented agriculture, and their crops clearly suffered the ravages of an ever-increasing and ravenous game population. Herein lies one of the anomalies to be found in the region

---

1   E. Selley, *Village Trade Unions in Two Centuries* (London, 1919), p. 2.

for, on the one hand, Norfolk and Suffolk were renowned for their agricultural progressiveness and, on the other, they were the nation's game larder. This inconsistency only made sense from the game-preserving landlords' viewpoint, as their willingness to invest in agrarian improvements was counterbalanced by their desire to use the countryside as a place of leisure and recreation, not simply profit. Thus farmers and labourers extracted capital and charity but at the price of allowing game preservers to dictate the terms in the numbers of game reared. The pheasant became as indigenous as the 'peasant', whatever the social cost to the latter. Furthermore, game benefited from far greater care, protection, and legislative reform than many of its hunters. It is doubtful whether any of the repressive legislation had any effect in stamping out the crime; rather, changing moral values and improved material conditions after 1870 more than likely contributed to poaching's decline towards the end of the century.

As for animal maiming, this was an individualistic crime of the most covert nature which never elicited nor even required a collective response from the rest of the community. Grievances where they existed — one should recall the accidental nature of some of the cases — were probably of a more private and personal nature between victim and maimer. Its effectiveness lay more in the psychological terror it could produce than as a vehicle for the initiation of social and economic improvements. It was a retrospective individualistic response to some personal harm and was merely intended to show that the powerless were indeed capable of striking back, often with terrifying and bloody effect.

Arson possessed similar traits but, unlike maiming, the results were often public, an advertisement which could and did, especially between 1830 and 1851, elicit responses of support for the incendiary. The psychological terror in these instances was magnified, for not only was an individual prepared to strike at the very heart of a farmer's livelihood but, as we have seen, the entire labouring population was equally prepared to stand by him in mute support. When the volume of incendiary attacks reached epidemic proportions, as in the early 1830s in Norfolk, the mid-1840s, and the mid-century, farmers and landlords were forced into making some kind of response, nor was it necessarily the knee-jerk reactions of bigoted reactionaries. Capital punishment, for example, was never reintroduced, despite petitions calling for its return. By way of compensation, rural constabularies in West Suffolk and Cambridgeshire were established and often with telling effect. On occasions wages ceased to fall and employment rose for fear of offending the labouring community. In the long term many landowners were forced to re-examine their roles and position in their rural kingdoms, and discovered that they had been usurped by the cash nexus and the farmers for whom the traditions of *noblesse oblige* and paternalism were largely meaningless concepts from an earlier age. At this realization landlords, in quite a few cases, attempted to claw back their status as community leaders. Apart from a flurry of model cottage building, they left behind one permanent monument to the rural war, the garden allotment. Thus, for a minority of the rural population, very real improvements were made thanks to the fearless actions of a few, especially young single unemployed men, for whom little was gained other than the growing awareness that their futures lay anywhere but on the land.

Arson created a climate of fear which the gentry tried to combat by what some historians have called the introduction of 'pseudo-paternalistic' methods of social control. Their moral crusade through allotments, better housing, harvest homes, education, charity, and village societies still awaits further investigation but it probably was, in part, successful. Many villagers remained amenable to such forces and within some communities one can discern divisions between 'respectable' and 'rough' elements becoming evident after 1850. But it can only be counted a partial success — why else should trade unionism emerge with such force in the 'Revolt of the Field' just two years after the terminal date of this study?

Rural England may well have been picturesque to those who could afford to look, but the reality for its indigenous poor was far different; it was for many years a mean and unpleasant land. To reiterate Glyde's words: 'The simplicity and innocence of peasant life exists only in [the] imagination.'[2]

---

2   Glyde, *Suffolk*, p. 145.

Bibliography

I. MANUSCRIPT SOURCES

Public Record Office, London

ASSI 33/12-14: Norfolk Circuit Gaol Delivery Books 1831-52.
ASSI 35/276-90: Assize Papers South-East Circuit 1836-50.
HO 27/12-76: Criminal Registers 1816-45.
HO 40/17-18, 27, 29, 39, 46, 48, 53, 56, 59: Disturbances: Correspondence and Papers 1822-44.
HO 41/6-7, 9, 18: Disturbances: Entry Books 1822-47.
HO 43/24, 63-8: Domestic Letter Books 1816-44.
HO 45/OS 2410, OS 3200, OS 3823, 3472H: Disturbances 1840-50.
HO 48/36, box 1: Police Commission.
HO 52/1-3, 6-12, 14-15, 19-30, 37-40, 42-6: Municipal and Provincial Correspondence 1820-1840.
HO 64/1-6: Rewards 1820-36.
HO 73/2, 5-9: Returns from Local Guardians to Constabulary Commission.
MH 12/8185, 8616, 12064: Poor Law Union Papers.
MH 32/48-9, 60, 80, 83: Poor Law Commission, Assistant Commissioners and Inspectors Correspondence 1835-6.

Norfolk and Norwich Record Office

Aylsham Poor Law Union, C/GP1 /459.
Bacon, R. N.: Papers for 1844 Agricultural Report, 2 vols., MS 4363 T138B.
Barton Collection: BAR 49.
Boileau Papers: Boi 62/117X4 (1830 letters), Boi 69/117X5 (Diaries 1842-6), T.140D MS 21470 (Diaries 1847), Boi 69/117X6 (Diaries 1851).
Depwade Union Papers: C/GP3/192, C/GP3/231.
Kimberley Papers: LLC/3/1, 4, 14.
North Elmham Association for the Prosecution of Felons: PD 209/445.
Norfolk Return for First and Second Offences Against Night Poaching 1829-70: C/S6/I.
Norfolk Quarter Sessions 1830: C/S1/24.

Norfolk and Norwich Local History Library

Broadsheets: C343 (Clarke), N343 (Knockolds).
Memoir of J. Hudson, farmer of Castleacre: C.631 C.Hud.
Reepham Parish Council, 1832 Vestry Meeting: Rec 331.763.
Tunstead and Happing Association, Rewards and Premiums: C.331.2 (06).
Assorted Papers and Calendars on Norfolk Assizes: not indexed.

Ipswich and East Suffolk Record Office

Ashburnham Papers: HA 1/HB6/1b/4, 6, 14, 24-32, 36, 57-63, 66, 80-1; HA
   1/HB6/3/4, 23.
Edgar Papers: HA 247/5/47-8, 54, 85-7, 91-2, 103.
Loraine Papers: HA 61/436/16.
Rous Papers: HA 11/A13/10, HA 11/B1/1 1/2, 7-8, HA 11/B1/23/17,
   HA 11/B1/24/1-2, 6, HA 11/B2/12, HA 11/B5/5, 25, HA 11/C4/12.
Gosbeck Baptismal Records 1813-80: FBA 43/D2/6.

West Suffolk Record Office

Brandon Association for the Prosecution of Felons: EL 110/1/14.
Hengrave Arson: 449/3/11.
Newmarket Poor Law Union: 611/2.
List of Suffolk Fire Office Records: NRA 13.

Norwich Union Insurance

Norwich Union Fire Office Minutes of Directors' Meetings 1840-51.

II. BRITISH PARLIAMENTARY PAPERS

Hansard, 1844.
1821-71, *Census Reports*.
1835-52, *Criminal Returns and Statistics*.
1834-47, *Annual Reports of the Poor Law Commissioners*.
1818, XVI, *Criminal Returns*.
1823, IV, *Report from Select Committee on Laws Relating to Game*.
1824, VI, *Select Committee on Agricultural Labourers' Wages*.
1826-7, VI, *Select Committee on Criminal Commitments and Convictions*.
1826-7, XIX, *Criminal Returns*.
1828, VIII, *Report from Select Committee on Laws Relating to Game*.
1829, XVIII, *Criminal Returns*.
1831-2, XXXIII, *Number of Persons now Confined in the Gaols of England and
   Wales, Scotland and Ireland for Offences Against the Game Laws*.
1833, V, *Select Committee on the Present State of Agriculture*.
1833, XXIX, *Return of Number of Commitments under the Game Laws in England
   and Wales*.
1834, XXX-XXXIV, *Answers to Rural Queries*, pts. 1-5.
1834, XLVII, *Return of Number of Commitments under the Game Laws in England
   and Wales*.
1836, VIII, *Select Committee of the House of Lords on the State of Agriculture*.
1836, XLI, *Return on Number of Commitments, Prosecutions etc. under the Game
   Laws in England and Wales*.
1837, V, *Select Committee of the House of Lords on Agriculture*.
1837-8, XVIII, *Select Committee on the Administration of the Relief of the Poor*, pt.

I.

1839, XIX, *First Report of the Commissioners Appointed to Inquire as to the Best Means of Establishing an Efficient Constabulary Force.*

1840, XXIII, *Reports from the Assistant Commissioners on Handloom Weavers.*

1842, XXI, *Seventh Report of the Inspector of Prisons for Northern and Eastern Division.*

1843, VII, *Select Committee on the Labouring Poor (Allotments of Land).*

1843, XII, *Reports of Assistant Commissioners on the Employment of Women and Children in Agriculture.*

1843, XLII, *Lists of Names of all Persons Killed or Wounded in Affrays with Poachers 1841-42.*

1844, III, *Bill to Amend the Law as to Burning Farm Buildings.*

1844, XXXIX, *Return of all Inquests Held by Coroners of England and Wales since 1833, upon the Bodies of Gamekeepers and Verdicts of Juries.*

1844, House of Lords 258, *Return of Ages and Descriptions of Persons Committed for Trial for Incendiary Offences in Norfolk and Suffolk.*

1846, VI, *Select Committee on the Burdens Affecting Real Property.*

1846, IX, *Select Committee on the Game Laws,* pts. 1 and 2.

1846, XXXIV, *Returns of all Inquests in England and Wales upon the Bodies of Gamekeepers; the Verdicts of the Juries. Returns of Number of Persons Convicted under the Game Laws.*

1846, XXXVI, *Report on Certain Alleged Abuses in the Administration of the Poor Law in Norfolk and Suffolk.*

1847-8, VII, *Select Committee on Agricultural Customs.*

1849, XXVI, *Fourteenth Report on Prisons in Northern and Eastern Divisions.*

1849, XLIV, *Return of Number of Persons for Offences against the Game Laws and Number of Keepers Killed since 1832.*

1850, XXVII, *Reports to the Poor Law Board of Settlement and Removal.*

1850, XXVIII, *Fifteenth Report on Prisons in Northern and Eastern Divisions.*

1851, XXVII, *Sixteenth Report on Prisons in Northern and Eastern Divisions.*

1852-3, XXV, *Second Report of Select Committee on the Police.*

1852-3, XXXVI, *Rural Constabulary First Report to the Select Committee.*

1857-8, XLVII, *Return of Number of Persons in Gaol in England and Wales for Poaching in 1856.*

1857-8, XLIX, *Number of Women and Children Chargeable to Poor Law Unions in England and Wales during 1856 in Consequence of Persons by Whom They were Maintained Being Confined in Gaol for Offences against the Game Laws.*

1860, LVII, *Number of Persons Committed to Prison in the United Kingdom, Year Ended June 1859, for Game Law Offences.*

1861, L, *Return on the Earnings of Agricultural Labourers.*

1862, XVI, *Report on Game Law Amendment Bill (Night Poaching Prevention Bill).*

1862, XLV, *Memorial in 1861 by Chief Constables of Twenty-Eight Counties in England and Wales on Game Laws.*

1862, XLVII, *Number of Persons Committed to Gaol in England and Wales during Last Seven Years on Charge of Felony.*

1862, XLVII, *Number of Murders or Murderous Assaults on Servants Legally Appointed to Prevent Violation of Game Laws.*

1864, XLIX, *Return of Prosecutions in England and Wales under the Game Laws, 1857-62.*

1865, XLV, *Number of Cases Committed under the Provisions of Poaching Prevention Act.*

1867, X, *Select Committee on Fire Protection.*

1867, XVI, *Sixth Report of the Commissioners on the Employment of Children.*

1867-8, XVII, *Report of the Commissioners on the Employment of Children, Young Persons and Women in Agriculture.*

1870, LVII, *Return of the Number of Convictions under the Game Laws.*

1871, LVIII, *Return of the Number of Convictions under the Game Laws.*

1872, X, *Select Committee on the Game Laws.*

1872, L, *Return of the Number of Convictions under the Game Laws.*

1873, XIII, *Select Committee on the Game Laws.*

1893-4, XXXV, *The Royal Commission on Labour*, general report from the Senior Assistant Agricultural Commissioner, W. C. Little.

1900, LXXXII, *Report on the Wages and Earnings of Agricultural Labourers in the United Kingdom.*

III. PERIODICALS

Annual Register, 1843-4.
Bury and Norwich Post, 1820-70.
Cambridge Chronicle, 1849-52.
East Anglian, 1830-3.
Eastern Weekly Press, 1872.
Essex Mercury, 1838.
Fraser's Magazine, 1844.
Gentleman's Magazine, 1860.
Ipswich Journal, 1850-2.
The League, 1843-5.
Mark Lane Express, 1845.
Morning Advertiser, 1844.
Morning Chronicle, 1844, 1849.
Norfolk Chronicle, 1815-70.
Norfolk News, 1845-70.
Norfolk and Norwich Monitor and Police Gazette, 1840-4.
Northern Star, 1843-4.
Norwich Mercury, 1820-70.
Notes to the People, 1851-2.
Political Register, 1835 .
Punch, 1844.
Quarterly Review, 1867.
Red Republican and Friend to the People, 1850-1.

Star in the East, 1836.
Suffolk Chronicle, 1815-51.
The Times, 1843-4.

IV. CONTEMPORARY PRINTED WORKS (pre-1900)

ANON., 'Incendiarism, its Causes and Cure', *Fraser's Magazine*, 30 (Aug. 1844), 243-52.

—— *Biographical Sketch of the Revd John Stevens Henslow* (London, 1861).

ADAMS, S., *A Letter to Lord Suffield recommending Adoption of a Labour Rate* (Norwich, 1831).

ALMACK, B., 'Agriculture of Norfolk', *JRAS* 5 (1845).

ARCH, J., *The Story of His Life told by Himself* (London, 1898).

BACON, R. M., *Address to Rick Burners* (Norwich, 1822).

—— *A Memoir of the Life of Edward, Third Baron Suffield* (Norwich, 1838).

BACON, R. N., *Report on the Agriculture of Norfolk* (Norwich, 1844).

BALLACHEY, G. B., *A Letter to the Editor of the Norwich Mercury Respecting a Reduction of Wages in the Parish of Edgefield* (Norwich,1833).

BAXTER, G. R. W., *Book of the Bastiles* (London, 1841).

BAYNE, A. D., *A Comprehensive History of Norwich* (London, 1869).

BIDDELL, H., *The Suffolk Stud Book* (Diss, 1880).

BLOOM, J. H., *Notices, Historical and Antiquarian of the Castle and Priory of Castleacre* (London, 1843).

BOWLEY, A. L., 'The Statistics of Wages in the United Kingdom during the Last Hundred Years', *JRSS* 61-2 (1898-9), 702-22.

BROUGHAM, H. P., *Speeches*, 4 vols. (Edinburgh, 1838).

BUNBURY, C. J. F., ed., *Memoir and Literary Remains of Lt. Gen. Sir H. G. Bunbury Bart.* (London, 1868).

BUNBURY, H., 'On the Allotment System', *JRAS* 1 (1845), 391-4.

CAIRD, J., *English Agriculture in 1850-51* (London, 1852).

CLIFFORD, F., *The Agricultural Lock Out of 1874* (London, 1875).

COBBETT, W., *Rural Rides* (London, 1830), ed. G. D. and M. Cole, 2 vols. (London, 1930).

COBBOLD, REVD R., 'Parochial Features of Wortham 1828-1870', IESRO, HA 11/A13/10.

COLCHESTER, B., *Hints on the Employment of Agricultural Labourers* (Ipswich, 1849).

COLMAN, H., 'The Agricultural Labourers of England', *Labourers' Friend* (Aug. 1844), 58-63.

DAY, C., *An Address to Those whom it may Concern — an Account of the Late Trials* (Ipswich, 1831).

ENGELS, F., *The Condition of the Working Class in England in 1844* (London, 1969 edn.),

EVERETT, Z., *A Sketch of the Life of Z. Everett, a Notorious Poacher* (Norwich, 1867).

FITZROY, G. H., *A Letter to the Magistrates of the Western Division of Suffolk on the Preservation of Game* (London, 1844).

FLETCHER, M., *Migration of Agricultural Labourers* (Bury St Edmunds, 1836).

GLYDE, J., *Suffolk in the Nineteenth Century* (London, 1856).

———— 'Localities of Crime in Suffolk', *Journal of the Statistical Society*, 19 (1856), 102-6.

———— *The Norfolk Garland* (London, 1872).

———— *The Benefit Societies of Suffolk, Their Present Position and Future Prospects* (1874).

———— 'The Autobiography of a Suffolk Farm Labourer', *Suffolk Mercury* (1894).

GREEN, J. L., *Allotments and Small Holdings* (London, 1896).

HEATH, F. G., *The English Peasantry* (London, 1874).

HENSLOW, REVD J. S., *Suggestions towards an Enquiry into the Present Condition of the Labouring Population of Suffolk* (Hadleigh, 1844).

JEFFERIES, R., *The Gamekeeper at Home* (London, 1878).

———— *Hodge and his Masters*, 2 vols. (London, Fitzroy edn., 1966).

JESSOPP, A., *Arcady for Better or Worse* (London, 1887).

JOHNSON, W., *England as It is* (London, 1851).

JONAS, S., 'On the Farming of Cambridgeshire', *JRAS* 7 (1846), 35-50.

KAY, J. P., 'Earnings of Agricultural Labourers in Norfolk and Suffolk', *Journal of the Statistical Society*, 1 (1839), 179-83.

KENT, J. H., *Remarks on the Injuriousness of the Consolidation of Small Farms and the Benefit of Small Occupations and Allotments: With Some Observations on the Past and Present State of the Agricultural Labourers* (Bury St Edmunds, 1844).

———— *On the Physical and Moral Condition of the Agricultural Labourers* (Bury St Edmunds, 1844).

LAING, S., *National Distress: Its Causes and Remedies* (London, 1844).

MABERLEY, F. H., *To the Poor and their Friends* (London, 1836).

MASON, R. H., *The History of Norfolk* (London, 1884).

PAGE, L. F., *Incendiarism: Its Causes, Call, Wickedness, Folly and Remedy* (Bury St Edmunds, 1844).

PETTY, L., *The History of the Primitive Methodist Connexion* (London, 1864).

PLACE, F., 'Place Papers: Free Trade, Distress, Fires' (British Library, 1844).

PURDY, F., 'On the Earnings of Agricultural Labourers in England and Wales', *Journal of the Statistical Society*, 24 (1861), 328-73.

RAYNBIRD, H., 'On Measure Work', *JRAS* 7 (1846), 119-40.

———— and W., *The Agriculture of Suffolk* (London, 1849).

READ, C. S., 'Recent Improvements in Norfolk Farming', *JRAS* 19 (1858), 265-311.

RITCHIE, J. E., *Christopher Crayon's Recollections: The Life and Times of the Late James Ewing Ritchie, as Told by Himself* (London, 1898).

SPENCER, J. C., 'On the Improvements which have taken place in West Norfolk', *JRAS* 3 (1842), 1-9.

TRIMMER, K., *Folly, Sinfulness and Consequences of Stackburning* (Kings Lynn, 1833).

WAKEFIELD, E. G., *Swing Unmasked* (London, 1830).

WATTS, T., *The Present State and Alarming Prospects of the Agricultural Population* ... (Norwich, 1831).

WEYLAND, J., *Thoughts submitted to the Employers of Labour with a few Words to the Employed* (Norwich, 1830).

WHITE, W., *History, Gazetteer and Directory of Norfolk 1845* (Newton Abbot, David and Charles repr., 1970).

——— *History, Gazetteer and Directory of Suffolk 1844* (Newton Abbot, David and Charles repr., 1970).

WILSON, E., *A Parish Priest's Address to his Congregation on the Present Disorders* (Norwich, 1830).

WILSON, M., *Rural Cyclopedia*, 2 vols. (Edinburgh, 1849).

YELLOLY, J., *Some Account of the Employment of Spade Husbandry on an Extensive Scale in the County of Norfolk* (London, 1838).

YOUNG, A., *General View of the Agriculture of Suffolk* (London, 1797).

——— *General View of the Agriculture of Norfolk* (London, 1804).

V. SECONDARY SOURCES

ABBIATECI, A., 'Arsonists in Eighteenth-Century France: An Essay in the Typology of Crime', in R. FORSTER AND O. RANUM, eds., *Deviants and the Abandoned in French Society: Selections from the Annales*, iv (Baltimore, 1978), 157-77.

ARCHER, J. E., 'The Wells-Charlesworth Debate: A Personal Comment on Arson in Norfolk and Suffolk', *JPS* 9 (1982), 277-84.

——— 'Rural Protest in Norfolk and Suffolk 1830-1870', in A. Charlesworth, ed., *Rural Social Change and Conflicts since 1500* (Hull, 1983), 83-95

——— '"A Fiendish Outrage"?: A Study of Animal Maiming in East Anglia, 1830-70,, *Ag. Hist. Rev.* 33/11 (1985), 147-57.

——— 'Under Cover of Night: Arson and Maiming', in G. E. Mingay, ed., *The Unquiet Countryside* (London, 1989).

ARMSTRONG, A., *Farmworkers: A Social and Economic History 1770-1980* (London, 1988).

ARMSTRONG, H. B. J., *A Norfolk Diary* (London, 1949).

ASHBY, M. K., *Joseph Ashby of Tysoe, 1859-1919* (London, 1974).

BALDRY, G., *The Rabbit Skin Cap* (Ipswich, 1939).

BARKER, T., ed., *The Long March of Everyman* (London, 1975).

BARNETT, D. C., 'Allotments and the Problem of Rural Poverty 1780-1840', in G. E. MINGAY AND E. L. JONES, eds., *Land, Labour and Population in the Industrial Revolution* (London, 1967), 162-83.

BEATTIE, J. M., *Crime and the Courts in England 1660-1800* (Oxford, 1986).

BECKETT, R. B., *John Constable's Correspondence* (Ipswich, 1962).

Bell, C., and Newby, H., 'The Sources of Variation in Agricultural Workers Images of Society', *Sociological Review*, 21 (1973), 229-53.

Bennett, E. N., *Problems of Village Life* (London, 1914).

Beresford, J., ed., *The Diary of a Country Parson 1758-1802* (Oxford, 1978).

Best, G., *Mid-Victorian Britain 1851-1870* (London, 1979).

Blaug, M., 'Myth of the Old Poor Law and the making of the New', *Journal of Economic History*, 23 (1963), 151-84.

Bloomfield, B. C., ed., 'The Autobiography of Sir James Kay Shuttleworth', *Education Libraries Bulletin Supplement*, 7 (1964).

Bovill, E. W., *English Country Life, 1780-1830* (Oxford, 1962).

Brown, A. F. J., *Chartism in Essex and Suffolk* (Chelmsford, 1982).

Brundage, A., 'The English Poor Law of 1834 and the Cohesion of Agricultural Society', *Agricultural History*, 48 (1974), 405-17.

Bunney, S., ed., *The Illustrated Book of Herbs* (London, 1984).

Bushaway, B., *By Rite: Custom, Ceremony and Community in England 1700-1880* (London, 2011).

Carter, I., 'Agricultural Workers in the Class Structure: A Critical Note', *Sociological Review*, 22 (1974), 271-9.

Carter, M. J., *Peasants and Poachers* (Woodbridge, 1980).

Chadwick, O., *Victorian Miniature* (London, 1960).

Chambers, J. D., and Mingay, G. E., *The Agricultural Revolution 1750-1850* (London, 1966).

Charlesworth, A., *Social Protest in a Rural Society: The Spatial Diffusion of the Captain Swing Disturbances of 1830-31* (Historical Geography Research Ser.; Norwich, 1979).

—— 'The Development of the English Rural Proletariat and Social Protest, 1700-1850: A Comment', *JPS* 8 (1980), 101-11.

—— *An Atlas of Rural Protest in Britain 1548-1900* (London, 1983).

—— ed., *Rural Social Change and Conflicts since 1500* (Hull, 1983).

Checkland, S. G. and E. O. A., *The Poor Law Report of 1834* (London, 1974).

Chenevix Trench C., *The Poacher and the Squire* (London, 1967).

Christian, Garth, ed., *James Hawker's Journal: A Victorian Poacher* (Oxford, 1978).

Clapham, J. H., 'The Transference of the Worsted Industry from Norfolk to the West Riding', *Economic Journal*, 20 (1910), 195-210.

Cole, G. D. H., *The Life of William Cobbett* (London, 1927).

Coleman, D., C., 'Growth and Decay during the Industrial Revolution: The Case of East Anglia', *Scandinavian Economic History Review*, 10 (1962), 115-27.

Collins, E. J. T., 'Harvest Technology and Labour Supply in Britain, 1790-1870', *Econ. Hist. Rev.*, 2nd ser., 22 (1969), 453-73.

Critchley, T. A., *A History of the Police in England and Wales, 1900-66* (London, 1978).

Darnton, R., *The Great Cat Massacre and Other Episodes in French Cultural History* (Harmondsworth, 1985).

DARROCK, E., and Taylor, B., edd., *Bibliography of Norfolk History* (Norwich, 1975).

DAVIS, J., 'The London Garotting Panic of 1862: A Moral Panic and the Creation of a Criminal Class in Mid-Victorian England', in V. A. C. GATRELL, B. LENMAN, AND G. PARKER, eds., *Crime and the Law: The Social History of Crime in Western Europe since 1500* (London, 1980), 190-213.

DIGBY, A., 'The Labour Market and the Continuity of Social Policy after 1834: The Case of the Eastern Counties', *Econ. Hist. Rev.*, 2nd. Ser., 28 (1975). 69-83.

——— 'The Rural Poor Law', in D. Fraser, ed., *The New Poor Law in the Nineteenth Century* (London, 1976), 149-70.

——— *Pauper Palaces* (London, 1978).

DREW, B., *The Fire Office, being the History of the Essex and Suffolk Equitable Insurance Society Limited, 1802-1952* (London, 1952).

DUNBABIN, J. P. D., 'The Revolt of the Fields: The Agricultural Labourers Movement in the 1870s', *Past and Present*, 26 (1963), 68-97.

——— *Rural Discontent in Nineteenth-Century Britain* (London, 1974).

EDSALL, N. C., *The Anti-Poor Law Movement 1834-44* (Manchester, 1971).

EDWARDS, G., *From Crow-Scaring to Westminster* (London, 1922).

EDWARDS, J. K., 'The Decline of the Norwich Textiles Industry', *Yorkshire Bulletin of Economic and Social Research*, 16 (1964), 31-41.

——— 'Chartism in Norwich', *Yorkshire Bulletin of Economic and Social Research* (1967).

EMSLEY, C., *Policing and its Context 1750-1850* (London, 1983).

——— '"The Thump of Wood on a Swede Turnip": Police Violence in Nineteenth-Century England', *Criminal Justice History*, 6 (1985), 125-49.

——— *Crime and Society in England 1750-1900* (London, 1987).

ERNLE, R. E. P., *English Farming Past and Present* (London, 1912).

EVANS, E. J., 'Some Reasons for the Growth of English Anti-Clericalism, c.1750-c.1830', *Past and Present*, 66 (1975), 84-109.

——— *The Contentious Tithe: The Tithe Problem and English Agriculture 1750-1850* (London, 1976).

EVANS, G. E., *The Horse in the Furrow* (London, 1960).

——— and Thomson, D., *The Leaping Hare* (London, 1972).

Everyman's Encyclopedia, 6th edn. (London, 1978).

FEARN, H., 'Chartism in Suffolk', in A. Briggs, ed., *Chartist Studies* (London, 1959), 147-73.

FINER, S. E., *The Life and Times of Sir Edwin Chadwick* (London, 1952).

FOX, A. W., 'Agricultural Wages in England and Wales during the Last Fifty Years', *Journal of the Statistical Society*, 66 (1903), 273-348.

FOX, N. E., 'The Spread of the Threshing Machine in Central Southern England', *Ag. Hist. Rev.* 26 (1978), 26-8.

FUSSELL, G. E., *From Tolpuddle to the TUC* (Slough, 1948).

——— *The English Rural Labourer* (London, 1949).

GARNIER, R. M., *Annals of the British Peasantry* (London, 1908).

GATRELL, V. A. C., AND HADDEN, T. B., 'Criminal Statistics and Their Interpretation', in E. A. Wrigley, ed., *Nineteenth-Century Society* (Cambridge, 1972), 336-96.

GEORGE, M. D., *Political Caricature: A Study of Opinion and Propaganda*, 2 vols. (Oxford, 1959).

GOODWYN, E. A., *A Suffolk Town in Mid-Victorian England, Beccles in the 1860s* (Ipswich, n.d.).

GRACE, D. R., AND PHILLIPS, D. C., *Ransomes of Ipswich: A History of the Firm and Guide to its Records* (Reading, 1975).

GREEN, F. E., *A History of the English Agricultural Labourer 1870-1920* (London, 1920).

GROVES, R., *Sharpen the Sickle: The History of the Farm Workers Union* (London, 1949).

HAGGARD, L. R., ed., *I Walked by Night* (London, 1952).

———— AND WILLIAMSON, H., *Norfolk Life* (London, 1943).

HAMMOND, J. L. AND B., *The Village Labourer*, 3rd edn. (London, 1920).

HARRISON, B., 'Animals and the State in Nineteenth-Century England', *English Historical Review*, 88 (1973), 786-809.

HARVEY, LT. COL. J. R., *Records of the Norfolk Yeomanry Cavalry 1780-1908* (London, 1908).

HASBACH, W., *A History of the English Agricultural Labourer* (London, 1908)

HAY, D., LINEBAUGH, D., J. G. RULE, THOMPSON, E. P., AND C. WINSLOW, *Albion's Fatal Tree: Crime and Society in Eighteenth-Century England* (London, 1975).

HENSLOW, G., *Reminiscences of a Scientific Suffolk Clergyman* (London, 1901).

HOBSBAWM, E. J., *Primitive Rebels* (Manchester, 1959).

———— AND RUDÉ, G., *Captain Swing* (Harmondsworth, 1973).

HOLDERNESS, B. A., 'Open and Close Parishes in England in the Eighteenth and Nineteenth Centuries', *Ag. Hist. Rev.* 20 (1972), 126-39.

HOPKINS, H., *The Long Affray: The Poaching Wars 1760-1914* (London, 1985).

HORN, P., *Joseph Arch 1826-1919, the Farm Workers' Leader* (Kineton, 1971).

———— *The Rise and Fall of the Victorian Servant* (Dublin, 1975).

———— *Labouring Life in the Victorian Countryside* (Dublin, 1976).

———— *The Rural World, 1780-1850: Social Change in the English Countryside* (London, 1980).

HOWKINS, A., 'Economic Crime and Class Law: Poaching and the Game Laws, 1840-1880', in S. E. Burman and B. H. Bond, edd., *The Imposition of Law* (New York, 1979), 273-87.

———— *Poor Labouring Men: Rural Radicalism in Norfolk 1870-1923* (London, 1985).

HUNT, E. H., 'Labour Productivity in English Agriculture, 1850-1914', *Econ. Hist. Rev.* 2nd ser., 20 (1967), 280-92.

———— *Regional Wage Variations in Britain 1850-1914* (Oxford, 1973).

JOHNSON, D., *Victorian Shooting Days: East Anglia 1810-1910* (Ipswich, 1981).

JONES, D. J. V., *Chartism and the Chartists* (London, 1975).

———— 'Thomas Campbell Foster and the Rural Labourer: Incendiarism in East Anglia in the 1840s', *Social History*, I (1976), 5-43.

———— 'The Second Rebecca Riots: A Study of Poaching on the Upper Wye', *Llafur*, 2 (1976), 32-56.

———— '"A Dead Loss to the Community": The Criminal Vagrant in Mid-Century Wales', *Welsh Historical Review*, 8 (1977), 312-43.

———— 'The Poacher: A Study in Victorian Crime and Protest', *Historical Journal*, 22 (1979), 825-60.

———— *Crime, Protest, Community and Police in Nineteenth-Century Britain* (London, 1982).

———— 'The New Police, Crime and People in England and Wales, 1829-88', *Transactions of the Royal Historical Society*, 5th ser., 33 (1983), 151-68.

———— and Bainbridge, A., *Crime in Nineteenth-Century Wales*, SSRC Report (1975).

JONES, E. L., *The Development of English Agriculture* (London, 1968).

———— 'The Agriculture Labour Market in England, 1793-1872', *Econ. Hist. Rev.* 2nd ser., 17 (1964-5), 322-38.

JONES, E. L., AND MINGAY, G. E., *Land, Labour and Population in the Industrial Revolution* (London, 1967).

KERR, B., 'The Dorset Agricultural Labourer 1750-1850', *Proceedings of the Dorset Natural History and Archaeological Society*, 84 (1962), 158-77.

———— *Bound to the Soil* (London, 1968).

KIRBY, C., 'The Attack on the English Game Laws in the Forties', *Journal of Modern History*, 4 (1932), 18-37.

———— 'The English Game Law System', *American Historical Review*, 38 (1933). 240-62.

KITTERINGHAM, J., 'Country Work Girls in Nineteenth-Century England', in R. Samuel, ed., *Village Life and Labour* (London, 1975), 73-138.

KUSSMAUL, A., *Servants in Husbandry in Early Modern England* (Cambridge, 1981).

LOWERSON, J., 'The Aftermath of Swing: Anti-Poor Law Movements and Rural Trade Unions in the South East of England', in A. CHARLESWORTH, ed., *Rural Social Change and Conflicts since 1500* (Hull, 1983), 55-82.

McCORD, N., *The Anti-Corn Law League* (London, 1958).

MACKIE, C., *Norfolk Annals* (Norwich, 1901).

MANN, E., 'Shipmeadow Union House: Extracts taken from the Diary of an Inmate', *Suffolk Institute of Archaeology*, 23 (1939), 42-9.

MARLOW, J., *The Tolpuddle Martyrs* (London, 1971).

MARSHALL, J. D., 'The Nottinghamshire Reformers and their Contribution to the New Poor Law', *Econ. Hist. Rev.* 2nd ser., 13 (1961), 382-96.

MARTIN, E. W., *The Secret People* (London, 1954).

MINCHINTON, W., *Essays in Agrarian History*, 2 vols. (Newton Abbot, 1968).

MINGAY, G. E., *Rural Life in Victorian England* (London, 1977).

———— ed., *The Victorian Countryside*, 2 vols. (London, 1981).

Mitchell, B. R., and Deane, P., *Abstracts of British Historical Statistics* (Cambridge, 1976).

Montmorency, J. E. G. de, 'State Protection of Animals at Home and Abroad', *Law Quarterly Review*, 18 (1902), 31-48.

Morgan, D. H., 'The Place of Harvesters in Nineteenth-Century Village Life', in R. Samuel, ed., *Village Life and Labour* (London,1975), 27-72.

Munby, L. M., ed., *The Luddites and other Essays* (London, 1971).

Munsche, P. B., 'The Game Laws in Wiltshire, 1750-1800), in J. S. Cockburn, ed., *Crime in England, 1550-1800* (London, 1977), 210-28.

———— *Gentlemen and Poachers: The English Game Laws 1671-1831* (Cambridge, 1981).

Murphy, M. J., *Poverty in Cambridgeshire* (Cambridge, 1972).

Muskett, P., 'The East Anglian Riots of 1822,, *Ag. Hist. Rev.* 32 (1984), 1-13.

Newby, H., 'Agricultural Workers in the Class Structure', *Sociological Review*, 20 (1972), 413-39.

———— 'Deference and the Agricultural Worker', *Sociological Review*, 23 (1975), 51-60.

———— 'The Deferential Dialectic', *Comparative Studies in Society and History*, 17 (1975), 139-64.

———— *The Deferential Worker* (London, 1977).

Obelkevich, J., *Religion and Rural Society: South Lindsey 1825-75* (Oxford, 1976).

Orwin, C. S. and Whetham, E., *History of British Agriculture 1846-1914* (London, 1964).

O'Sullivan, G. H., and Kelleher, M. J., 'A Study of Firesetters in the South-West of Ireland', *British Journal of Psychiatry*, 151 (1987), 818-23.

Palmer, S. H., *Police and Protest in England and Ireland 1780-1850* (Cambridge, 1988).

Parker, R. A. C., *Coke of Norfolk: A Financial and Agricultural Study, 1707-1842* (Oxford, 1975).

Peacock, A. J., *Bread or Blood: A Study of the Agrarian Riots in East Anglia in 1816* (London, 1965).

———— 'Village Radicalism in East Anglia 1800-50', in J. P. D. Dunbabin, *Rural Discontent in Nineteenth-Century Britain* (London,1974), 27-61.

Perkin, H., *The Origins of Modern English Society, 1780-1880* (London, 1969).

Philips, D., *Crime and Authority in Victorian England* (London, 1977).

Prescott, C., 'The Suffolk Constabulary in the Nineteenth Century', *Suffolk Institute of Archaeology*, 31 (1967-9), 1-46.

Radzinowicz, L., *A History of English Criminal Law and its Administration from 1750*, 4 vols. (London, 1948-68).

Reaney, B., *The Class Struggle in Nineteenth-Century Oxfordshire: The Social and Communal Background to the Otmoor Disturbances of 1830-35* (Oxford, 1970).

Redford, A., *Labour Migration in England 1800-50* (Manchester, 1964).

Riches, N., *The Agricultural Revolution in Norfolk* (London, 1967).

Roberts, D., *Paternalism in Early Victorian England* (New Brunswick, 1979).

ROGERS, P. G., *Battle in Bossenden Wood: The Strange Story of Sir William Courtenay* (London, 1961).

ROSE, M. E., *The Relief of Poverty 1834-1914* (London, 1972).

RUBIN, G. R., AND SUGARMAN, D., eds., *Law, Economy and Society* (Abingdon, 1984).

RUDÉ, G., 'Protest and Punishment in Nineteenth-Century Britain', *Albion*, 5 (1973), 1-23.

———— *Ideology and Protest* (London, 1980).

———— *Protest and Punishment: The Story of the Social and Political Protesters Transported to Australia 1788-1868* (Oxford, 1980).

———— *Criminal and Victim: Crime and Society in Early Nineteenth-Century England* (Oxford, 1985).

RULE, J. G., 'Social Crime in the Rural South in the Eighteenth and Early Nineteenth Centuries', *Southern History*, 1 (1979), 135-53.

———— *The Labouring Classes in Early Industrial England, 1750-1850* (London, 1986).

———— ed., *Outside the Law: Studies in Crime and Order 1650-1850* (Exeter, 1982).

RUSSELL-GEBBETT, J., *Henslow of Hitcham* (Lavenham, 1977).

SALAMAN, R., *The History and Social Influence of the Potato* (Cambridge, 1949).

SAMBROOK, J., *William Cobbett* (London, 1973).

SAMUEL, R., ed., *Village Life and Labour* (London, 1975).

SAVILLE, J., *Rural Depopulation in England and Wales 1851-1951* (London, 1957).

SCOTLAND, N., *Methodism and the Revolt of the Field: A Study of the Methodist Contribution to Agricultural Trade Unionism in East Anglia, 1872-96* (Gloucester, 1981).

SELLEY, E., *Village Trade Unions in Two Centuries* (London, 1919).

SMITH, F., *The Life and Work of Sir James Kay Shuttleworth* (London, 1923).

SNELL, K. D. M., *Annals of the Labouring Poor: Social Change and Agrarian England 1660-1900* (Cambridge, 1985).

SPIERS, E. M., *The Army and Society 1815-1914* (London, 1980).

SPRINGALL, L. M., *Labouring Life in Norfolk Villages 1834-1914* (London, 1936).

STEEDMAN, C., *Policing and the Victorian Community: The Formation of English Provincial Police Forces 1856-80* (London, 1984).

STEVENSON, J., *Popular Disturbances in England 1700-1870* (London, 1979).

STORCH, R. D., 'The Plague of Blue Locusts: Police Reform and Popular Resistance in Northern England, 1840-57', *International Review of Social History*, 20 (1975), 61-90.

———— 'The Policeman as Domestic Missionary: Urban Discipline and Popular Culture in Northern England, 1850-80', *Journal of Social History*, 9 (1976), 481-509.

STYLES, J., AND INNES, J., 'The Crime Wave: Recent Writing on Crime and Criminal Justice in Eighteenth Century England', *Journal of British Studies*, 25 (1986), 380-435.

SWIFT, R., 'Urban Policing in Early Victorian England, 1835-56: A Reappraisal', *History*, 73 (1988), 211-37.

TATE, W. E., 'A Handlist of Suffolk Enclosure Acts and Awards', *Proceedings of the Suffolk Institute of Archaeology*, 25 (1952) 248-61.

———— *The English Village Community and the Enclosure Movement* (London, 1967).

THIRSK, J., AND IMRAY, J., *Suffolk Farming in the Nineteenth Century* (Ipswich, 1958).

THOMAS, K., *Man and the Natural World: Changing Attitudes in England 1500-1800* (London, 1983).

THOMPSON, E. P., *The Making of the English Working Class* (Harmondsworth, rev. edn., 1968).

———— 'The Moral Economy of the English Crowd in the Eighteenth Century', *Past and Present*, 50 (1971), 76-136.

———— *Whigs and Hunters: The Origin of the Black Act* (London, 2013).

THOMPSON, F. M. L., *English Landed Society in the Nineteenth Century* (London, 1971).

TILLY, C., *Collective Violence in European Perspective* (Washington, 1969).

———— 'The Changing Place of Collective Violence', in M. Richter, ed., *Essays in Theory and History* (Cambridge, Mass., 1970), 139-64.

TOBIAS, J. J., *Crime and Industrial Society in the Nineteenth Century* (Harmondsworth, 1967).

UNWIN, E. F., *The Hungry Forties* (London, 1906).

Victoria County History, Norfolk, ed. W. Page, (London, n.d.).

Victoria County History, Suffolk, ed. W. Page, (London, 1906).

WEA EASTERN DISTRICT, *Chartism in East Anglia* (Cambridge, 1952).

WEBB, S. AND B., *The English Poor Law History* (London, 1963 repr.).

WELLS, R. A. E., 'The Development of the English Rural Proletariat and Social Protest, 1700-1850', *JPS* 6 (1979), 115-39.

———— 'Social Conflict and Protest in the English Countryside in the Early Nineteenth Century: A Rejoinder', *JPS* 8 (1981), 514-30.

———— 'Sheep-Rustling in Yorkshire in the Age of the Industrial and Agricultural Revolutions', *Northern History*, 20 (1984), 127-45.

———— 'Rural Rebels in Southern England in the 1830s,, in C. EMSLEY AND J. WALVIN, eds., *Artisans, Peasants and Proletarians* (Beckenham, 1985), pp. 124-65.

WIENER, M. J., *English Culture and the Decline of the Industrial Spirit* (Cambridge, 1981).

WILLIAMS, R., *The Country and the City* (London, 1973).

VI. DISSERTATIONS

AMOS, S. W., 'Social Discontent and Agrarian Disturbances in Essex 1795-1850', MA diss. (Univ. of Durham, 1971).

ARCHER, J. E., 'Rural Protest in Norfolk and Suffolk 1830-70,, Ph.D. thesis (Univ. of East Anglia, 1982).

BAILLIE, T., 'Rural Protest in Lincolnshire 1842-50,, BA diss. (Edge Hill College of Higher Education, 1989).

BEAMES, M. R., 'Peasant Disturbances and their Control, Ireland 1798-1852', Ph.D. thesis (Univ. of Manchester, 1976).

COLLINS, E. T. J., 'Harvest Technology and Labour Supply in Britain 1790-1870'; Ph.D. thesis (Univ. of Nottingham, 1970).

DIGBY, A., 'The Operation of the Poor Law in the Social and Economic Life of Nineteenth-Century Norfolk', Ph.D. thesis (Univ. of East Anglia, 1971).

EDWARDS, J. K., 'The Economic Development of Norwich 1750-1850 with Special Reference to the Worsted Industry', Ph.D. thesis (Univ. of Leeds, 1963).

FEARN, H., 'Chartism in Suffolk', MA diss. (Univ. of Sheffield, 1952).

HARBER, J., 'Incendiarism in Suffolk 1840-45', MA diss. (Univ. of Warwick, 1975).

LLOYD PRITCHARD, M. F., 'The Treatment of Poverty in Norfolk 1700-1850', Ph.D. thesis (Univ. of Cambridge, 1949).

MACNAB, K. K., 'Aspects of the History of Crime in England and Wales between 1805 and 1860', D.Phil. (Univ. of Sussex, 1965).

ROE, P. J., 'The Revolution of Norfolk Agriculture in the Nineteenth Century 1815-1914', M.Phil. thesis (Univ. of East Anglia, 1975).

SPRINGALL, L. M., 'The Norfolk Agriculture Labourer 1834-84', Ph.D. thesis (Univ. of London, 1935).

TAYLOR, R., 'The Development of the Old Poor Law in Norfolk, 1795-1834', MA thesis (Univ. of East Anglia, 1970).

WADE-MARTINS, S., 'The Holkham Estate in the Nineteenth Century', Ph.D., thesis (Univ. of East Anglia, 1975).

Index of Places

Index of Subjects

Ralph Anstis, WARREN JAMES AND THE DEAN FOREST RIOTS, *The Disturbances of 1831*
£17.00 • 242pp *paperback* • 191x235mm • ISBN 978-0-9564827-7-8

Victor Bailey, CHARLES BOOTH'S POLICEMEN, *Crime, Police and Community in Jack-the-Ripper's London*
£17.00 • 162pp *paperback* • *2 colour and 8 b/w images* • 140x216mm • ISBN 978-0-9564827-6-1

Victor Bailey, ORDER AND DISORDER IN MODERN BRITAIN, *Essays on Riot, Crime, Policing and Punishment*
£15.00 • 214pp *paperback* • 5 *b/w images* • 191x235mm • ISBN 978-0-9570005-5-1

Roger Ball, Dave Beckwith, Steve Hunt, Mike Richardson, STRIKERS, HOBBLERS, CONCHIES & REDS, *A Radical History of Bristol, 1880-1939*
£18.50 • 366pp *paperback* • *101 b/w images* • 156x234mm • ISBN 978-0-9929466-0-9

John Belchem, 'ORATOR' HUNT, *Henry Hunt and English Working Class Radicalism*
£17.50 • 248pp *paperback* • 191x235mm • ISBN 978-0-9564827-8-5

Alastair Bonnett & Keith Armstrong (eds.), THOMAS SPENCE: THE POOR MAN'S REVOLUTIONARY
£15.00 • 214pp *paperback* • 156x234mm • ISBN 978-0-9570005-9-9

Bob Bushaway, BY RITE, *Custom, Ceremony and Community in England 1700-1880*
£16.00 • 206pp *paperback* • 191x235mm • ISBN 978-0-9564827-6-1

Norah Carlin, REGICIDE OR REVOLUTION?, *What Petitioners Wanted, September 1648 - February 1649*
£18.50 • 358pp *paperback* • 156x234mm • ISBN 978-1-9161586-0-3

Malcolm Chase, THE PEOPLE'S FARM, *English Radical Agrarianism 1775-1840*
£12.00 • 212pp *paperback* • 152x229mm • ISBN 978-0-9564827-5-4

Malcolm Chase, EARLY TRADE UNIONISM, Fraternity, *Skill and the Politics of Labour*
£17.00 • 248pp *paperback* • 191x235mm • ISBN 978-0-9570005-2-0

Nigel Costley, WEST COUNTRY REBELS
£20.00 • 220pp *full colour illustrated paperback* • 216x216mm • ISBN 978-0-9570005-4-4

James Epstein, THE LION OF FREEDOM, *Feargus O'Connor and the Chartist Movement, 1832-1842*
£17.00 • 296pp *paperback* • 156x234mm • ISBN 978-0-9929466-1-6

James Epstein, RADICAL EXPRESSION, *Political Language, Ritual, and Symbol in England, 1790-1850*
£15.00 • 220pp *paperback* • 156x234mm • ISBN 978-0-9929466-2-3

Chris Fisher, CUSTOM, WORK & MARKET CAPITALISM, *The Forest of Dean Colliers, 1788-1888*
£14.00 • 198pp *paperback* • 156x234mm • ISBN 978-0-9929466-7-8